BOCCONI
UNIVERSITY
PRESS

Giuseppe Mayer

INSPIRED BY DATA

AI's Transformative Role in Corporate Communication

Foreword by **Vittorio Carlei**

Cover: Cristina Bernasconi, Milan
Typesetting: Laura Panigara, Cesano Boscone (MI)

Copyright © 2023 Bocconi University Press
EGEA S.p.A.

EGEA S.p.A.
Via Salasco, 5 - 20136 Milano
Tel. 02/5836.5751 – Fax 02/5836.5753
egea.edizioni@unibocconi.it – www.egeaeditore.it

First edition: December 2023

ISBN Domestic Edition	979-12-80623-26-3
ISBN International Edition	979-12-81627-13-0
ISBN Digital Domestic Edition	979-12-81627-14-7
ISBN Digital International Edition	978-88-238-8749-7

Table of Contents

Foreword

by *Vittorio Carlei*[*]

When Giuseppe first discussed this book with me, we actually started talking about something else. It is characteristic of the human mind to embark on reasoning and dialogues without adhering to a predetermined plan. Every word, every thought evokes images within us, driving us to new thoughts, new words. It's a flow we experience daily, a phenomenon that, until recently, seemed exclusive to humans. When we interact with others, our flow melds with theirs, altering its direction and quality. We meet people every day, and let's be honest, sometimes we feel enriched by these encounters, sometimes not so much. Meeting Giuseppe was like a meeting of three; it was as if we were discussing a mutual friend. This time, the third entity in our discussion was ChatGPT. Both of us being pioneers and enthusiasts of new technologies and innovation, the conversation naturally veered toward this topic, and the idea for this book was already in Giuseppe's flow, so he asked for my opinion and invited me into his stream.

I waited until the last possible moment to write this preface for several reasons: firstly, I work best under the pressure of a deadline; secondly, I needed time to observe and scrutinize what I needed to convey to others (so I waited for Giuseppe to finish the first draft); finally, I needed to find the right moment when I felt attuned to the flow that would line up the words.

This book speaks of many things, but most importantly, it signifies the realization that "something has changed." I had this thought while

_____

[*] LUISS Professor – Artificial Intelligence for Decision Processes.

lecturing my students in Pescara, a university where I have been teaching for nearly twenty years, in my personal "coast to coast" with LUISS in Rome. During the lecture, as my mental flow merged with the course program, a question suddenly emerged from the confluence of flows, which I immediately posed to the classroom.

The course on Economics of Innovation primarily deals with paradigm shifts and the economies of scale introduced by new technologies; however, in discussing the LLMs, or large language models, we use with ChatGPT and other similar tools, the emerging paradigm shift is particularly subtle. Take, for example, the invention of the printing press. The cost of reproducing a book decreased dramatically with this invention (and even more with the advent of digital technologies, becoming almost zero). But how much did, and does, writing the first copy cost? I believe this book mainly speaks about this. How will the world of communication (and also of teaching) change now that generating content has become so fast and low-cost? Will we still write theses (hopefully not, or at least hopefully they will change profoundly)?

This question raises even more uncomfortable ones: How much will originality cost? Will it still have value? What will originality become in a world offering us the possibility to orchestrate a plethora of generative algorithms of all kinds? Maybe (as this book suggests), we will choose how much we want to be instrumentalists and how much conductors of this orchestra, in a world where technology provides us with increasingly complex and fast tools.

In writing this preface, I preferred to be an instrumentalist, even though I was tempted to use a generative algorithm up to the very end; but writing and reading one word after another is not only a cost but also a pleasure, especially when done for a friend and an important project.

Happy reading!

1 Generative AI and Value Creation for the Company

1.1 Unpacking generative AI: Core concepts and mechanisms

The invention of photography, a seemingly simple process of capturing light and shadow, has had far-reaching implications across a multitude of sectors. It all began in 1826, with a blurred, grainy image captured by Joseph Nicéphore Niépce. This first photograph, while far from perfect, was the initial spark that ignited a new universe of opportunities.

The introduction of the Kodak No. 1 by George Eastman in 1888 democratized photography. No longer was it a pursuit limited to artists and chemists; now, anyone could capture a moment in time. This shift had a profound impact especially on the art world, liberating painting from the need for precise representation of reality. Artists such as Picasso were free to explore new forms of expression, leading to the birth of movements such as Cubism. The advent of color photography in the 1930s, thanks to Eastman Kodak's Kodachrome film, added another layer to this evolving scenario. The ability to capture vivid, lifelike images opened new possibilities in fields as diverse as advertising, journalism, fashion, and many more.

The emergence of generative AI (artificial intelligence) parallels the inception of modern photography in several fascinating ways. Just as photography altered our perception and documentation of reality, generative AI is reshaping how we conceive and produce content. Initially, both fields demanded specialized knowledge – photography in light and chemistry, and generative AI in complex algorithms and neural networks.

The invention of photography democratized the capture of special moments, eliminating the need for an artist and an extended period of time. Similarly, generative AI is leveling the playing field in content creation. It empowers individuals to produce not just text and images but also music and intricate designs or code, thereby broadening the scope for creativity and innovation. As digital technology made photography accessible to all, advancements in AI are making generative technologies increasingly user-friendly and frictionless.

This democratization allows businesses, irrespective of size or industry, and individuals to harness the capabilities of generative AI at a fraction of the previous cost. This has been made possible due to the increasing accessibility of AI platforms, open-source contributions, and flexible pricing models that make AI more affordable for everyone.

Generative AI, like photography, is not monolithic; it has diverse applications requiring specialized approaches. Just as photography includes genres such as portrait and landscape, generative AI serves various sectors, each demanding a unique skill set. Nevertheless, the future implications of generative AI adoption are both exhilarating and unfathomable. Drawing a parallel with photography helps us appreciate and welcome the forthcoming opportunities with open-mindedness and optimism. Just as photography expanded our creative boundaries, generative AI holds the promise of unlocking unprecedented realms of innovation and opportunities.

1.1.1 *AI and Generative AI: From Data Driven to Data Inspired*

When the world first heard of artificial intelligence, it seemed like something straight out of a science fiction novel or the musings of forward-thinking visionaries. It was in the middle of the 20th century that the seeds of AI were planted, thanks to Alan Turing's groundbreaking work that laid the foundation for a technological revolution.[1] Fast-forward to today, and AI is no longer an abstract idea but a tangible reality that has become an integral part of our everyday lives in many ways. Not only is it visibly present, but it also operates subtly and seamlessly within many of the digital services and products we use, often without us even realizing it.

---

[1] https://it.wikipedia.org/wiki/Alan_Turing.

At its core this technology refers to the replication of intelligence in machines programmed to think and learn just like humans. This concept has been expanding over several decades, making its way into various industries; from healthcare to finance, transportation to entertainment, AI's impact is extensive and diverse. As we explore further in this book, big tech companies such as Amazon have been harnessing these technologies for over twenty-five years, utilizing AI and specifically machine learning to optimize their operations, improve customer experiences, and foster innovation.[2]

Within the realm of AI lies a specialized field that warrants particular attention and is the main focus of the subsequent chapters about the evolution of corporate communication: generative AI. While conventional AI models are designed to analyze and interpret data effectively, generative AI takes it a step further; it goes beyond merely comprehending existing patterns and ventures into creating something new from them.

To simplify, the distinction between AI and generative AI can be likened to the contrast between reading a book and writing one. Traditional AI, much like reading, involves absorbing and interpreting information, comprehending patterns, and making decisions based on that comprehension and understanding. It revolves around processing what already exists; that's all. Generative AI, meanwhile, takes this understanding a step further by crafting something that, in a way, is entirely new. It employs the patterns and knowledge acquired from existing data to generate content, ideas, or solutions – similarly to how an author draws on inspiration and employs creativity in weaving a unique narrative. So, while AI can comprehend and interpret the words on a page, generative AI has the capability to compose a chapter by crafting sentences and ideas that are in part its own. It represents a leap from comprehension to creation, from following established paths to forging new ones.

---

[2] Machine learning, in a nutshell, is a subset of artificial intelligence that focuses on the development of algorithms and statistical models that enable computers to perform specific tasks without being explicitly programmed to do so. Instead of writing detailed instructions for every action, machine learning allows a system to learn from data, identify patterns, and make decisions or predictions. It's like teaching a computer to think and learn from experience, much as a human would. Whether it's recommending a movie on a streaming platform or detecting fraudulent activity in banking transactions, machine learning is at the core of many modern technologies, automating complex processes and enhancing efficiency.

This is made possible through machine learning models that undergo training on vast amounts of data, allowing them to grasp underlying patterns and structures. This training phase plays a key role in generative AI. In sum, it is akin to a student delving into a subject, absorbing knowledge, grasping principles, and then applying that knowledge in an innovative manner. Through ongoing processes and continuous refinement, the model learns how to produce new content based on its learning that not only makes sense but also might generate new ideas. The algorithms and neural networks employed in generative AI imitate the brain's ability to learn, create, and innovate. They employ techniques that go beyond mere analysis toward synthesis and surpass comprehension to reach creation itself.

This distinction between AI and generative AI highlights how this technology has evolved from being a tool that helps us understand the world to one that actively contributes to creating it. It signifies a shift from making decisions based on data to using data as inspiration for innovation and creativity, paving the way for new possibilities.

However, it's important to note that this practice is not without significant issues, such as those related to copyright laws; these concerns will be discussed in detail later in the book.

In communication and marketing, generative AI goes beyond traditional boundaries, providing a dynamic platform for fostering creativity and driving innovation. It's no longer just about analyzing consumer behavior or following market trends; it's about harnessing insights to craft unique narratives, create personalized experiences, and pioneer new approaches to brand storytelling. It's about how we can transform that data into captivating messages and forward-thinking strategies that resonate with audiences and shape the future of our business.

1.1.2 *The ChatGPT moment*

In the history of technology, there are a few defining "moments" that mark the emergence of certain innovations, catapulting them from obscurity to enormous popularity. These moments transform the way we interact with the world and shape our daily lives in many ways.

One such milestone was the "Netscape moment" in the 1990s. Netscape Navigator was one of the first web browsers that made the internet accessible to a public without specific tech knowledge. With Netscape, the internet became, almost instantly, a place for everyone to explore and discover. That was the beginning of the modern digital age.

The "iPhone moment" represents another significant shift. Launched in 2007, the iPhone redefined mobile communication by integrating in a single device a phone, an iPod (an mp3 player), and an internet communication device. Its intuitive design and innovative features set a new standard for smartphones, making advanced technology accessible and appealing to the masses. As a direct consequence of this launch, the app economy skyrocketed in subsequent years. Services such as social media, food delivery, and micropayments were made possible by this "moment," creating a tremendous economic impact.

The "AWS moment" in the 2000s marked a real revolution in the way businesses handle IT (information technology) infrastructure. Amazon Web Services (AWS) introduced cloud computing, allowing companies to rent computing resources rather than owning and maintaining physical and expensive servers. This not only reduced costs but also provided flexibility and scalability, enabling startups and large enterprises alike to innovate and grow without heavy investments in hardware and fixed costs.

These peculiar moments in recent history symbolize profound shifts in technology, where a particular innovation transcends its niche to become a global phenomenon. They represent not merely the launch of a product or service; they are cultural milestones that have changed our relationship with technology, making it more accessible, functional, and integral to everyone's life.

The "ChatGPT moment" is one such defining instance; it may turn out to be the most important. It all began with the launch of GPT (Generative Pre-trained Transformer), a generative AI language model developed by OpenAI, in late 2022. This tool quickly became a global sensation, captivating the attention of millions around the world virtually overnight; it is easy to use, free, and ... surprisingly good. The reason behind its meteoric rise lies in its ability to mimic real human language patterns and structures so convincingly that it blurs the line between man and machine.

The user base growth of GPT was immediately exponential. According to an analyst's note from Reuters,[3] ChatGPT reached 100 million

---

[3]   https://www.reuters.com/technology/chatgpt-sets-record-fastest-growing-user-base-analyst-note-2023-02-01/.

monthly active users in January 2023 (less than three months after its launch), setting a record for the fastest-growing user base for any product.

What makes this specific generative AI model particularly captivating is its high accessibility and low friction; for consumers, it offers text- and image-based interfaces at an affordable price. At the same time, companies benefit from application programming interface (API) access from leaders such as OpenAI and enterprise and private models provided by giants including Amazon and Microsoft.[4] This democratization of technology enables a wide range of individuals and organizations to harness the power of AI, experimenting and discovering new ways to implement it.

But it's the efficiency of this particular generative AI model that truly sets it apart. Unlike the old world of AI, where a project required a budget of millions and a team of engineers working for years, generative AI has reduced these requirements to $20 a month,[5] one knowledge worker, and less than a week to achieve significant value. This dramatic reduction in cost and time has revolutionized how businesses approach AI, making it a viable option for a wide range of projects and organizations. In the realm of corporate communication, where conveying complex messages accurately and engagingly is paramount, the ability of GPT to understand and generate content tailored to specific contexts becomes invaluable. These AI technologies, being capable of processing large amounts of data and producing relevant content efficiently, represent a precious asset for communication professionals. Particularly since the release of ChatGPT, publishers, agencies, and companies have begun experimenting with the potential activations of this tool to enhance the performance of corporate communication. ChatGPT's ability to generate coherent and well-structured text allows for more effective and personalized communication, meeting the audience's needs and expectations more precisely. This not only improves the efficacy of communication but can also contribute to building stronger and more meaningful relationships with various stakeholders.

---

[4] https://en.wikipedia.org/wiki/API.
[5] This is the price at which, at the time of going to print, OpenAI makes its flagship product available to the end consumer.

1.1.3   *Understanding generative AI: A nontechnical introduction*

This technology, which represents a significant advancement in our ability to create specific and generic outputs, is no longer the domain of experts and engineers. Its core principles should be understood by everyone, particularly in the business cohort.

As previously mentioned, at the heart of generative AI are machine learning models known as generative models, but how do they work? These models are like artists, learning the subtle patterns of a given dataset and then crafting new data that mirrors these learned patterns. It's a process that might seem complex but can be seen as collaborative work between creativity and critique.

Take generative adversarial networks (GANs), for example; imagine a pair of artists – one creating original pieces and the other critiquing them.[6] The "artist" or generator crafts new data instances, while the "critic" or discriminator evaluates their authenticity and rates them. They then work together, refining and enhancing each other's abilities at every step until the generator can create data that the discriminator can't tell apart from the original dataset. Variational autoencoders (VAEs) offer another alternative perspective; they act like translators, encoding input data into a different form and then decoding it to generate new data.[7] This dual process allows VAEs to create new data that closely resembles the original input.

Among the notable advancements in generative AI are LLMs (large language models) such as GPT, which are capable of understanding and generating human-like text, images, and video at a vast scale. These models, built on transformer architectures, have shown a remarkable ability to produce coherent, contextually relevant content over extended sequences, making them incredibly valuable for a wide range of applications including content creation, language translation, and interactive conversational agents. These models employ a mechanism known as attention, allowing them to weigh the relevance of different words in a sentence when crafting new text. This attention mechanism enables them to create sentences that are not only grammatically correct but also

---

[6] https://en.wikipedia.org/wiki/Generative_adversarial_network.

[7] https://towardsdatascience.com/understanding-variational-autoencoders-vaes-f70510919f73.

contextually relevant. The process of generating new text based on the learned patterns from training data is often carried out during a phase known as inference. During inference, the models utilize the learned parameters to make predictions or generate new data without any further learning. While we often interpret the coherent and contextually relevant text generated as a form of "intelligence," at its core, it's a result of statistical patterns learned from vast amounts of data.

The learning process, known as training, is where these models learn their skills. Having been exposed to vast amounts of data, they understand the underlying patterns and structures within that data. This training involves a careful adjustment of the model's parameters to minimize the difference between the generated data and the real data, a process known as inference.

While these core concepts of generative AI may appear complex and designed for technical experts, they are far from inaccessible and should be understood by anyone who interacts with these powerful tools. For instance, for those aspiring to work in the field of communication or marketing, embracing these technologies is becoming as crucial as understanding the transformative influence of innovations such as the iPhone or AWS. Just as these breakthroughs revolutionized our daily interactions and professional landscapes, generative AI is poised to have a similar, if not greater, impact.

The cultural effect of these new technologies has led many to fear the potential loss of jobs due to the increased efficiency in various processes made possible by generative AI. However, the focus should not be on the fear that AI will replace human labor: rather, it should be on recognizing that those who learn to harness the power of AI will be the ones leading the way – the new AI class. The future, as always, belongs to those who can adapt and innovate, leveraging generative AI not as a mere tool but as a partner in creativity and business. The challenge is in realizing its potential to redefine how we work, communicate, and create.

1.2   The current landscape: AI in today's business world

From the way we search for information to the way we connect with friends, listen to music, or interact with businesses, AI is subtly transforming our everyday lives. It's a revolution that's happening behind the scenes, driven by complex algorithms and machine learning models that are continually learning and adapting to our behaviors and preferences. This AI revolution is not confined to the tech giants or cutting-edge research labs; it's permeating every aspect of our society. Whether it's a small business leveraging AI to compete with larger corporations or a music streaming service connecting independent artists with their audience, AI is democratizing opportunities and redefining success.

1.2.1 *The democratization of information*

In the digital landscape, where information is sought and consumed at an unprecedented pace, the way we access and interact with knowledge is continually evolving. One of the key players in this transformation is Google, but what makes this search engine so effective and adaptive? The answer lies in its utilization of AI.[8]

Google's search engine, a lifeline for information seekers around the globe, is more than a mere collection of algorithms. It's a learning entity, powered by AI, that continually refines and improves the quality of its answers with each query. By analyzing user behavior, clicks, and engagement with the content, Google's AI doesn't just respond to searches; it learns from them and adapts for the next search and the next users.

Whether you're a student delving into historical research, a legal professional seeking precedent, or an individual exploring the latest culinary trends, Google adapts to your needs and improves while delivering results. It understands the nuances of your queries and personalizes the search rankings accordingly. This adaptability ensures that the information it provides is not only relevant but also valuable to the individual searcher.

The profound transformation brought about by Google's use of AI extends beyond mere convenience. It has democratized information access, turning the once arduous task of finding accurate information into a dynamic and ever-improving experience. No longer confined to rigid algorithms, the search engine evolves with the user, making each search more precise and personalized. But the impact doesn't stop at personalization. By making information access more intuitive and efficient, Google's AI

---

[8] https://blog.google/technology/ai/9-ways-we-use-ai-in-our-products/.

is breaking down barriers that once hindered the free flow of knowledge. It's leveling the playing field, ensuring that information is accessible to all, regardless of background or expertise or geographic location.

In a world where information is power, Google's use of AI to enhance access is a game changer that express the potential of generative AI to not only meet our needs but also to anticipate them, connecting us with the knowledge we seek and fostering a more informed and engaged global community.

1.2.2 *Personalization and polarization in social media*

Personalization has become a defining feature of our online experiences. Meta, the tech giant behind platforms including Facebook and Instagram, stands at the forefront of this transformation, leveraging the power of AI to create highly personalized digital environments on our mobile feeds.[9]

Through meticulous analysis of user behaviors, from the posts we like to how long we linger on a photo, Meta's algorithms curate a bespoke digital tapestry for each user. This isn't just about showing you content that might interest you; it's about creating a digital space that reflects and resonates with your beliefs, interests, and values. It's an area where your views are not just acknowledged but also echoed and amplified.

This level of personalization has undeniable allure. It enhances user engagement, making social media platforms more appealing and, in a way, addictive. It creates a sense of belonging, a feeling that the digital world understands and caters to you – fundamental premises to allow advertisers to leverage users' attention and effectively position their campaign. But this personalized experience carries with it profound implications.

As these algorithms become more adept at discerning our preferences, they inadvertently narrow the spectrum of content we're normally exposed to. Instead of a diverse and challenging array of opinions, we find ourselves in echo chambers, insulated from viewpoints that might contradict or challenge our beliefs. This, combined with the pervasiveness that these platforms have achieved in recent years, could lead to significant consequences from a social, economic, and political standpoint.

---

[9] https://about.fb.com/news/2023/06/how-ai-ranks-content-on-facebook-and-instagram/.

For the younger generation, for example, this is particularly concerning. Adolescence and young adulthood are pivotal periods of cognitive and social development. Exposure to a variety of perspectives is crucial in shaping a well-rounded, critical, and empathetic worldview. Yet if young individuals are consistently fed a diet of homogenized content, they risk developing a myopic view of the world. This can foster intolerance, reduce critical thinking abilities, and diminish the capacity for constructive discourse.

The phenomenon of polarization, where individuals gravitate toward extreme viewpoints and become less receptive to middle-ground opinions, is exacerbated by such echo chambers. In a world already rife with divisions, these AI-driven platforms could inadvertently deepen societal fissures.

The implications here are vast, from shaping electoral outcomes to influencing public opinion on critical issues such as climate change, healthcare, or human rights. The power of personalization in social media is a force to be reckoned with. It's about how we think, how we interact with others, and ultimately, how we shape our society.

In the development of projects with intense use of AI, the famous quote from the movie Spiderman must always be kept in mind: "with great power comes great responsibility." As we delve deeper into the world of AI-driven personalization, we must be mindful of the ethical considerations and potential consequences. It's about fostering a healthy and diverse digital ecosystem that respects and nurtures our shared humanity. (We go deeper into this topic in Chapter 9, "Transparency, Ethics, and Responsibility.")

1.2.3 *AI's impact on artists and listeners*

In the world of music, discovery has always been a key part of the listener's experience. Spotify, the widely used music streaming service, has taken this sense of discovery and transformed it into an exciting adventure powered by AI.[10] This transformation is revolutionizing our daily connection with music.

---

10   https://shabbiraliofficial.medium.com/the-spotify-artificial-intelligence-synergy-transforming-music-discovery-96ae259c8797.

By truly understanding your unique musical preferences, from specific beats and instruments to your favorite artists, Spotify's AI opens up a whole new realm of songs and hidden treasures for you to explore. It's like embarking on a personalized musical expedition guided by an AI companion that truly comprehends your tastes. It surprises you with relevant recommendations that delight your senses. This innovative approach to discovery represents a fundamental shift in how we interact with music; it's about embracing curiosity, venturing into unexplored territories, and experiencing that exhilarating feeling when we stumble upon something fresh and deeply meaningful.

This AI-powered approach also provides valuable insights for musicians themselves, allowing them to gain a deeper understanding of what songs, beats, or lyrics resonate the most with their audience or even how they can further refine their artistic direction. This creates a cycle of feedback that empowers artists to grow and develop in ways that were previously unattainable. It also enables them to monetize their fan base in innovative and unprecedented ways, not only enhancing the music experience but also shaping the music industry itself. By breaking down old barriers and forging new connections, Spotify's AI brings together artists and audiences, transforming the way music is shared and enjoyed. This transformation is redefining success in the music world by allowing talent to shine regardless of financial support or industry connections. For young independent musicians, this represents a significant game changer. They can now upload their music on the platform and connect with listeners who genuinely appreciate their style, establishing personal connections with individuals for whom their music resonates on a deep level. This personalized bond between artists and listeners contributes to a more diverse and vibrant musical landscape. In this manner, Spotify's AI impact extends beyond personal enjoyment alone; it is democratizing the music industry by leveling the playing field for emerging young musicians who lack major record label support.

To keep users engaged and excited, Spotify consistently introduces them to new music that aligns with their preferences. Each time users log in, they are greeted with fresh recommendations, thoughtfully curated playlists, and surprising musical connections. This dynamic engagement creates a sense of connection and loyalty to the platform. Switching to another service becomes more challenging not just in terms of cost but also because users would miss out on the personalized experience of discovering a new set of music that evolves over time. While other platforms may offer similar music catalogs, Spotify's AI understands individual tastes in a way that consistently surprises and delights listeners with new discoveries.

This functionality taps into psychological principles such as curiosity and reward. By consistently providing fresh and relevant musical content, Spotify ignites listeners' curiosity. The joy of finding a new favorite song or artist acts as a reward, reinforcing the user's engagement with the platform. It's an ingenious and effective method to ensure that users remain engaged and thoroughly enjoy their AI-enabled Spotify experience.

1.2.4   *Customer interaction and AI*

In the realm of customer service, the emergence of AI-powered solutions has brought about a significant change in how businesses engage with their customers on different levels. Among these tools are the so-called chatbots, which are essentially software applications designed to engage in online conversations, simulating interactions much like a human would. These chatbots aim to understand and respond to written or spoken language, quickly addressing customer inquiries. This functionality is enabled by natural language processing (NLP), a specialized field within AI that allows chatbots to comprehend, interpret, and generate human language.[11]

These tools, driven by specific AI algorithms, have become increasingly commonplace and offer immediate assistance across various domains and contexts. One notable advantage of chatbots is their ability to provide 24/7 support; in contrast to human agents, they do not require rest or breaks. They can deliver round-the-clock help, ensuring customers from different time zones can receive immediate support consistently. This proves especially advantageous for businesses with a global customer base. Moreover, chatbots can continuously learn and enhance their performance over time. By analyzing previous interactions, they can identify common queries or issues and adjust their responses accordingly.

This ability of AI-powered chatbots to learn and adapt makes them incredibly valuable for enhancing customer service. They can continu-

---

[11]   https://en.wikipedia.org/wiki/Natural_language_processing.

ously evolve to meet the changing needs of various user segments. In many cases these chatbots also serve as a valuable source of insights on customers. Through their interactions with customers, they gather a wealth of data that can be analyzed to gain a deeper understanding of customer behavior, preferences, and perceptions.

One significant aspect that can be extracted from chatbot data is how customers discuss a company's product or service. By examining the language used by customers, businesses can identify the keywords and phrases commonly employed when referring to their offerings. This information can shape marketing and communication strategies by aligning messaging with the language, tone of voice, and words preferred by customers. For example, if customers frequently describe a product as "innovative," the business may choose to highlight this aspect in their marketing materials. Similarly, if customers often express confusion about a specific feature, the business might opt to provide clearer instructions or explanations.

Furthermore, real-time reputation analysis becomes possible using chatbot data. By monitoring chatbot interactions, businesses can track shifts in customer sentiment and perceptions over time. If there is a sudden increase in negative comments, it could indicate a potential issue with the company's reputation that needs to be addressed. At the same time, positive comments may suggest a successful marketing campaign or a well-received product update.

In contrast to traditional surveys or focus groups, which can take weeks or even months to gather and analyze data, chatbots offer immediate feedback. This enables businesses to respond swiftly to emerging trends or concerns, enhancing their agility and responsiveness.

However, integrating AI models into business goes beyond customer service and reputation analysis. As an illustration, in the field of e-commerce, generative AI has the power to redefine product descriptions and catalogs in an efficient and effective way. By analyzing customer behavior and preferences, AI can create product descriptions that resonate with the target audience and make them more compelling and relevant. This personalized approach leads to higher conversion rates and an overall more satisfying shopping experience. Furthermore, generative AI can automate the creation of product images that align with customer preferences and current trends. This scalability in image development saves businesses time and resources while allowing them to adapt quickly to market changes.

As previously mentioned, this adoption of AI is no longer limited to large corporations with extensive resources. In today's world, small and medium-sized businesses (SMEs) are also realizing the transformative capabilities of AI. By suggesting products based on past purchases and tailoring marketing messages to individual preferences, AI empowers small businesses to offer a personalized experience to their customers. This level of customization can foster stronger customer loyalty and boost conversion rates, enabling SMEs to stand out in a competitive market.

1.3 Generative AI as a new creative frontier

At a point where creativity has become both a highly sought-after talent and a vital business commodity, the advent of generative AI is heralding a new and fascinating era. As discussed earlier, these large language models and specialized tools are doing more than just automating content creation; they are weaving a new tapestry of creative expression.

Standing at the threshold of this innovative frontier, we are faced with profound implications and limitless possibilities. The mastery of prompt engineering, the elegance of human-like text generation, and the crafting of search engine optimization (SEO)-optimized content are not mere technological feats; they are the precursors to a novel creative age. In this section, we delve into how generative AI is not only augmenting the creative process but also forging a future where human ingenuity and AI meld together in extraordinary harmony.

The once exclusive terrain of human intuition and inspiration in creativity is experiencing a tectonic transformation. In this context, generative AI emerges as a partner, a collaborator, and at times even an inspiring muse. Let's explore the different kinds of generative AI that are pioneering new pathways across various creative fields.

1.3.1 *Text-based generative AI*

The written word has found a new ally in generative AI, which is reshaping the landscape of content creation in many ways. In the realm of text-based generative AI, a fascinating convergence of technology and creativity is taking place. These AI models, such as OpenAI's GPT, are not just mimicking human-like text; they are enhancing the creative process, providing personalized and effective solutions across various domains. But how does text-based generative AI work?

At the heart of this technology lies the ability to predict the next word in a sequence. Imagine reading the beginning of a sentence and instinctively knowing what word comes next. That's what these models do, but on an incredibly sophisticated scale. They begin their learning journey by immersing themselves in vast oceans of text data, gathered from every conceivable corner of the internet, books, articles, and more. This extensive reading helps them grasp the structure, grammar, and subtle nuances of human language. It's similar to a child learning to speak by listening to adults but at an exponentially accelerated pace.

It is important to underline that human supervisors play a crucial role in this learning process. They act as teachers, providing correct answers to prompts and guiding the model toward understanding the right responses. They also rank different answers, instilling in the model a sense of quality and relevance. It's a collaborative dance between human intuition and machine learning, each step fine-tuned to create a harmonious blend of artificial and human intelligence.

But the learning doesn't stop there. These models can be tailored for specific tasks, whether writing in Shakespearean prose or generating content for a tech blog. This fine-tuning is achieved through a delicate process known as "prompt engineering," where the input is artfully crafted to steer the model's response in the desired direction. And the models continue to evolve, adapting and improving over time. They are not static entities but dynamic learners, constantly refining their understanding of language and their ability to generate text that resonates with human readers.

The already mentioned ChatGPT is a prime example of this technology and has been designed to assist a wide range of users. From small business owners crafting personalized marketing campaigns to academics summarizing dense research content, the applications are diverse and impactful. The art of prompt engineering, fine-tuning the model's responses, is becoming a vital skill, allowing for more targeted and relevant outputs. But the integration of GPT technology is not confined to OpenAI. Other tech giants, such as Microsoft with Bing Chat and Google with Google Bard, are also exploring this terrain. They offer different response modes, such as conversational interfaces and real-time access to current events, providing accurate and context-aware results. These variations reflect the diverse applications and the competitive landscape of generative AI.

Specialized AI writing assistants such as Jasper AI take this innovation a step further.[12] They have been fine-tuned for specific business and marketing applications, resulting in optimized and SEO-friendly content. Unlike generic AI models, these apps/tools are tailored to industry-specific needs, enhancing the creative process without replacing human creativity. They serve as collaborative tools that augment human abilities rather than supplant them.

The implications of text-based generative AI are profound. It's about empowerment and democratization. By leveling the playing field, it enables small businesses to compete with larger corporations, providing them with tools previously accessible only to well-funded entities. Moreover, it allows individuals to express themselves more eloquently, bridging the gap between professional writers and those who may lack the relevant skills or resources.

1.3.2 Text-to-image generative AI

Visual creativity is reaching new heights with text-to-image generative AI. The process is similar to that already covered for text-based generative AI and begins with training the model on vast datasets comprising both text descriptions and corresponding images. This dual understanding of language and visual cues allows the model to form connections between words and the visual elements they represent.

The model's learning process is akin to an artist studying under various masters, absorbing different styles, techniques, and interpretations. It learns not just what a tree looks like, but also how different words can represent a tree's various aspects, from its gnarled bark to the way its leaves flutter in the wind.

Human guidance, once again, plays a vital role in this learning journey. Supervisors provide feedback, correct misunderstandings, and help the model refine its visual vocabulary. It's a collaborative effort that melds human creativity with machine precision.

---

[12] https://www.jasper.ai/.

Once trained, the model can take a textual prompt and begin the process of visual creation. However, it does not involve a linear path from words to image; it's an iterative process where the model generates multiple drafts, each one a step closer to the final visual representation. In this way tools such as DALL-E by OpenAI can create images based on text prompts, offering a wide variety of concepts, tones, and styles.[13] Whether you're a marketing professional needing an eye-catching graphic or a student wanting to illustrate a concept, Dall-E can transform your words into visuals, bridging the gap between imagination and realization. It's a tool that transcends traditional boundaries, enabling people with various backgrounds and skill levels to engage in artistic expression. But this landscape is far from monolithic.

There are other models, including Stable Diffusion and Midjourney, each of which has unique fine-tuning controls and artistic capabilities.[14] Stable Diffusion, on the one hand, offers an approach that is focused on the generation of high-quality images through a controlled random process. It's a playground for experimentation, where users can explore textures, colors, and forms, guided by the underlying intelligence of the algorithm. It's not just about producing an image; it's about discovering new aesthetic possibilities and pushing the boundaries of visual language. Midjourney, on the other hand, represents another facet of this democratization, providing a platform for both creation and collaboration. It's a space where artists and non-artists can come together, leveraging AI to enhance their creativity, share ideas, and build upon each other's work. It's a community-driven approach that fosters innovation and inclusivity.

These are not just incredible tools; they are artistic partners, enabling creators to explore new horizons of visual expression. But this is not just a game for new players or startups: Adobe's Firefly AI generator integrates seamlessly with Creative Cloud apps, providing impressive control over style, color, tone, and more.[15] This integration is particularly noteworthy in the context of Adobe's flagship product, Photoshop, a tool that millions of people around the world use every day. By embedding this AI-powered functionality within a platform already familiar to design-

---

[13] https://openai.com/dall-e-2.

[14] https://stablediffusionweb.com/; https://www.midjourney.com/app/.

[15] https://www.adobe.com/sensei/generative-ai/firefly.html.

ers, photographers, and hobbyists, Adobe has made sophisticated image manipulation and generation accessible to a broader audience.

Users who have honed their skills on Photoshop can now explore new creative horizons without the need to learn a completely new tool. Firefly's capabilities, such as style transfer, color adjustment, and texture manipulation, are available right within the Photoshop interface. This allows for a more intuitive and efficient workflow, where AI-enhanced features can be leveraged alongside traditional Photoshop tools.

These tools cater to various creative needs, from research and ideation to final results, each with its unique flair and functionality.

Text-to-image generative AI can be used in education to illustrate complex concepts, turning abstract theories into tangible visuals. In healthcare, it can visualize medical conditions, providing a new perspective on patient care. In entertainment, it creates immersive virtual worlds, redefining the boundaries of storytelling.

1.3.3 *Image-to-image generative AI*

By taking existing images and transforming them into new visuals, models such as DALL-E and Stable Diffusion have opened up a new realm of possibilities. These tools operate by employing deep learning algorithms that understand and interpret visual data. By analyzing existing images, they learn the intricate relationships between various visual traits such as shape, color, texture, and lighting. This learning process requires substantial computational resources and a vast dataset to train the models, enabling them to generate new, realistic imagery that adheres to specific parameters or artistic styles.

The applications of this technology are vast and multifaceted. From artistic creation to face filters, lighting scenarios, image restoration, and style transfer, image-to-image generative AI offers specific results that empower creators to add or remove elements within an image. Artists can now experiment with shapes and textures in ways previously unimaginable, while designers can manipulate lighting and color to create stunning visual effects. The ability to restore damaged images or transfer styles from one image to another has also brought new dimensions to photography and graphic design.

Beyond individual creativity, image-to-image generative AI is redefining entire industries. In architecture, it's enhancing designs by allowing architects to visualize different lighting scenarios or material textures. Personalized fashion collections can be created by integrating individual preferences and styles, making fashion more accessible and tailored to individual tastes.

While the technology offers immense potential, it also of course raises ethical considerations. The ability to manipulate images so precisely can lead to misuse, such as creating deepfakes or altering historical images. Ensuring responsible use and creating clear guidelines for ethical practices is paramount.

Moreover, the technology's complexity and the need for significant computational resources may limit its accessibility to a broader audience. Bridging this gap and making image-to-image generative AI available to all while considering ethical and legal issues will be a critical challenge moving forward.

1.3.4 *Audio-based generative AI*

From voice cloning technology, such as Respeecher,[16] to text-to-speech software that creates natural-sounding human voices, the applications of audio-based generative AI are diverse and far-reaching. Over the past decade, significant advancements in AI-powered audio generation techniques have been witnessed, including music and speech synthesis. With foundational ideas from large language models and text-to-image generation being adapted into the audio modality, AI-powered audio-generative systems are reaching unprecedented levels of quality. Google's audio-generative model MusicLM, for instance, can generate a guitar solo in a matter of seconds.[17] Audio signals represent one of the most multifaceted data types that we regularly encounter. Creating synthetic audio that convincingly mirrors real-world sounds requires systems that can understand and encode various types of information uniformly. This includes semantic aspects such as the consistency of speech or melodic/harmonic consistency in music, and acoustic aspects including the unique tone of a voice or the timbre of a musical instrument.

The main difference between audio and other modalities such as text and image lies in the amount of high-quality data available for training.

---

[16] https://www.respeecher.com/.
[17] https://blog.google/technology/ai/musiclm-google-ai-test-kitchen/.

While image and text data is abundant, audio data is comparably scarce or expensive. Text-to-audio AI models used to depend almost entirely on acoustic models, which transform text into mel-spectrograms. While these models have demonstrated some degree of effectiveness, they require high-quality audio data for training, which is both scarce and costly.

The applications of audio-based generative AI are indeed diverse, from enhancing accessibility for the visually impaired to revolutionizing the music industry by enabling young and independent artists to create professional-quality compositions.

Sir Paul McCartney, in late 2023, utilized AI to craft what he refers to as "the final Beatles record."[18] The technology was employed to extract John Lennon's voice from an old demo, allowing McCartney to complete a song likely to be a 1978 Lennon composition called "Now and Then." Use of this song had previously been considered for a Beatles reunion in 1995 but was abandoned due to sound quality issues and a lack of verses. The turning point came with Peter Jackson's "Get Back" documentary, where AI was used to separate the Beatles' voices from background noises. McCartney described the AI process as "scary but exciting" and acknowledged the potential concerns about other applications of AI.

1.3.5 Video-based generative AI

Today the way we consume and interact with moving images is constantly evolving. Video-based generative AI is at the forefront of this revolution, adding the dimension of time to image creation and offering possibilities including upscaling, deinterlacing, motion interpolation, and more. But how does this technology work, and what are its implications?

The process starts with the selection of a dataset containing images, videos, and audio clips that correspond to the desired theme. The AI model is then trained on this dataset using neural networks and computer vision. Once trained, it can generate new videos by combining and manipulating elements from the dataset according to specified parameters. These videos can be further refined and optimized through additional training and editing. For example, text-to-video is a common AI

---

[18] https://www.bbc.com/news/entertainment-arts-65881813.

generation tool that allows people to write a text prompt and convert it into video. The AI video generation tool takes the text prompt, crawls the internet, and interprets the information, contextualizing it to fit the prompt and condensing billions of options into one neat, digestible video. HeyGen serves as an example of harnessing the prowess of generative AI in the realm of video creation. This platform effortlessly transforms text into video, employing AI-generated avatars and voices. Users can choose from a vast array of avatars or craft their own and select voices from a rich library spanning over forty languages. With HeyGen, the once formidable barriers of costly equipment and complex editing tools crumble, ushering in a new era of accessible, efficient video production.[19]

Deepfake technology, a complex form of AI, can replace a person's likeness in a video, leading to both beneficial and controversial applications. Digital video avatars offer low-budget ways to create marketing content, and the impact of video-based generative AI is far-reaching. It enhances film production, creates personalized educational content, and changes how we consume and interact with moving images.

In architecture, AI-generated video content enhances designs by allowing visualization of different lighting scenarios or material textures. In the fashion industry, personalized collections can be created by integrating individual preferences and styles.

The technology also threatens to disrupt big players in video streaming such as Netflix, TikTok, and YouTube, changing the power and economics of video streaming. Content creators can create smarter content, and the potential number of content creators explodes as barriers to creating video content fall.

While the technology offers immense potential, it also raises, once again, ethical considerations. The ability to manipulate images so precisely can lead to misuse, such as creating deepfakes or altering historical images. Ensuring responsible use and creating clear guidelines for ethical practices is paramount.

---

[19] https://www.heygen.com/.

1.4 The new frontier: How generative AI is reshaping corporate communication

I consider myself extremely lucky. Throughout my life, I have had the privilege of witnessing the three truly transformative moments in the business world that we discussed earlier: the advent of browsers, the introduction of the first iPhone, and the emergence of cloud services such as AWS. I have actively participated in these revolutions, and they have become integral components of both my personal and professional life.

The arrival of browsers brought about a rapid expansion of the internet's capabilities and gave birth to e-commerce and, later, to streaming services. This was during a time when society was just beginning to explore the immense potential offered by the digital landscape. Our shopping habits, education methods, and even communication styles were forever transformed.

Then came the iPhone. Not only did it redefine personal communication, but it also paved the way for technological breakthroughs such as GPS integration and 5G connectivity. These advancements laid the foundations for services and features that were once considered no more than fantasies. From navigation assistance to streaming entertainment content to mobile banking solutions, smartphones revolutionized our day-to-day lives by making technology an indispensable part of our existence.

Lastly, we cannot overlook the significance of cloud services such as AWS in this narrative. Their development marked yet another major milestone in shaping our modern business and technology world.

The democratization of technology has been a game changer, allowing businesses of all sizes to access powerful computing resources. The advent of the cloud has completely transformed how we store, process, and share information, fostering innovation and adaptability in a rapidly evolving world.

Speaking from personal experience, I've noticed a common pattern in these transformations. They typically begin with resistance from the industries, followed by curiosity and interest that eventually lead to widespread adoption and integration into our daily lives. However, these transitions are far from easy or painless. I distinctly remember engaging in heated debates with a CEO back in the early 2000s who doubted the effectiveness of email as a work tool. Instead, they preferred traditional messaging systems within their company's network. Unfortunately, that company's refusal to embrace change ultimately led to its downfall, and numerous others have faced similar fates due to an inability to accept and navigate the impacts of change within their organizations.

It is through experimentation, trial and error, and hands-on experience that we can truly understand the opportunities, limitations, and challenges presented by these tools. Although this process can be time consuming and demanding at times, it is not merely a luxury but rather an absolute necessity. It serves as our pathway toward innovation and adaptation in a world that never ceases moving forward.

In the world of communication, it's extremely important to be effective and avoid being superficial. Adapting to change, learning from mistakes, and moving forward are not just strategies; they are essential skills for survival in the ever-changing landscape of business and technology.

Generative AI is already transforming how we communicate both within and outside our organizations. It unlocks new possibilities and efficiencies, reshaping our professional interactions to be more dynamic, responsive, and personalized.

This technology enhances productivity in ways that we have not yet fully grasped. It automates repetitive tasks, giving employees more time to focus on strategic and creative endeavors. Additionally, it facilitates real-time collaboration by seamlessly integrating with existing collaboration platforms. This enables team members to work together effortlessly across different time zones and locations. For instance, it can analyze project conversations, suggest responses based on previous interactions, and even predict the needs of team members, fostering a connected and efficient work environment.

Enhanced writing tools powered by generative AI are revolutionizing every aspect of content creation. Whether it's composing emails, writing reports, or crafting marketing materials, these tools provide suggestions, corrections, and stylistic enhancements that align with the brand's voice and target audience.

Automating and customizing content creation not only saves time but also ensures consistency and quality across various communication channels. The impact of AI is noticeable in the field of public relations as well. From automating press release distribution to utilizing predictive analytics for identifying PR prospects, AI aids businesses in effectively communicating with the media and the public.

In investor relations, one significant advantage of AI is the automation of financial reporting. For example, the Associated Press has successfully utilized AI to increase their quarterly production of articles on earnings reports from 300 to an impressive 3,700. Such automation enhances efficiency while guaranteeing accurate and comprehensive financial reports, providing investors with reliable and timely information.

Generative AI also plays a crucial role in engaging customers. By analyzing customer behavior, preferences, and feedback, it can create personalized messages, offers, and support that align with marketing strategies. This level of customization leads to more meaningful interactions with customers, fostering trust and loyalty. In crisis communication scenarios as well, AI proves to be an invaluable ally. Real-time monitoring of social media and news outlets by AI tools alerts companies about potential crises before they escalate. This enables businesses to respond swiftly and effectively, minimizing harm to their reputation.

Furthermore, the ability of generative AI to process and analyze large volumes of data in real time is providing unprecedented insights into market trends, customer opinions, and competitive landscapes. These valuable insights empower businesses to make decisions based on data, refine their communication strategies, and adapt quickly to emerging opportunities and challenges.

However, what we are witnessing now is just the beginning. The impact of generative AI in corporate communication is comparable to the early stages of internet browsing or the launch of the first iPhone. We couldn't have predicted the immense potential of the App Store when the iPhone was initially released, and similarly, we may only be scratching the surface of what generative AI can offer.

The future possibilities are vast and largely unexplored. Like with any groundbreaking technology, diving in headfirst and experimenting is our best strategy for success. It's crucial that we get involved hands on, learn through trial and error, and remain open to unexpected innovations that may arise.

And that's where our journey begins.

Insight
Pioneering Generative AI in Commercial Real Estate

by *Barbara Cominelli*[*]

My journey with AI began at Vodafone roughly a decade ago when we launched a pioneering big data platform and a natural language processing chatbot called Tobi. Through the implementation of Tobi we revolutionized customer interaction, allowing customers to access Vodafone services in a simpler, faster, and richer way and providing customer care consultants with a powerful tool to support them in their job and improve their capabilities to serve, upsell, and cross-sell.

Subsequently, during my tenure at Microsoft, I had the privilege of assisting numerous clients in their digital transformation journeys by implementing AI solutions. I vividly recall the opportunity to share insights on the potential benefits of AI during our Microsoft innovation summit in Milan, where I took the stage after Satya Nadella's captivating keynote address to launch the Microsoft program "Ambizione Italia." The program aimed at making AI available to companies and institutions in Italy, as well as training 1.5 million people in the country on AI and digital technologies.

Now, at JLL, where I am the CEO for Italy, we have an ambitious plan to be the front runner in generative AI for commercial real estate (CRE). In August 2023, we made a significant breakthrough with the introduction of JLL GPT™, a pioneering language model designed exclusively for the CRE sector. This cutting-edge generative AI model is poised to transform how JLL's global workforce of over 103,000 professionals offers CRE insights to clients. Generative AI will enable consultants to

[*] CEO, JLL Italy and Retail lead EMEA.

provide data-driven and smarter insights, in less time, that are fully compliant with privacy policies, improving workplace planning strategies and space utilization and optimizing investment opportunities. By leveraging a combination of JLL's comprehensive internal data and external sources specific to CRE, we also plan to provide tailor-made solutions to clients in the near future.

In the past ten years, I have witnessed an exponential advance in technology, but I have also realized that some key leadership and management principles remain crucial to harness the potential of AI and embrace a successful transformation journey.

Indeed, in the past decade, we have seen incredible advancements in AI technology in terms of capabilities and performance, thanks to the intersection of machine learning, data, and computing power. Today, it's not just about simple digitalization and automation; it's about a completely new way of getting work done, with a technology that can help not only with productivity but also with generating new content, designs, or solutions with an unprecedented proficiency in writing, drawing, coding, and composing.

And we have seen the science move from niche to mainstream, making a quantum leap in terms of accessibility and ubiquity: AI can be used by anyone in an infinite number of scenarios and is being embedded everywhere, as using it requires virtually no technical training. This democratization of AI is and will be a key factor contributing to its future impact.

While the transformative potential of generative AI is increasingly evident, and its impact on organizations and the economy is projected to be profound, there are some leadership and managerial principles that underpin its successful application and utilization; technology is the enabler but not the only ingredient of a successful transformation.

The first principle is human centricity. The focus should be on augmenting, not replacing, human capabilities. We need to put people, not technology, at the center of our AI strategy, designing and deploying AI systems with a focus not on what the machine can do, but on how generative AI amplifies human skills and capabilities - how to empower people and increase organizational capabilities. This is at the core of our strategy in JLL: we recognize the value of AI as a tool that enhances human capabilities rather than replacing them outright. With the capacity to harness and analyze the immense volumes of data, AI has the potential to generate remarkable insights that will shape the future of the real estate industry. Our core mission is to empower our most valuable asset - our people - by equipping them with AI tools and leveraging their expertise in conjunction with AI-driven insights to deliver unparalleled value to our clients.

The second principle comprises vision and strategy. Today, if you do not have an AI and data strategy, you simply do not have a strategy. Technology is just an enabler; the competitive advantage lies in how you supercharge and augment your business through AI. As leaders, we are asked to have a vision and a roadmap of how we can augment our business, disassembling and reassembling it, like Lego bricks, but augmenting each Lego brick with data and AI in the process: decision-making, workplace experience, customer experience, operations, and ultimately the business model, product, and services we offer.

The third principle concerns ethics and responsibility, incorporating in our projects a broad set of principles that should make AI projects trustworthy: ethical use, privacy and security, transparency, fairness and avoidance of biases, risk management, and avoidance of unintended consequences. We should always ask ourselves not only what AI can do, but also what it should do, in an ethical and responsible way. Responsible AI extends beyond technical considerations. It requires a multidisciplinary approach, involving not only technologists but also ethicists, policymakers, and society as a whole. Establishing ethical frameworks, codes of conduct, and regulatory mechanisms can help ensure that AI technology aligns with human values and promotes the greater good.

Finally, the focus should be on competences, skills, and change management. For an AI project to be successful, we need to address some fundamental questions: What talent and skills do we need? Where do we find the right talent to support our AI projects? How do we address the skill mismatch and upgrade existing resources through upskilling and reskilling? How should each business line and function be organized to collaborate with AI? How do we redefine roles, responsibilities, and ultimately our entire organizations?

The knowledge and skills gap represents a major potential obstacle to successful implementation. For example, in our latest global technology survey, we found that AI and generative AI are considered among the top three technologies that corporate occupiers, investors, and developers predict will have the biggest influence on real estate in the next three years. However, in comparison with other technologies such as virtual reality and blockchain, AI and generative AI have the lowest level of understanding[1].

Implementing AI is ultimately a huge transformation program, and we need to address it from a broad perspective, focusing not only on technology but also, with a 360-degree view, on strategy, capabilities, and change management.

In conclusion, embracing AI and the core principles of human centricity, vision and strategy, ethics and responsibility, and addressing talent and skills gaps are essential for successfully harnessing the potential of AI in our transformation journey. By adopting a holistic approach and a strategic perspective, we can navigate the challenges and leverage the transformative power of AI in creating a better future for our organizations, our people, and society at large.

---

[1] JLL conducted research among 1,006 senior real estate decision-makers during May and June 2023.This included over 600 CRE (corporate real estate) leaders at major occupiers and over 400 leaders at real estate investors, landlords and developers. All respondents have responsibility for making or influencing decisions regarding real estate within their organization and hold senior leadership roles including department heads, executive management and C-level positions.

2   AI for Process Management, Internal Communication, and HR

2.1   AI in business processes: Enhancing efficiency and adaptation

As businesses seek to streamline processes and foster innovation, generative AI offers a promising avenue to explore. Its ability to analyze historical data allows it to identify patterns, uncover bottlenecks, and detect inefficiencies within business processes. This leads to actionable insights and recommendations that ensure optimal resource allocation and overall efficiency. But the promise of generative AI extends beyond mere optimization. Its standout feature is the ability to automate repetitive or mundane tasks. By training AI models on existing data and leveraging generative capabilities, decision-making processes can be automated, and tasks can be executed with increased efficiency, accuracy, and speed. This not only saves valuable time but also minimizes human error, paving the way for a more streamlined workflow.

Beyond optimization and automation, generative AI also fuels innovation in many ways. By generating new ideas, concepts, or designs, it opens up creative solutions and alternative approaches. This can lead to improved customer experiences, novel product development, and competitive differentiation.

2.1.1   *A Technology with a different DNA*

Throughout human history, groundbreaking inventions have not only transformed sectors but also redefined our very lives. The steam engine, telephone, and internet each marked a turning point, ushering in new ways of thinking, working, and living. Unlike the rigid, transactional technologies of the past, AI is a fluid, dynamic force. It transcends mere data capture and transfer; it's about understanding, learning, and adapting, serving as a general-purpose technology that enables better, faster, and automated decisions, essentially embodying a different technological DNA. For the knowledge workers who have dominated the job market in recent decades, these innovations are generating significant impacts from many viewpoints.

The transformative prowess of AI elevates meetings by automating administrative tasks, boosts sales and marketing through analytics and chatbots, assesses and improves customer service with automatic quality checks, revolutionizes product development processes through generative design, automates content generation, enhances manufacturing with collaborative robots, and refines recruitment processes. This new technological DNA isn't solely about automation and efficiency; it's about redefining the human–machine relationship, promoting collaboration, and unlocking new avenues for creativity and innovation.

A study by Boston Consulting Group disclosed that consultants utilizing AI complete 12.2 percent more tasks on average, perform tasks 25 percent faster, and produce 40 percent higher quality results.[1] AI-based virtual assistants can alleviate many tedious, repetitive tasks typically delegated to human assistants. Based on a survey conducted by Salesforce,[2] it was discovered that marketers have the potential to save five hours of repetitive tasks every week. The survey further revealed that a significant obstacle to adopting generative AI for better personalization is the lack of data, as acknowledged by 61 percent of marketers.

The integration of AI into business operations significantly benefits knowledge workers also by overcoming human biases, offering more objective viewpoints, and drawing on cross-domain knowledge. Its infinite patience and ability to generate multiple options make AI an exemplary "thought partner." As AI becomes increasingly integrated into our workflows, we should expect a seismic shift in performance metrics. Those who embrace AI will skyrocket in productivity, leaving the skeptics behind. The introduction of this innovation in the work environment will soon mark the end of interface friction. As AI streamlines user experiences, our tolerance for clunky, unintuitive interfaces will plummet.

---

[1] https://papers.ssrn.com/sol3/papers.cfm?abstract_id=4573321.
[2] https://www.salesforce.com/blog/personalization-challenges/.

Businesses that fail to adapt will find themselves becoming obsolete. However, joining the AI revolution comes with its challenges. One must be prepared to navigate through initial bugs, hallucinations, and other growing pains. It's the tax for early adoption, but the return on investment is invaluable.

As we explore AI's untapped potential, it's fascinating to realize that the AI we interact with today is the most primitive version we'll ever encounter. The evolution promises AI that's exponentially more efficient and user-friendly. Moreover, regularly auditing workflows will become an essential "work hygiene" to leverage AI effectively in daily tasks. Consumer services are already integrating AI through features such as chatbots, ushering AI into our daily interactions. Similarly, enterprise software that powers our daily work tasks is embracing AI; major platforms from Adobe to Salesforce to Google Docs will have AI embedded within them more and more in the coming years. This integration heralds an explosion not only in capabilities, which are astonishing yet at times alarming, but also in user engagement. This increased usage will further refine AI as user interactions help train these models, propelling us from early adopters to the early majority within the next several months.

To grasp the authenticity of this evolution, let's start by delving into the initiatives and innovations of one of the world's largest companies in this domain, as its AI endeavors provide a clear and compelling illustration of this transformative potential.

2.1.2   *The Amazon case study: From logistics to white collars*

Let's turn our attention to the retail giant Amazon, a prime example of AI implementation through its subsidiary Amazon Robotics, formerly known as Kiva Systems. This venture has revolutionized Amazon's logistics and operations, particularly in inventory management and delivery processes, setting a precedent for efficiency and automation in the retail sector. Traditionally, goods in distribution centers were moved using conveyor systems or human-operated machines. However, Amazon's acquisition of Kiva Systems in 2012 for $775 million marked a significant shift.[3] Kiva's approach involves mobile robotic fulfillment systems that

---

[3]   https://techcrunch.com/2012/03/19/amazon-acquires-online-fulfillment-company-kiva-systems-for-775-million-in-cash/.

navigate around the warehouse, following computerized barcode stickers on the floor. These robots, capable of lifting loads as heavy as 1,300 kilograms, retrieve items and carry them to human operators for picking.

This system has proven to be much more efficient and accurate than traditional methods. The robots' maximum velocity of 1.3 meters per second, coupled with their ability to recharge every hour for just five minutes, ensures that they are always ready to assist. By June 2019, Amazon had more than 200,000 robots working in their warehouses, a proof to the scale and success of this integration.

The advent of generative AI has propelled this technological evolution from the warehouses and factories into the white-collar realms of Amazon, impacting the way they operate. Beyond just managing logistics, generative AI, such as GPT models, is being leveraged by Amazon employees across various business operations. From enhancing customer service with AI-driven chatbots, to automating content generation for marketing, analyzing customer feedback for product development, and integrating tools such as ChatGPT for improved internal communication, the scope is extensive. This automation of routine tasks and intelligent assistance in decision-making processes is redirecting human resources toward more creative and strategic pursuits, heralding a modernized operational framework.

Amazon's exploration of AI technologies extends into the very core of its decision-making processes. For example, the company's unique approach to innovation, known as PRFAQ (Press Release and FAQ), requires employees to envision and articulate new ideas through a hypothetical press release and FAQ announcement.[4] This method ensures that the focus remains on customer needs and the potential impact of the innovation. Amazon has been planning to leverage generative AI to enhance this critical part of the decision-making process. Utilizing the natural language processing capabilities of LLMs, the staff believes they can speed up the PRFAQ process, allowing for more rapid development and assessment of new ideas. By automating the generation of press releases and FAQs, employees can concentrate on the creative and strategic aspects of their proposals, ensuring that the essence of the idea is captured without getting bogged down in the writing process.

---

[4] https://medium.com/intrico-io/strategy-tool-amazons-pr-faq-72b3e49aa167.

This potential application within Amazon's decision-making framework is yet another example of how the company is harnessing the power of AI to streamline operations and foster innovation. It reflects a broader trend within Amazon to integrate cutting-edge technologies into every facet of the business, from warehouse management to product development and internal decision-making processes.

Clearly Amazon has also harnessed generative AI across various functions of its e-commerce platform, enhancing operational efficiency and customer experience. Here's a more in-depth exploration of how generative AI is utilized within Amazon.

- **Product recommendations**: Amazon leverages generative AI to tailor product recommendations to its customers based on their browsing and purchase history. This technology enables the analysis of vast amounts of data to identify behavioral patterns, providing relevant suggestions that might appeal to the user.[5]
- **Content creation**: The platform employs generative AI for crafting product descriptions and titles, as well as generating images and videos. This automated process aids in maintaining a consistent and appealing presentation of products, enhancing product discovery by customers.
- **Customer service**: Amazon deploys generative AI to develop chatbots and virtual assistants capable of answering customer queries and providing support. These AI tools can handle a wide range of customer interactions, freeing up human personnel to handle more complex issues.
- **Fraud detection**: Utilizing generative AI, Amazon can identify fraudulent activities on its platform, such as fake reviews and counterfeit products. This technology scrutinizes data to detect anomalies that might indicate fraudulent behaviors.
- **Inventory management**: Generative AI aids Amazon in optimizing inventory management, forecasting demand, and ensuring that products are available when customers wish to purchase them. This reduces wait times and improves customer satisfaction.

---

[5] https://aws.amazon.com/it/blogs/machine-learning/announcing-new-tools-for-building-with-generative-ai-on-aws/.

Overall, Amazon's adoption of generative AI has contributed to delivering a more personalized and efficient shopping experience for its customers, in addition to improving business operations and reducing fraud. The integration of generative AI exemplifies how emerging technologies can be leveraged to enhance both operational efficiency and customer interaction in the e-commerce domain.

2.1.3 Creativity and business process management through AI

Once again – and we are going to repeat this concept a lot in this book – AI is not just a tool; it's a partner, a collaborator, a catalyst for change. How is that possible?

To understand how the revolutionary wave of generative AI is reshaping the business landscape, it may be useful to draw on another similitude. In the first chapter, we made a comparison with modern photography; now, we turn our attention to modern art. Artists such as Jackson Pollock have embraced randomness and spontaneity, allowing natural forces and chance to guide their creative process. This approach to art, though seemingly chaotic, has given birth to masterpieces that continue to inspire and challenge our understanding of creativity. Today, a similar revolution is taking place in the world of business, driven by generative AI. This revolution involves a philosophical shift that is redefining creativity, innovation, and optimization in business. Just as Pollock's drip paintings broke away from conventional artistic norms, generative AI is breaking away from traditional business practices. It offers a new toolkit for creative exploration, expanding the boundaries of what is creatively possible. The algorithms that generate new ideas and designs are akin to Pollock's paintbrush, guided by data rather than emotion but equally capable of producing something novel and valuable.

Generative AI's role in redefining optimization in business parallels the way modern art has redefined artistic creation. From supply chain management to customer engagement, AI algorithms are transforming traditional business operations, making them more agile and aligned with the ever-changing business landscape. The parallels between modern photography, modern art, and the business world highlight a universal truth: that true creativity often lies in the willingness to explore the unknown. It's a lesson that transcends disciplines and continues to resonate as we navigate the complex and ever-evolving landscape of business innovation. The fusion of art and technology, randomness and strategy, emotion and data paints a picture of a future where creativity knows no bounds. It's a future that beckons us to think beyond conventional boundaries and embrace the potential of the unexpected.

Consider the world of product design. In the past, designers would sketch, model, and iterate, constrained by the limitations of human imagination and physical laws. Today, generative AI algorithms can explore thousands of design possibilities in a fraction of the time, optimizing for specific criteria such as strength, weight, or cost. It's a process that's not just faster but also more innovative, unlocking design potentials that were previously unimaginable. By leveraging the creative capabilities of generative AI, companies are discovering innovative approaches to problem-solving, enhancing efficiency, and forging more personalized and engaging connections with their clientele.

Indeed, the beauty of generative AI lies in its ability to combine the precision of machines with the creativity of humans. It's a synergy that's empowering businesses to explore, experiment, and excel. It's a collaboration that's breaking down the silos between departments, fostering a culture of innovation and adaptation.

By harnessing AI's capabilities, intricate and monotonous tasks are transformed into smooth, efficient processes. This technological synergy liberates human minds from the mundane, unlocking their potential to explore the creative, strategize the innovative, and connect on a more profound human level.

2.1.4 *Leading AI-Enabled Process Change: Strategy and Implementation*

The integration of AI into business processes, especially within the daily routines of knowledge workers, unlocks immense potential for growth and innovation. However, navigating the path to successful AI implementation poses challenges, necessitating a well-orchestrated strategy. As illustrated by the Amazon case, leading AI-enabled process change transcends mere technology adoption; it entails aligning AI with business objectives, nurturing collaboration, and maintaining a vigilant eye on performance. Here's a deep dive into these pivotal facets.

Step 1. Alignment with business goals
   • **Understanding objectives**: Before diving into AI implementation,

it's crucial to have a clear understanding of what the business aims to achieve. Is it about enhancing customer experience, improving efficiency, or driving innovation? Example: A logistics company wants to reduce delivery times. By clearly defining this objective, they can implement AI algorithms that optimize routing, taking into account traffic, weather, and other variables.

- **Tailoring AI solutions:** AI is not a one-size-fits-all solution. It must be tailored to meet specific business needs and objectives. This requires a deep understanding of the industry, the challenges, and the opportunities. Example: A bank wants to enhance fraud detection. It will need to tailor AI solutions specifically to analyze transaction patterns, recognize suspicious activities, and alert the security team, rather than using generic AI models.

- **Measuring success:** Setting clear and measurable key performance indicators (KPIs) ensures that the AI implementation is aligned with business goals and provides a benchmark for success. Example: An e-commerce platform implements AI for personalized recommendations. Success can be measured through KPIs such as increased conversion rates, average order value, and customer satisfaction scores.

Step 2. Collaboration and building a diverse team

- **Breaking silos:** AI implementation is not just an IT (information technology) project; it's a business transformation that requires collaboration across various departments, including marketing, sales, operations, and HR (human resources). *Example*: In a manufacturing firm, the production, quality control, IT, and sales departments must collaborate to implement AI that synchronizes production schedules with sales forecasts and quality standards.

- **Building a diverse team:** A successful AI project requires a mix of skills, including data scientists, business analysts, IT professionals, and domain experts. Building a cross-functional team fosters creativity and ensures that all aspects of the business are considered. *Example*: A healthcare provider implementing AI for patient care would need a team comprising medical experts, data scientists, IT professionals, and ethical compliance officers to ensure a holistic approach.

- **Fostering a culture of innovation:** Collaboration is not just about working together; it's also about fostering a culture of innovation and continuous learning. Encouraging open communication, experimentation, and failure can lead to groundbreaking solutions. *Example*: A tech startup encourages its employees to experiment with new AI algorithms, even if they fail initially. This culture of innovation leads to the development of cutting-edge solutions.

Step 3. Continuous monitoring and adaptation

- **Real-time performance tracking**: AI is dynamic, and its performance must be monitored in real time. This includes tracking accuracy, efficiency, and alignment with business goals. *Example*: A stock trading platform uses AI for real-time market analysis. Continuous monitoring of the system's accuracy and responsiveness ensures that it keeps up with rapid market changes.
- **Adaptation to changing needs**: The business landscape is ever changing, and AI solutions must adapt to meet new challenges and opportunities. Continuous monitoring allows for timely adjustments and ensures that the AI system remains relevant. *Example*: A retail chain uses AI for inventory management. As consumer preferences shift, the AI system must adapt to new trends, requiring ongoing adjustments to algorithms and data inputs.

The integration of AI into business processes is a present-day reality, filled with potential but also complex challenges. Success in this endeavor requires more than just adopting new technology; it demands a strategic alignment with business goals, robust collaboration across various departments, and continuous monitoring and adaptation. By understanding the specific objectives, such as enhancing customer experience or improving efficiency, businesses can tailor AI solutions to their unique needs. Building diverse, cross-functional teams fosters creativity and ensures that all aspects of the business are considered. Continuous real-time monitoring, adaptation to changing needs, and adherence to ethical guidelines and regulations are vital for sustained success. Leading AI-enabled process change is a rewarding journey that can lead to enhanced efficiency, innovation, and a competitive edge in today's dynamic business landscape. Whether it's a small startup aiming for disruptive innovation or a multinational corporation seeking to streamline global operations, these principles can serve as a comprehensive guide to harnessing the transformative power of AI.

2.2   Revolutionizing internal communication

So far, we have understood that the integration of AI into various aspects of business is no longer merely a concept; it's a reality that's shaping the future of all industries in many areas, from logistics to business meetings. One of the most significant areas where AI is making a profound impact is in internal communication and collaboration within organizations. Traditional communication methods rely on manual processes, hierarchical structures, and siloed information. These conventional models have led to significant challenges, including time-consuming procedures, loss of critical information, and a profound inefficiency that hampers innovation and responsiveness. In contrast, AI's ability to streamline communication, break down barriers, and provide real-time insights is revolutionizing the way organizations operate. By replacing outdated methods with intelligent, adaptive systems, businesses are unlocking new potentials for collaboration, agility, and growth. This transformation is akin to the invention of the printing press, marking a revolution in knowledge dissemination and accessibility.

2.2.1   *Redefining a Company's Internal Knowledge*

In the typical company, knowledge has traditionally been tribal and elusive, often passed down through apprenticeship without proper documentation. This informal transfer of information has led to a lack of structure and consistency, making it challenging to define where knowledge resides within an organization. The result has been a fragmented and inefficient system where vital insights and expertise can be lost or overlooked.

But with the advent of AI, we are witnessing a paradigm shift that is transforming the way companies manage and disseminate knowledge. For the first time, we can train AI models such as LLMs on everything that has ever been written, said, or published within a company. This includes not only formal documents but also emails, chat logs, and even recorded conversations.

This ability to codify and embody an organization's collective knowledge is transformative. It's akin to the transition from the oral transmission of knowledge to the printing of books, where knowledge became accessible to the masses. It's a shift that democratizes information, making it available to everyone within the organization, regardless of rank or role.

Just as the printing press allowed a mathematician to share his knowledge with millions through printed books, AI enables us to interact with something that represents the collective knowledge of an organization. This knowledge, accumulated over the years, can be passed on to the next generation through AI, redefining the way we accumulate, codify, and distribute it. But what does this mean for businesses, and how is AI shaping the way we communicate within organizations? The implications are profound and far-reaching.

One of the first examples of what can be done in this area is provided by McKinsey, the nearly century-old consulting behemoth.[6] The consulting firm launched in mid-2023 its own generative AI tool named "Lilli" for its employees. Designed by McKinsey's "ClienTech" team, Lilli is not just another chat application. It's a tool that serves up information, insights, data, and plans and even points employees to the most suitable internal experts for consulting projects. All of this is based on a vast reservoir of over 100,000 documents and interview transcripts. Named in honor of Lillian Dombrowski, the first woman McKinsey hired for a professional services role in 1945, Lilli represents a significant leap in the firm's commitment to innovation, and since its beta launch the tool has already demonstrated its value, slashing research and planning times from weeks to mere hours or even minutes in some cases.

It's easy to envisage that the example of McKinsey will not remain an isolated one. Among consulting firms, EY has already taken strides in this domain by announcing the launch of EY.ai, a platform aimed at assisting clients in ramping up AI adoption.[7] The platform encapsulates an AI ecosystem endowed with a spectrum of capabilities, thanks to partnerships with notable corporations including Microsoft (which granted EY early access to Azure OpenAI capabilities) and others. Observing the expansive scope of EY, with 360,000 personnel and a broad spectrum of tools and capabilities, it's evident that the organization possesses a vast reservoir of knowledge. However, this knowledge appears to be dispersed, lacking a tangible form, despite representing the essence of the organization. The

---

[6] https://venturebeat.com/ai/consulting-giant-mckinsey-unveils-its-own-generative-ai-tool-for-employees-lilli/.

[7] https://venturebeat.com/ai/ey-launches-ai-platform-and-llm-after-1-4-billion-investment/.

challenge lies then in transitioning this immaterial wealth of knowledge into a structured ontology through these new technologies.

AI's role in internal communications and knowledge sharing, as McKinsey's and EY's forays into this space shows, is about more than just efficiency; it's about aligning these new technologies with the strategic goals of the organization. This alignment is crucial for ensuring that AI serves the broader objectives of enhancing engagement, personalizing experiences, and fostering a culture of collaboration.

By leveraging AI, companies can create a dynamic and responsive knowledge management system that adapts to the needs of the organization. It can provide real-time insights, facilitate cross-departmental collaboration, and empower employees with the information they need to make informed decisions.

Furthermore, AI can personalize the way information is delivered, tailoring content to individual preferences and roles. This personalization fosters a more engaged and satisfied workforce, enhancing productivity and innovation.

2.2.2 *Engagement and collaboration in an AI-enabled workplace*

Let's start with the basics: in the fast-paced world of business, real-time engagement is key to success. AI-powered tools enable organizations to communicate with employees instantaneously, providing them with timely updates, feedback, and support. This not only enhances efficiency but also builds a sense of connection and trust within the organization. Whether it's tailoring content to specific roles, interests, or needs, AI ensures that communication is relevant and resonant. This personalization fosters a more engaged and satisfied workforce.

That's the reason why the most critical aspect of AI's integration into internal communications is the alignment with business goals. Implementing AI without a clear understanding of what the organization aims to achieve can lead to disjointed efforts and missed opportunities. By aligning AI with specific objectives, businesses can ensure that technology serves the broader mission, whether it's enhancing customer experience, improving efficiency, or driving innovation.

Through this transformation we are redefining the way organizations engage with their employees. But what does this mean for the future of work, and how is AI shaping the landscape of employee engagement and collaboration?

The aim of AI in enhancing employee engagement and collaboration should represent a holistic approach to creating a more connected, responsive, and innovative workplace. By leveraging intelligent algorithms and data-driven insights, AI seeks to foster a culture of continuous learning, open communication, and creative problem-solving. It enables real-time collaboration across different teams and geographical locations, breaking down traditional barriers and silos. Furthermore, AI's adaptive learning systems can provide personalized support and development opportunities for each employee, recognizing individual strengths and areas for growth.

This not only enhances productivity but also contributes to employee satisfaction and well-being. In the age of remote work and digital transformation, keeping employees engaged is a challenge. AI-powered tools are bridging the gap, providing personalized experiences that resonate with individual needs and preferences. Some notable use case in this area include:

- **AI-powered communication tools**: Tools augmented with AI, such as SuperNormal's AI-driven note-taking functionality, facilitate seamless communication and collaboration. They help in automating mundane tasks such as note-taking, ensuring that key points discussed during meetings are captured and can be easily referenced later. This leaves team members free to engage in more meaningful interactions.[8]
- **Personalized learning**: AI's ability to personalize learning experiences is invaluable. It can curate and deliver relevant training materials to new hires, ensuring a smoother transition into their new roles. By assessing individual learning patterns and progress, AI can tailor training programs to meet the unique needs of each employee.[9]
- **Real-time feedback**: With AI, real-time feedback becomes attainable. AI algorithms can analyze an employee's performance and provide instant feedback, enabling individuals to reflect on their performance, identify areas of improvement, and make necessary adjustments swiftly.[10]

---

[8] https://resources.workable.com/stories-and-insights/how-ai-can-enhance-human-skills-and-collaboration-at-work.

[9] https://www.zavvy.io/blog/ai-employee-engagement.

[10] https://blog.shrm.org/sasia/blog/artificial-intelligence-and-employee-engagement-connecting-the-dots.

- **Automated collaboration**: Post-meeting collaborations are simplified with AI-enabled tools. They allow for the recording, transcription, and sharing of meeting information with both on-site and off-site employees, fostering a culture of inclusivity and ensuring everyone is on the same page.[11]
- **Identifying delays and challenges**: AI can monitor project timelines and individual performance to identify potential delays and challenges. By doing so, it enables managers to provide timely support to team members, ensuring projects stay on track.
- **Streamlining data-driven recruitment platforms**: AI streamlines the recruitment process by automating the screening of applicants, scheduling interviews, and even creating online orientation training programs. This ensures a more efficient and less biased recruitment process, and a smoother onboarding experience for new hires.
- **Enhancing productivity**: By fostering a culture of continuous learning, open communication, and creative problem-solving, AI enhances productivity. It enables real-time collaboration across different teams and geographical locations, breaking down traditional barriers and silos. This allows organizations to leverage diverse perspectives and skills, driving innovation and efficiency.

In summary, AI is a pivotal tool in modernizing the organizational workspace, ensuring employees are well equipped with the necessary skills and knowledge, nurturing a conducive learning and communication culture, and ultimately boosting productivity. Through these measures, AI significantly contributes to the creation of a more efficient and effective workplace environment. From tailored content to real-time feedback, this technology is ensuring that employees feel they are seen, heard, and valued.

2.2.3 *A step-by-step approach to integrating AI in an organization*

In many ways collaboration is the cornerstone of innovation, and AI is playing a pivotal role in fostering a culture of collaboration. By streamlining workflows and automating mundane tasks, AI is freeing up time

---

[11] https://leena.ai/.

and mental space for creative thinking and teamwork. Whether it's connecting cross-functional teams or facilitating brainstorming sessions, AI is enabling a more collaborative and dynamic work environment.

To effectively integrate these models and tools within a company with the aim of improving internal communication, knowledge sharing, and collaboration, it is necessary to follow a step-by-step approach (Tab. 2.1).

Table 2.1 Framework to integrate AI in the organization

Step	Description	Example	Action
1. Identify objectives and needs	Understand the specific challenges and objectives AI can address within the organization.	Multinational corporation faces time-zone differences hindering real-time collaboration.	Conduct surveys or workshops to gather insights on communication challenges, define goals such as reducing communication delays.
2. Assess current infrastructure and capabilities	Understand existing tools, systems, and capabilities to identify where AI can be integrated or where foundational changes are needed.	Organization heavily relies on email, leading to information silos.	Audit current communication tools, evaluate effectiveness, identify areas where AI can streamline processes.
3. Select appropriate AI technologies	Choose AI technologies that align with the organization's unique needs, understanding potential applications.	Need identified for real-time translation in video conferences.	Research AI-driven translation tools for integration into existing video conferencing platforms.
4. Develop and test prototypes	Experiment with AI solutions in a controlled environment to gauge effectiveness before broader rollout.	Prototype AI-driven internal social network developed to enhance employee interaction.	Launch prototype within a single department, gather feedback, refine based on user experience.
5. Roll out and train users	Ensure a smooth transition to new AI-driven solutions, with training and support for users.	AI-powered collaboration platform ready for company-wide adoption.	Organize training sessions, create user manuals, establish a help desk for assisting users in transition.
6. Evaluate and scale	Periodically evaluate AI implementation success, decide on expanding scope or introducing new functionalities for long-term sustainability and growth.	Successful pilot phase prompts consideration of expanding AI tools to external communication.	Conduct a feasibility study, evaluate potential benefits, plan a phased rollout to external stakeholders.

By focusing on a tailored approach that considers the unique needs and goals of each organization, this action plan encompasses not only the technological aspects but also, once again, the human factors, promoting a seamless blend of AI with existing workflows. It provides clear guidelines, milestones, and support mechanisms, all aimed at fostering innovation, efficiency, and effectiveness in organizational collaboration, ultimately leading to a transformative and successful integration of AI.

2.3   Human resource management in the age of AI

The conventional methodologies in recruitment, training, and development were fundamentally anchored in manual processes and human intuition. These methodologies exhibited inherent limitations; hiring managers engaged in manual screening of résumés, a process that was not only time-consuming but also susceptible to human biases and errors. The efficacy of gauging a candidate's suitability based solely on a resume was questionable, often leading to the allocation of valuable time to interviewing unsuitable candidates. Furthermore, the capacity for data analysis was circumscribed by the limitations of the tools and expertise available at the time. The insights derived were often superficial, falling short of providing the depth of understanding requisite for optimal decision-making.

Integrating AI, and particularly generative AI, into these domains transcends these structural limitations, ushering in a new era of efficiency and precision; it's a shift from intuition to precision, from guesswork to evidence-based decision-making.

2.3.1   *Skills analysis*

In traditional recruitment, defining the skills required for a role often relied on personal and subjective intuition, experience, and sometimes guesswork. AI transforms this process by employing data-driven algorithms that analyze the specific needs and demands of a position. By examining historical data, performance metrics, and industry trends, AI can pinpoint the exact competencies and attributes that are crucial for success in a given role. It's a move from subjective judgment to objective analysis, providing a more accurate and comprehensive understanding of what a job truly entails. Generative AI can then assist managers in crafting more precise job requirements by identifying the necessary skills for a particular role. However, human judgment is still essential to ensure the quality of the job requirement.

Once the essential skills are identified, AI can assist in matching candidates to those skills. By scanning résumés, social media profiles, and other digital footprints, AI can create a detailed skills profile for each candidate. This profile is then matched against the skills requirements of the role, ensuring that the candidates selected for interviews are those whose abilities align most closely with the needs of the position. It's a targeted approach that minimizes the risk of overlooking qualified candidates or selecting those who are not a good fit.

Skills analysis through AI also offers the potential to reduce biases in hiring. By focusing on the specific skills and competencies required for a role, rather than subjective factors such as appearance, background, or personal connections, AI promotes a more equitable selection process. It's a shift toward merit-based hiring, where candidates are evaluated on their abilities, not their identities.

AI's skills analysis is not a static process; it's dynamic and adaptive. As industry needs change, as new technologies emerge, and as organizational goals evolve, the AI algorithms can continuously learn and update the skills requirements for various roles. It's a responsive system that stays in tune with the changing landscape of the business world, ensuring that recruitment practices remain relevant and effective. Generative AI can also be used in this context to identify emerging skills in the following ways:

- Analyzing job market trends and skills needs to identify emerging skills and integrate them into training programs;[12]
- Analyzing employee data to identify hidden skills or interests that could be useful to the company, allowing companies to leverage existing talent and offer new opportunities for employees to develop their skills and contribute to the company's success;[13]

---

[12] https://www.mckinsey.com/capabilities/people-and-organizational-performance/our-insights/generative-ai-and-the-future-of-hr.

[13] https://jeremy-lamri.medium.com/generative-ai-hr-what-are-the-use-cases-dbd2e2cb068.

- Helping HR and managers quickly draft job requirements by analyzing data to determine which skills are critical to success in a role;[14]
- Providing real-time feedback to employees during their learning process, analyzing their progress, and adjusting training paths accordingly;
- Analyzing employee sentiment and engagement, finding patterns and trends in data from employee surveys, social media, and email correspondence, to identify emerging skills and create focused interventions that address particular concerns while increasing employee engagement and happiness.[15]

Generative AI can help HR identify emerging skills and integrate them into training programs, allowing employees to stay up to date and prepare for future changes in their field. It can also help companies leverage existing talent and offer new opportunities for employees to develop their skills and contribute to the company's success.

2.3.2 Competency-based hiring

Traditional recruitment often emphasizes degrees, titles, and years of experience. Competency-based hiring shifts the focus to the actual abilities and potential of the candidates. It's about what they can do, not what they have already done. AI plays a pivotal role in this shift by analyzing the specific competencies required for a role and evaluating candidates' potential based on those competencies. It's a more nuanced and targeted approach that recognizes talent for its intrinsic value.

AI algorithms can scan a wide array of data sources, from résumés and LinkedIn profiles to online portfolios and even coding repositories, to create a detailed competency profile for each candidate. This profile is not simply a list of skills but an in-depth analysis of how those skills have been applied and developed over time. It's a dynamic picture of a

---

[14]   https://www.mckinsey.com/capabilities/people-and-organizational-performance/our-insights/the-organization-blog/how-generative-ai-could-support-not-replace-human-resources.

[15]   https://www.hrexchangenetwork.com/hr-tech/articles/generative-ai-in-human-resources-what-you-need-to-know.

candidate's abilities, one that goes beyond static credentials to capture the essence of their potential. Generative AI's ability to tag unstructured data can help in identifying skills rather than relying on credentials such as degrees. This could open doors for candidates with on-the-job learning experiences, emphasizing skills over formal education.

Competency-based hiring through AI also enables a more personalized and relevant interview process. By understanding the specific competencies required for a role, interview questions and tasks can be tailored to assess those competencies directly. It's a move away from generic interviews to targeted evaluations, where candidates have the opportunity to demonstrate their abilities in meaningful and relevant ways.

By focusing on competencies rather than credentials, AI-driven competency-based hiring opens doors for a more diverse pool of candidates. It recognizes nontraditional career paths, self-taught skills, and unconventional experiences as valid indicators of ability. It's a more inclusive approach that values diversity of thought and experience, fostering a richer and more innovative workplace.

AI's role in competency-based hiring is not a one-time intervention; it's an ongoing partnership. The algorithms can continuously calibrate the competency criteria based on performance outcomes, industry trends, and organizational changes. It's a living process that evolves with the needs of the business, ensuring that hiring practices remain aligned with strategic goals.

2.3.3 Customized training and development

Traditional training programs often follow a one-size-fits-all approach, offering the same content and methods to all employees. AI revolutionizes this by analyzing individual performance data, learning styles, and career goals to understand the unique needs and potential of each employee. It's a shift from uniformity to individuality, recognizing that each person's path to growth is distinct.

Based on the understanding of individual needs, AI can create personalized learning paths that align with each employee's abilities, interests, and aspirations. These paths are not static but dynamic, adapting to the employee's progress, feedback, and changing goals. It's a responsive and flexible approach that fosters genuine growth rather than mere compliance.

AI's ability to analyze big data enables it to integrate various learning resources, from online courses and tutorials to mentorship programs and peer collaboration. It can match employees with the resources that are most relevant and effective for them, ensuring that learning is not just efficient but also engaging.

Beyond formal training, AI can provide real-time performance support, offering guidance, feedback, and resources at the moment of need. It's a move from episodic training to continuous learning, where development is an ongoing process, woven into the fabric of daily work.

Generative AI adds another layer of personalization and adaptability. It can generate content, scenarios, and simulations that are tailored to each employee's specific context and needs. It's not just about selecting the right resources but creating them, crafting learning experiences that are truly individualized.

AI's role in customized training and development extends to monitoring and evaluation. It can track progress, assess outcomes, and provide insights into the effectiveness of the training. It's a feedback loop that ensures continuous improvement, both in the training content and in the employee's performance.

2.3.4 *Performance monitoring and evaluation*

In the pre-AI world, performance evaluations often occurred at fixed intervals, such as annual reviews. Generative AI introduces a continuous assessment model, where performance is monitored and evaluated in real time. It's a shift from periodic snapshots to a continuous stream of insights, providing a more accurate and nuanced understanding of an employee's performance.

AI algorithms can analyze data from task completion rates and collaboration metrics to client feedback and self-assessments. By integrating and interpreting this data, AI provides a holistic view of performance, one that captures the complexity and multifaceted nature of modern work. Based on continuous assessment and data-driven insights, AI can provide personalized feedback to employees. This feedback is not generic but tailored to the individual's specific strengths, weaknesses, goals, and learning styles. It's a targeted approach that fosters growth by addressing the unique needs and potentials of each person.

Generative AI adds another dimension to performance monitoring and evaluation. It can generate customized reports, simulations, and scenarios that reflect an employee's specific performance context. It's a move from standardized evaluations to individualized explorations, where feedback is not just informative but also interactive and engaging.

AI's performance monitoring and evaluation are not isolated processes; they are aligned with organizational goals and strategies. By understanding the broader context of the business, AI ensures that performance assessments are not just about individual achievements but also about contributions to the collective mission. It's a holistic approach that recognizes the interconnectedness of individual and organizational success.

Beyond immediate feedback, AI's performance monitoring and evaluation support long-term career development. By tracking progress over time, identifying emerging strengths, and recognizing growth opportunities, AI can guide employees in their career paths, helping them make informed and meaningful choices. It's a partnership in growth, where technology serves as a mentor and a guide.

2.3.5 *AI and bias: Something we need to talk about*

The question of bias in HR management is as old as the field itself. Traditional hiring practices have often been marred by unconscious biases, leading to unequal opportunities and a lack of diversity. Enter AI, with its promise of objective, data-driven decision-making. By analyzing patterns and correlations, AI can help identify and correct biases in recruitment and performance evaluation. It's a step toward a more equitable workplace, where decisions are made on merit, not stereotypes.

But this promise comes with a caveat. AI is only as unbiased as the data it's trained on. If that data reflects societal biases, AI can inadvertently perpetuate those biases, replicating and even amplifying existing inequalities. It's a paradox at the heart of AI's potential: The very tool that can correct bias can also propagate it. The solution lies in mindful implementation and continuous monitoring. AI algorithms must be trained on diverse and representative data, and their decisions must be regularly reviewed for signs of bias. It's not a one-time fix but an ongoing commitment to fairness and integrity.

In the realm of HR, AI offers a path to a more just and inclusive workplace. But that path must be trodden with care, with an awareness of the potential pitfalls and a determination to avoid them. The promise of unbiased AI is not a given; it's a goal to be pursued with diligence and dedication.

2.3.6 *Keeping the human in the loop*

What is the role of HR professionals in this brave new world? The answer lies in a concept that is both profound and pragmatic: the human in the loop.

Generative AI is a powerful tool, capable of analyzing vast amounts of data, generating content and recommendations, and even personalizing communications with applicants. These algorithms may learn, but they do not understand; they need guidance, the insight, the intuition, the nuanced understanding that only a human being, HR professionals in this case, can provide. Algorithms lack the empathy, the creativity, the ethical compass that defines our humanity. The human in the loop then is not just a guide but also a gatekeeper, a safeguard against potential biases, errors, and ethical lapses that can occur when machines operate without human oversight.

Moreover, in an era when mental health is finally receiving the attention and care it deserves, the role of AI in supporting mental health in the workplace is a topic of growing interest and importance. The integration of AI into mental health support systems is a compassionate approach to understanding and nurturing the human mind.

Of course, mental health is complex, multifaceted, and deeply personal; traditional approaches to mental health support in the workplace often fall short in providing personalized care and understanding. Enter AI, with its ability to analyze patterns, understand behaviors, and provide tailored support.

AI's role in mental health support is about leveraging data and insights to provide empathetic care. It's about recognizing the unique needs of each individual and providing support that resonates with their specific situation. AI, as has been shown, can play a vital role in enhancing internal communication within organizations. By analyzing communication patterns and employee interactions, it can identify areas where mental health support may be needed. It can facilitate open and honest communication, creating a supportive environment where employees feel comfortable sharing their mental health concerns.

One of the key advantages of AI in mental health support is its ability to provide personalized care. By analyzing data such as communication patterns, work habits, and social interactions, AI can identify signs of stress, anxiety, or depression. This enables organizations to provide timely and targeted support, whether it's counseling, therapy, or simply a compassionate conversation.

Mental health still carries a stigma in many workplaces, and employees often hesitate to seek help. AI-powered mental health support systems can provide a confidential and nonjudgmental space for individuals to express their feelings and seek help. It's a safe haven that encourages openness and breaks down the barriers that often prevent people from seeking support.

Being able to make people feel more connected and involved in the company organization can also help improve not only people's well-being, but also the company's overall results. Searching for information within an organization, for example, can be a daunting task in many companies. Whether it's finding the right person for a specific project, locating a document, or understanding a particular process, traditional search methods often fall short. The integration of AI in HR offers tremendous efficiencies, from drafting job requirements to analyzing performance data, but efficiency is not the only goal. The human touch, the ability to connect, empathize, and inspire, remains irreplaceable. It's a balance that honors both the power of technology and the value of humanity.

As we navigate this complex and exciting landscape, let us do so with the wisdom to recognize the limits of machines and the courage to assert the value of the human spirit. Let us forge a partnership where human and AI not only coexist but thrive together, guided by the understanding that the human in the loop is not a constraint but a vital ingredient, a touchstone of integrity, empathy, and wisdom.

Insight
Artificial Intelligence and HR:
What Will the Combination Generate?

by *Manlio Ciralli**

I am firmly convinced that Albert Einstein was almost right when he affirmed, a long time ago, that "computers are incredibly fast, accurate, and stupid. Human beings are incredibly slow, inaccurate, and brilliant. Together they are powerful beyond imagination." Of course, since then, much progress has been made in tech and ICT (information and communication technology) and we have experienced an incredible number of exponential disruptions. Nevertheless, the essence of that sentence, which I particularly love, is that it clearly points to the need to integrate humanity and technology, because it should never be humanity versus technology. A well-blended combination of the two can bring significant benefits, create value for society at large, and improve health, well-being, productivity, and welfare on a large scale.

Moreover, history shows that major transformational disruptions – such as electric light, automobiles, telephones, radio, television, computers, and smartphones – have enhanced human development, improved our knowledge, boosted our communication, led to significant advancements in life sciences, and consequently created millions of jobs.

Looking back, I am strongly convinced that AI will not only create many good jobs but also transform how current jobs are performed. It is highly likely that AI already represents the most significant business opportunity of the next decade. It is already automating manual and repetitive tasks, and it is advancing so quickly that it will soon augment human decision-making. Simply put, AI will help us focus on more stra-

---

* Senior Vice President Global Marketing Adecco.

tegic aspects of our businesses, reduce lead times, and allow for a better work–life balance.

What is extremely important is the attitude and approach that we adopt to fully embrace and capitalize on the opportunities AI will create. Leaders will have to understand how AI will impact their workforces and ensure they are prepared by upskilling some workers to do existing jobs, but with AI, and by retraining and hiring others for the new roles that AI will demand. Both schools and parents will need to instill in children not only STEM (science, technology, engineering, and math) skills but also a culture of humanism, creativity, and lifelong learning. For individuals, enterprises, and countries equipped with the right skills, AI-powered automation poses no threat. Its economic boost offers a gigantic prize.

With all this in mind, I foresee that humans will continue to be central to work in the future. We are living in an extraordinary era in which several diverse trends and phenomena have already heavily impacted the way we work, live, think, shop, and make decisions.

So how can we "surf" the momentum – as leaders, as individuals – of these fascinating disruptions? What are the key elements to be taken into consideration to stay relevant, up to date, and decisive?

Firstly, I believe we need to invest in skills that are uniquely human. Human skills will remain more influential than AI in the workplace, especially emotional intelligence, empathy, and interpersonal skills. Cultivating these human skills will require connecting workers to coaching, leadership development, and training.

Next, upskilling programs and tailored employee-based plans will shape better workplaces. According to several studies on next-generation expectations, it is evident that the majority of Gen Z employees plan to stay with a company only if they have access to training and career progression opportunities. To retain and engage workers, it's crucial for employers to encourage and support lifelong learning and internal mobility opportunities, which are more important to workers than salary when deciding whether to stay with or leave a company.

Skills that are concretely present are now transferable to other roles or industries. Employees in tech, professional, and financial services possess skills that can be more easily transferred, in contrast to workers in the insurance, automotive, and defense sectors, whose skills are less transferable.

The shift from a job-based economy to a skills-based one is unfolding rapidly. Thus, it's clear that leading a company or even a team in the coming years will require a focus on aspects that will redesign the culture and attitude of the entire organization.

People primarily need to be engaged, motivated, nurtured, and equipped with a vision that encompasses not only the future but also the "what" and the "how" each organization responds to changes imposed by digital disruptions.

That's why I believe a leader should consider the following tips for reflection:

1. **Embrace technology and transformation**
   Workers need the tools, guidance, and education to thrive during profound technological transitions.
   – Assess existing skills and experience of all employees;
   – Check existing access to tools and technology and eliminate inequality;
   – Provide training and guidance to ensure workers use AI appropriately;
   – Ensure that AI-related policies consider safety, privacy, and accountability;
   – Adopt a people-centric approach to tech and digital transformation, protecting employability.

2. **Boost workers' mobility**
   In an increasingly dynamic environment, people must be ready to shift roles and even industries. This mobility is empowered by transferable skills.
   – Train managers to challenge traditional career paths and employment models.
   – Motivate employees to embrace internal mobility (cross-functions).
   – Create nonlinear skills-based career pathways for all employees.
   – Create a culture that promotes internal mobility to make the organization more resilient and attractive.
   – Celebrate transferable skills by onboarding employees from different functions, industries, and backgrounds.

3. **Enhance skills and capabilities**
   We are moving to an economy based on skills rather than jobs. Workers need support to build up their human and technical skills.

- Continuously assess employees' skills and whether they match the organization's needs and top their career path (transferable skills).
- Provide regular upskilling, not only in tech but also in human skills.
- Make training formal and informal, multi-modular and continuous.
- Align with a fundamental shift to a skills-based economy and away from a job-based one.
- Create a culture that incentivizes continuous upskilling and rewards employees who take ownership of their own training.

4. Protect workers' well-being

Without a healthy workforce there can be no future-proof organization. Protecting well-being must be a priority.

- Annual leave is not optional!
- Encourage employees to take time off with clear guidelines and communications.
- Use one-on-one manager meetings to conduct regular well-being check-ins with each employee.
- Invest in employee listening tools to understand individual needs.
- Address organizational challenges inclusively, putting employees at the center of all decisions.

3 The Impact of AI on the World of Information

3.1 From print to pixels: The digital transformation in media

While the technique of movable type can be traced back to China's 9th century, it was Johannes Gutenberg's refinement of this technology around the year 1440 that unleashed a tidal wave of change across Europe and beyond. He took a concept that had existed for centuries and elevated it to a level of sophistication that allowed for the mass production of books. It was a leap that transcended the limitations of time and place, turning a localized practice into a global phenomenon.

The ripple effects of Gutenberg's revolution were immediate and profound. New professions were born, languages flourished, and the very fabric of society was altered. The press evolved to become the "Fourth Estate," a central pillar of our democracies, and a beacon of truth.

The media industry then became a world unto itself, with its own rules, dynamics, and power structures. It was dominated by traditional channels such as print (newspapers, magazines), broadcast (television, radio), and outdoor advertising (billboards, posters). These forms of media held significant influence and control over the dissemination of information and entertainment, shaping public opinion and cultural norms.

The reach and distribution of media content in this era were limited by physical constraints. Newspapers and magazines were tangible objects, printed on paper and distributed through a network of trucks, newsstands, and door-to-door carriers. Television and radio broadcasts were confined to specific regions or areas, their signals fading at the edges of their designated territories.

Advertising played a crucial role in sustaining this media ecosystem. It was the lifeblood of the industry, the engine that drove both content creation and distribution. Advertisers relied on traditional media channels to reach their target audiences, and media companies generated revenue through carefully curated advertising placements. The relationship between media and advertisers was symbiotic, each depending on the other for survival and success.

In sum, this was a world where information had both a physical presence and a price. Media moguls and publishing giants held sway, their empires built on a foundation of ink, airwaves, and advertising dollars.

In this predigital age, the media was both a business and a public trust, a delicate balance between commercial interests and civic responsibility. Journalists were gate keepers, curators of truth in a world where information was a tangible commodity.

3.1.1   *The illusion of free information*

The tension between the value of information and the desire for accessibility reflects a complex reality. Information is both a precious commodity and a ubiquitous resource, a paradox that continues to shape the digital landscape. On the one hand, the desire for information to be free has driven innovation, opened doors to education, and fostered global connection. In the early years of mass digitalization, this vision of free information led to new experiments and solutions, with sometimes unexpected consequences.

A notable example was Napster, the pioneering peer-to-peer (P2P) file-sharing service that revolutionized the music industry, which was launched in 1999.[1] By enabling users to share music freely, Napster challenged traditional models of distribution and ownership of content. It sparked a debate about intellectual property rights, the value of creative work, and the very nature of access and control in a digital world. Napster's rise and eventual legal battles were emblematic of a broader struggle to reconcile the ideals of free information with the realities of commerce, law, and ethics.

---

[1] https://www.lifewire.com/history-of-napster-2438592.

But the evolution of the digital landscape took a decisive turn with the entry of a new major player, which, in its early stage, set its mission to "organize the world's information" and make it universally accessible and useful: Google.[2]

3.1.2 *Google's impact on media economics*

I vividly recall being present when Google was launched in Italy in the early 2000s. At that time, the internet was becoming an increasingly tangible reality in Italy, and the first "portals," as they were called back then, were gaining significant weight in the media industry. These portals were named as such because they provided access to content, sites, and news, organizing information in a manner akin to an encyclopedia.

Google was introduced by Virgilio.it, the leading Italian portal of those years, as a mere feature – an alternative to the directory, aimed at finding information more quickly. I also remember the example used by the presenters to demonstrate Google's algorithm's prowess. They wanted to show that by typing "Ferrari," the search results would prioritize the famous car manufacturer's website over information about the sparkling wine. It was a simple yet powerful illustration of how Google's search algorithm was designed to understand and prioritize user intent.

But what seemed like a clever addition soon turned into a self-inflicted wound. Users were drawn to Google's efficiency and began bypassing the portal altogether. Virgilio, once a dominant player, found itself relegated to the sidelines, a victim of its own miscalculation.

This misstep was just a microcosm of a much larger and more consequential error that would reverberate across the media landscape. The decision to let Google access and crawl media data (in this case quality content) was certainly driven by the allure of the digital age, a belief that embracing this new frontier would lead to untold riches and success.

Media companies were seduced by the promise of the internet, allowing Google to slice and dice their articles, selling them against search queries. This was a game changer, a shift that would redefine the economics of the media industry. Traditional advertising, once at the heart of every media company, was suddenly overshadowed by the far more

---

[2] https://www.google.com/search/howsearchworks/our-approach/.

lucrative world of search queries. But this brave new world came at a
steep price. Media companies soon found that their content was commoditized and devalued. They had unwittingly ceded control to Google,
allowing their hard-earned content to be repackaged and resold, with
Google reaping the rewards.

Many newspapers and magazines have struggled to adapt to this new
digital landscape, leading to a decline in print sales and advertising revenue. The gatekeepers of information were replaced by algorithms, and
the sanctity of the printed word gave way to the chaos of the digital
realm.

The impact on the media industry was profound, extending far beyond mere economics. It has fundamentally reshaped the very nature
of journalism, introducing new paradigms that have both enriched and
challenged the field.

The rise of Google has ushered in an era where SEO-oriented writing
has become paramount.[3] This shift has been driven by the need to rank
high in Google's search results, a coveted position that can translate into
increased visibility and revenue. But this pursuit of search engine su-
premacy has given birth to practices that are sometime at odds with the
traditional tenets of journalism.

Clickbait is perhaps the most notorious of these practices. Sensational
headlines, designed to attract clicks, have become commonplace. These
headlines often promise shocking revelations or tantalizing secrets, lur-
ing readers with the promise of the extraordinary. But all too often, the
content fails to deliver on these promises, leaving readers disappointed
and disillusioned.

An example of this can be seen in headlines such as "You Won't Believe
What Happened Next!" or "This One Trick Will Change Your Life!"
These headlines are crafted to pique curiosity, but the articles themselves
often contain mundane or widely known information. This trend toward
sensationalism is not confined to fringe websites or tabloids. Even repu-
table news organizations have been drawn into the clickbait game as the
pressure to compete in the crowded digital marketplace intensifies.

The SEO-driven approach has also led to a phenomenon known as
"keyword stuffing," where articles are laden with specific keywords to

---

[3] https://en.wikipedia.org/wiki/Search_engine_optimization.

improve their search engine ranking.[4] This can result in awkward and unnatural prose, as writers are forced to shoehorn keywords into their articles, sometimes at the expense of clarity and coherence.

Furthermore, the pressure to produce content that resonates with search algorithms has led to a homogenization of news. Topics that are deemed "trendy" or "viral" are prioritized, while important but less search-friendly subjects may be overlooked. This has the potential to narrow the scope of public discourse, as complex and nuanced issues are sidelined in favor of more clickable content.

The traditional values of journalism – truth, objectivity, and fairness – are at risk in this new landscape. The demands of the digital marketplace, with its relentless focus on clicks, views, and shares, can overshadow the core mission of journalism: to inform, educate, and hold power to account.

And after that came social media.

3.1.3 *The legitimization of fake news*

Social media platforms can connect us and divide us in ways we could never have anticipated. The algorithms that power these platforms are designed to engage users by showing them content that aligns with their existing beliefs and interests. On the surface, this creates a personalized and engaging user experience. But beneath this convenience lies a more insidious reality.

These algorithms lead to the creation of echo chambers where differing opinions are filtered out and extreme views are amplified. It's a phenomenon that has transformed our media environment, where nuance is lost and division is fostered. The result is a society increasingly polarized, with people entrenched in their beliefs, unwilling or unable to see the other side.

The spread of fake news on social media platforms further exacerbates this polarization. Misleading headlines and false information can quickly go viral, reaching vast audiences before corrections or retractions can be made. This rapid spread of misinformation not only undermines public trust in media but also creates a dangerous landscape where false

---

[4] https://www.linkedin.com/advice/1/what-benefits-drawbacks-using-keyword.

narratives are reinforced and legitimized. It becomes increasingly diffi-
cult for users to discern fact from fiction, leading to a distorted view of
reality.[5] This has profound implications for our democratic discourse.
An informed citizenry is the cornerstone of a healthy democracy, and the
erosion of trust in media and institutions undermines this foundational
principle.

Sensational headlines, clickbait tactics, and outright fabrications can
spread like wildfire, often outpacing the reach of factual and well-re-
searched reporting. Moreover, the economic pressures faced by traditional media outlets in the digital age can exacerbate these challenges. The
competition for clicks and advertising revenue may lead some publishers to compromise on journalistic standards, further contributing to the
spread of misinformation.

The interplay between publishers and social media platforms also
raises questions about responsibility and accountability. Who bears the
burden of fact-checking and combating fake news? How can platforms
balance the need for open discourse with the imperative to prevent the
spread of harmful misinformation? These are complex questions without
easy answers, and they highlight the delicate balance that must be struck
in navigating this new media landscape.

The rise of platforms such as Instagram and TikTok adds another layer of complexity; these platforms not only require particular attention
due to their unique nature but also impose the development of specific
formats, such as short videos, reels, and so on. While these formats can
be engaging and visually appealing, they are not always conducive to
conveying in-depth information. The push toward brief, visually driven
content can sometimes be at odds with the informational needs of readers. This leads to a potential dilution of substance and depth, favoring
style over substance and entertainment over enlightenment.

In the face of such a structural transformation in the media landscape, newsrooms cannot remain passive observers. As the boundaries
of content creation and dissemination evolve, so too must the strategies
and tools employed by journalists. The challenge is not just to adapt,
but to harness the full potential of emerging technologies, including
generative AI.

---

[5] On this topic I highly recommend the book James E. Katz and Kate K. Mays
(2019), *Journalism and Truth in an Age of Social Media*, Oxford: Oxford Unversity Press.

This technology, with its ability to analyze, generate, and even predict content trends, offers a promising avenue for newsrooms to maintain depth and substance in their reporting. By integrating AI tools, journalists can navigate the changing tides of content formats, ensuring that quality journalism doesn't get lost in the sea of fleeting trends. In essence, as the media world transforms, it's imperative for newsrooms to pivot, embracing new methodologies that amplify their core mission: delivering insightful, accurate, and impactful stories to their audience.

3.2 The algorithmic newsroom: Efficiency, creativity, and challenges

The advent of generative AI models has ignited fervent discussions among journalists regarding its prospective ramifications for the profession. Central concerns emerge: Will generative AI supplant journalists? Which facets of journalism are most vulnerable to this technological upheaval? Does this AI wave represent a hurdle or a boon? As with many technological breakthroughs, the enduring influence of these innovations will crystallize once the initial fervor subsides, allowing us to discern between authentic transformative shifts and transient fads.

Though the horizon is still nebulous, one aspect stands out distinctly: The confluence of journalism and AI is poised to sculpt the narratives of the future. This compels us not only to re-evaluate the core of storytelling and its foundational tenets but also to reconsider the very formats through which news is consumed and disseminated.

3.2.1 Beyond automation: AI's deepening role in news reporting and analysis

AI's initial embrace by journalism was a pragmatic one, targeting these very areas where repetitiveness met high stakes. With the sheer volume of data available in today's digital age, journalists often find themselves inundated, struggling to discern what's relevant. AI in this use case can act as a sophisticated filter, analyzing vast datasets in seconds, identifying patterns, and spotlighting crucial information. Imagine a tool that can instantly verify the authenticity of a viral video or cross-reference a breaking news story with historical data to provide context.

One of the most prominent areas that witnessed the immediate influence of AI is financial journalism. Financial reports, with their intricate details, numbers, and forecasts, demand utmost precision. A minor error in reporting a company's quarterly earnings or misinterpreting financial data can have significant repercussions, both for the news agency and for the stock market.

Before AI's intervention, journalists would sift through voluminous financial statements, extracting key data points to craft their reports. This process was not only time-consuming but also prone to oversights. With the introduction of AI, algorithms were trained to instantly parse these statements, extracting relevant data and even drafting preliminary reports. For instance, if Company X released its quarterly earnings, an AI system could quickly highlight its revenue, profit margins, and other key metrics, presenting a concise report within minutes of the release.

I guess this is a perfect example of what we should see next in this area; the automation didn't render financial journalists obsolete. Instead, it empowered them. With the grunt work handled by AI, journalists could focus on providing insightful analysis, contextualizing the numbers, and drawing connections to broader economic trends. They could interview industry experts, dissect the company's future strategies, and offer a more holistic view of the company's financial health.

Another domain that reaped the benefits of automation is sports journalism. Anyone who has followed a live sports event knows the dynamism it entails. Scores change in real time, players' statistics need constant updating, and game dynamics shift rapidly.

Before AI, journalists and editors would be glued to screens, manually updating scores and key events. With AI, algorithms could be fed data directly from the game – be it a goal in a soccer match or a home run in baseball. These systems would then instantly update live blogs and scores and even draft short match summaries, ensuring that readers always had real-time information.

But the influence of AI in sports journalism is not confined to real-time updates. With access to vast historical data, AI systems can provide instant comparisons – for instance, comparing a soccer player's current performance with past games or drawing parallels between teams' performances across seasons. This enriches the content, offering readers not just real-time data but also historical context and deeper insights.

The automation phase marked a pivotal shift in how newsrooms operate. Journalists, liberated from routine tasks, could channel their energies into more value-added activities. They could engage in investigative journalism, conduct in-depth interviews, and craft narratives that went beyond mere reporting.

But as with all technological advancements, AI's role in journalism will not remain static. Soon it will evolve from mere automation to play a more nuanced role. This shift isn't just about doing things faster; it is about doing things differently and doing different things, with a depth and precision previously unattainable.

3.2.2 *From creation to curation: AI's expanding role in modern journalism*

Several pioneering media outlets are already charting the course, integrating AI into their operations in innovative ways. BuzzFeed's use of AI for its popular personality quizzes offers a glimpse into how AI can be used to enhance user engagement, tailoring content to individual preferences.[6] The *New York Times'* experiment with ChatGPT for generating personalized Valentine's Day messages showcased the potential of AI in creating interactive and personalized content.[7] Meanwhile, global publishers such as Axel Springer and the UK's Reach are pushing the envelope, publishing articles crafted by AI, testing the waters to see how audiences respond to machine generated content (more on this topic below).[8]

But it's not just about content creation. AI can also play a pivotal role in content curation and distribution. Algorithms can analyze readers' behavior, preferences, and engagement patterns to tailor news feeds, ensuring that audiences receive content that's most relevant to them at the right moment. This could lead to a more personalized news experience, where stories are curated based on individual interests and preferences.

Here are some areas of interest for generative AI applications.

---

[6] https://www.theguardian.com/media/2023/jan/26/buzzfeed-artifical-intelligence-content-quizzes-chatgpt.

[7] https://www.nytimes.com/interactive/2023/02/13/opinion/valentines-day-chatgpt.html.

[8] https://www.theguardian.com/technology/2023/mar/01/german-publisher-axel-springer-says-journalists-could-be-replaced-by-ai.

- **Content personalization:** By studying user behavior, preferences, and reading patterns, algorithms curate newsfeeds, ensuring readers received stories most relevant to their interests. This not only enhances user engagement but also allows journalists to understand their audience better, shaping content strategies accordingly.

  Example: The *Washington Post* has used its in-house technology, called Heliograf, since 2016.[9] This AI-driven technology helps in automating short reports and tailoring content to suit individual readers based on their behavior and preferences.

- **Predictive analysis:** AI's prowess in data analysis enables it to forecast trends. For instance, by analyzing patterns in past news cycles, AI can predict spikes in interest for certain topics, allowing newsrooms to allocate resources proactively. This predictive capability is especially valuable in areas such as financial journalism, where understanding market sentiments ahead of time can provide a competitive edge.

  Example: In March 2023, Bloomberg unveiled BloombergGPT™, a cutting-edge generative AI model tailored for the financial sector.[10] This LLM is designed to enhance various natural language processing tasks within finance, such as sentiment analysis, news classification, and question answering.

- **Multimedia integration:** With the rise of multimedia journalism, AI tools have begun assisting in video and audio analysis. Transcribing interviews, extracting key soundbites from hours of footage, or even identifying potential viral video segments has become streamlined. This has allowed multimedia journalists to focus on crafting compelling narratives rather than getting bogged down by the logistics of content analysis.

  Example: CBS Interactive employs AI-driven video analysis tools to scrutinize each frame of a video, identifying and tagging objects within it. Similarly, the US National Football League harnesses

---

[9] https://www.washingtonpost.com/pr/wp/2016/08/05/the-washington-post-experiments-with-automated-storytelling-to-help-power-2016-rio-olympics-coverage/.

[10] https://www.bloomberg.com/company/press/bloomberggpt-50-billion-parameter-llm-tuned-finance/.

comparable technology to streamline and categorize its content, enhancing its searchability, usability, and monetization potential.

- **Real-time fact-checking**: In an era of "fake news," the credibility of a news outlet is its most valuable asset. AI has begun assisting journalists in real-time fact-checking. By cross-referencing statements, claims, or data against trusted sources, AI systems can flag potential inaccuracies, ensuring that stories maintain the highest standards of accuracy.

  Example: Full Fact, an independent team of fact-checkers and campaigners, is piloting a service that employs speech recognition technology to scan and verify misleading claims in real time.[11] This initiative is being tested in multiple languages with media partners in Argentina and Africa, and there are plans to expand to other countries.

- **Interactive storytelling**: AI has also ventured into enhancing the reader experience through interactive storytelling. Algorithms can generate dynamic content, such as interactive graphs, maps, or simulations, based on real-time data. This not only makes stories more engaging but also allows readers to delve deeper into topics, exploring data at their own pace.

  Example: BBC News Labs is leveraging AI to automate various aspects of news production, from graphical storytelling to summarizing content, ensuring that the content remains engaging and relevant for younger audiences while maintaining editorial integrity.[12]

- **Language translation and global reach**: For global news outlets, AI-powered translation tools have become indispensable. They allow stories to be instantly translated into multiple languages, ensuring that content reaches a global audience. Moreover, these translations are context-aware, ensuring that the essence of the story remains intact across linguistic boundaries.

In essence, AI's role in journalism is expanding to touch almost every facet of the newsroom. From content creation to distribution, from anal-

---

[11]   https://newsinitiative.withgoogle.com/dnifund/report/battling-misinformation/scaling-fact-checking-with-artificial-intelligence/.

[12]   https://wan-ifra.org/2021/06/how-bbc-news-labs-uses-ai-powered-content-automation-to-engage-young-audiences/.

ysis to engagement, AI has become an indispensable tool in the journalist's arsenal. Far from replacing the human touch, it has amplified it,
ensuring that stories are not only accurate and timely but also deeply resonant and insightful. It seems as if AI is helping to forge a future where
journalism reaches new heights, marrying the precision of machines with
the passion and intuition of human storytellers. But what are the limits
of this approach?

3.2.3 *The limits of AI storytelling*

Generative AI's prowess in churning out content, often at speeds incomprehensible to human writers, is proof of the technological advancements
of our age. Yet for all its capabilities, generative AI remains, at its core,
a tool – one that lacks the spark of originality and the depth of analytical insight that defines great journalism. Journalism is an exploration
of the human condition. It delves into the stories that shape our world,
seeking to shed light on the hidden corners of society and give voice to
the voiceless. Journalists are not just reporters; they are storytellers, analysts, and investigators. They probe, challenge, and dissect events, always
in pursuit of the truth. Their work is driven by curiosity, empathy, and
a commitment to public service. Each story they tell is imbued with a
unique human touch, capturing the nuances, emotions, and complexities
of the subjects they cover.

Generative AI operates on a fundamentally different plane. It is a
product of code, algorithms, and vast datasets. While it possesses the
computational power to analyze and generate content at an astonishing
pace, it lacks the intrinsic human qualities that define journalism. AI
doesn't experience curiosity or wonder. It doesn't feel empathy or outrage.
It operates within the confines of its programming, processing information based on predefined parameters.

Consider the process of crafting a narrative. A journalist, drawing
from their personal experiences, cultural background, and interactions,
will approach a story with a unique perspective. They'll seek out diverse
voices, ask probing questions, and strive to understand the broader implications of the events they're covering. Their narratives are enriched by
context, emotion, and a deep understanding of the human psyche.

Generative AI, in contrast, creates narratives based on patterns in the
data it's been fed. It can mimic the structure of a well-written article,

replicate stylistic elements, and even generate coherent and grammatically correct sentences. But it doesn't "understand" the stories it tells in the way humans do. It can't discern the emotional weight of a personal anecdote or the societal significance of a particular event. It's akin to a highly skilled artisan replicating a masterpiece without understanding the emotions and intentions behind the original work.

In essence, while generative AI can mirror the surface-level aspects of journalism, it cannot replicate the depth, passion, and soul that human journalists bring to their craft. It offers a reflection of the world as seen through the lens of data, but it lacks the illuminating insight that comes from genuine human experience and understanding. This isn't to downplay the transformative potential of AI in journalism. When used as a complementary tool, AI can free journalists from mundane tasks, allowing them more time for in-depth research, interviews, and on-the-ground reporting. The symbiosis of man and machine can lead to a richer, more informed journalistic landscape. Yet the road to this ideal integration is fraught with challenges. Generative AI, despite its sophistication, is not infallible. There have been instances where these models, in their quest to generate content, have inadvertently propagated factual inaccuracies. Their reliance on historical data makes them less adept at navigating the ever-evolving landscape of real-time events. Breaking news, with its fluidity and immediacy, remains a domain where the human touch is irreplaceable.

3.3   The business of AI in news: Licensing deals, revenue streams, and reader impacts

From the first printed newspapers to the digital behemoths of today, the underlying principle in this industry has remained consistent: the need to balance information dissemination with economic viability. It's therefore imperative to reflect, recalibrate, and reimagine our strategies in this area of interest.

The digital age has been both a boon and a bane for the world of publishing; the democratization of information, while empowering, has also led to a deluge of content, often drowning out the voices that matter.

But recognizing the value of content is just the beginning. The traditional models of revenue, often reliant on advertising and subscriptions, are being challenged. The status quo, comfortable as it may seem, is a quagmire. For publishers to thrive, they must break free from the shackles of convention. Embracing innovation, exploring alternative revenue streams, and being open to uncharted territories are not just options; they are necessities.

Lastly, we must turn our gaze to the most crucial stakeholder in this ecosystem: the reader. In a world where AI scripts news stories and algorithms dictate reading lists, how does the reader's relationship with information evolve? Understanding this dynamic is pivotal. After all, in the grand tapestry of information dissemination, it is the reader who weaves the narrative.

3.3.1 *Publishers' digital lesson decoded*

The first wave of digital transformation, epitomized by giants such as Google and Facebook, brought with it lessons that are invaluable for the industry. Publishers, in their pursuit of relevance, often found themselves at the mercy of algorithms, sacrificing the very essence of their existence – content. The takeaway here is clear: Also in the AI world, content remains king. Publishers must recognize and leverage their primary asset, ensuring it's not lost in the cacophony of the digital world. Now, as we transition into this new era, the value of authentic, quality content is magnified even further, becoming the linchpin for training sophisticated algorithms and shaping the future of information dissemination.

This is why the world's leading AI tech companies have been engaging throughout 2023 in hush-hush meetings with leading media moguls. Their goal? To hash out a landmark deal on the use of news content for training generative AI. Representatives from AI companies OpenAI, Google, and Amazon have been in talks with news executives from notable publishers such as News Corp, the *New York Times*, Axel Springer, the *Financial Times*, and *The Guardian*.[13] The aim is to craft a milestone agreement that would have media companies receiving fees for providing continued access to their content used to train AI models.

Much of the early discussions have centered around a potential pricing model for news content access, with one option in the form of an "un-

---

[13] https://www.ft.com/content/79eb89ce-cea2-4f27-9d87-e8e312c8601d.

limited use" model priced between $5 million and $20 million annually. Critics of this approach argue that this payment model may exclude smaller media organizations and regional news publications.

These discussions extend beyond just written content, deeply influencing other forms of media, especially music and imagery. The ongoing negotiations between tech platforms such as Google and prominent music labels, including Universal Music Group and Warner Music Group, highlight the shifting landscape of content rights and licensing in this digital age. The aim in this case is to secure licenses for artists' vocals and musical melodies to create AI-generated songs.[14]

This move is seen as an attempt by music labels to capitalize on the rising trend of "deepfake" songs, which employ generative AI technology to replicate artists' voices and produce musical compositions. Such advancements, while groundbreaking, have raised concerns, especially when these AI-generated tracks are created without obtaining proper consent from the original artists.

These talks are unfolding under a rapidly changing scenario for content. The use of copyrighted content without proper licensing or permission has led to a surge in lawsuits against AI companies.[15] These lawsuits highlight the legal gray areas surrounding the use of copyrighted material for training AI models. The core argument revolves around whether training an AI model using copyrighted content constitutes a violation of copyright laws. The outcome of these lawsuits could set significant precedents for how content is used in the AI industry.

Governments and regulatory bodies are stepping in to address the challenges posed by the AI-driven content landscape.[16] The European Union's AI Act is a prime example of such regulatory efforts. This act demands greater transparency from AI companies about how they use copyrighted content in their model training processes. The goal is to strike a balance between innovation and the rights of content creators, ensuring that the latter are adequately compensated and recognized for their contributions.

---

[14] Google and Universal Music Group in talks over licensing AI 'deepfakes' (report) – Music Business Worldwide.

[15] News outlets demand new rules for AI training data – The Verge.

[16] AI and Media titans quietly hash out future of content licensing – Artisana.

Recognizing the value of their vast datasets, platforms such as Reddit and StackOverflow have taken steps to monetize access. These platforms, which offer treasure troves of user-generated content, have been pivotal in training various AI models. By announcing that access to their datasets will now come at a cost, they are signaling a shift in how data is valued in the AI ecosystem. This move could pave the way for other platforms and content creators to seek compensation for the use of their data.

Media executives are confident of reaching a viable deal. Many are determined not to be caught off guard as they were in the early years of the internet era, when news organizations quickly found revenues shrink as consumption moved online. As Mathias Döpfner, Axel Springer's chief executive, puts it, AI companies "know that regulation is coming, and they are fearful of it." He added, "It is in the interest of all parties to come up with a solution for a healthy ecosystem. If there is no incentive to create intellectual property, there is nothing to crawl. And artificial intelligence will become artificial stupidity."

3.3.2 *Innovation and monetization: harnessing AI to carve out new revenue streams*

The generative AI market, overall, is poised for explosive growth, with projections indicating a near tenfold expansion by 2028, reaching a staggering $36 billion.[17] But while the revenue opportunities stemming from licensing agreements, as discussed in the previous section, are undoubtedly intriguing and signal a shift in the publisher–platform relationship, they are but a drop in the ocean compared to the digital tidal wave that has reshaped the industry over the past two decades. The digital revolution has not only transformed how content is consumed but has also upended traditional revenue models, challenging publishers to innovate and adapt in an ever-evolving landscape.

The tumult of 2023 in the media industry serves as a stark reminder of these transformations. Once celebrated digital-first platforms, which were heralded as the future of news, now find themselves in troubled waters. Vice's and Buzzfeed's challenges are emblematic of the broader

---

[17]   https://press.spglobal.com/2023-06-08-Generative-AI-Software-Market-Forecast-to-Expand-Near-10-Times-by-2028-to-36-Billion,-S-P-Global-Market-Intelligence-Says.

industry's struggles. Overambition, a saturated market, and the complexities of monetizing digital content have combined to create a perfect storm. The digital-first approach, which was their strength, has, in many ways, become their Achilles' heel. The advertising industry, traditionally the lifeblood of media, is in turmoil.[18] New regulations and changing user behaviors have disrupted that ecosystem. While ads are reaching more users than ever thanks to an increase in website visitors, their efficacy is in question. The cost of advertising has plummeted, but so has its impact. Fewer users are engaging with ads, leading to a concerning decline in conversion rates.

But perhaps the most poignant indicator of the industry's challenges is the human cost.[19] The number of media job cuts in 2023 has reached unprecedented levels, surpassing even the dark days of the 2020 Covid-19 pandemic. These layoffs represent talented professionals, each with stories, aspirations, and families. The reasons are manifold: a slowdown in the ad market, the burden of debt from consolidation efforts, and a phenomenon termed "subscription fatigue."[20]

The trajectory of generative AI's influence on digital publishing remains shrouded in uncertainty, but examining the features of this technology allows us to envision various incremental monetization models. Here are some illustrative examples.

- **Archives: The untapped goldmine**
  At the heart of every media house lies a treasure trove of content: archives. These vast repositories, often underutilized, hold the potential to be the bedrock of AI-driven innovations. By leveraging these archives, publishers can develop predictive models that anticipate audience preferences, curate content based on historical data, and even generate new content combinations that resonate with contemporary audiences. Imagine a world where a century-old article finds new relevance, intertwined with current events, offering

---

[18] https://www.digitalinformationworld.com/2023/05/advertising-cpm-sees-33-decrease-yoy.html.

[19] https://www.axios.com/2023/06/13/media-job-cuts-record.

[20] https://www.forbes.com/sites/pamdanziger/2022/05/10/as-retail-opens-up-and-inflation-closes-in-consumer-subscription-fatigue-is-on-the-rise/?sh=fabc-c062ede7.

readers a unique blend of historical context and modern perspective. Such AI-driven content recombination can not only enhance user engagement but also open up opportunities for incremental monetization.

- **Reimagining subscriptions: The recurring revenue bundle**
  The traditional subscription model, while still relevant, needs a facelift in the age of AI. Taking its cue from successful models such as Amazon Prime, the media industry can explore recurring revenue bundles. These bundles could offer readers a mix of content: AI-curated articles based on their reading habits, access to premium AI-generated content, virtual events, and even partnerships with other services, be it streaming platforms or e-commerce sites. Such a holistic approach ensures that subscribers see value beyond just content, fostering loyalty and ensuring a steady revenue stream.

- **Chatbots: The new gatekeepers of content**
  In an era where instant access is paramount, several publishers are turning to chatbots to simplify content access. These AI-driven assistants not only guide readers through vast content libraries but also offer personalized recommendations. As exemplified by platforms such as Skift's "Ask Skift,"[21] these AI-driven interfaces are revolutionizing the way readers interact with content. By intuitively guiding users through a plethora of information, chatbots ensure that readers find precisely what they're looking for, tailored to their unique interests and queries. Furthermore, by integrating features such as payment gateways, publishers can seamlessly transition readers from content discovery to content purchase. As these chatbots become increasingly sophisticated, they are evolving from simple tools for navigation into dynamic gatekeepers of content, enhancing user experience, and unlocking new monetization opportunities for publishers.

- **Personalized AI news assistants**
  Imagine a virtual assistant that not only curates news based on your preferences but also offers insights, background information, and even suggests further reading, all in real time.[22] Such a service,

---

[21] https://skift.com/ask-skift-faq/.

[22] https://medium.com/@akshat28vivek/unlocking-the-potential-of-ai-powered-personal-assistants-7d694ba07e0d.

available on a subscription basis, can revolutionize how we consume news. Beyond mere curation, this assistant provides contextual insights, drawing connections between current events and historical precedents, offering a richer understanding of the news. It doesn't stop there. The assistant can proactively provide background information on key figures, events, or terms mentioned in an article, ensuring readers are never out of their depth. And for those hungry for more, it suggests further reading, articles, and resources, ensuring a holistic understanding of the topic at hand.

The assistant adapts to your reading habits, learning and evolving with each interaction. Over time, it can anticipate your needs, pre-emptively providing information even before you realize you need it. It promises not just personalized content but a personalized experience, making news consumption more engaging, informative, and efficient. In a world where time is of the essence, such innovations ensure we stay informed without feeling overwhelmed.

- **Interactive AI-driven content**
  Imagine reading an article about a global event. Instead of a linear narrative, AI-driven platforms present you with an interactive canvas. As you read about specific incidents or regions, interactive maps and timelines pop up, allowing you to visually trace events as they unfolded. Hover over a term you're unfamiliar with, and a concise definition or background appears, ensuring you never feel lost. But the true magic of interactive AI-driven content lies in its adaptability. Based on your reading patterns and interests, the article can dynamically adjust its content. Want to delve deeper into a particular aspect? The AI seamlessly integrates related articles, videos, and infographics, allowing you to explore the topic from multiple angles.

  Beyond mere content exploration, these platforms also offer AI-moderated discussion forums. Here, readers can engage in meaningful discussions, share perspectives, and even pose questions that AI can instantly answer or direct you to expert sources. These discussions, curated to remain constructive and informative, elevate the reading experience from mere consumption to active participation.

- **AI-powered workshops or webinars**
  By analyzing reading habits, search behaviors, and even social media engagements, AI can pinpoint trending topics within a specific vertical, be it finance, economy, food, travel, or any other domain.

Once these trending topics are identified, publishers can curate content-rich workshops and webinars tailored to these verticals. For instance, if AI identifies a surge in interest around sustainable travel, a publisher can quickly organize a webinar featuring experts in ecotourism, sustainable accommodations, and green travel practices. Such targeted content not only ensures higher engagement rates but also opens up avenues for premium subscriptions or pay-per-access models.

Participants don't just passively consume content; they actively engage, pose questions, participate in AI-moderated discussions, and delve deeper into subtopics of interest. This interactive learning environment, coupled with the allure of niche topics, can command premium pricing, adding a lucrative revenue stream for publishers. Furthermore, these workshops and webinars can evolve into networking hubs. Participants, often professionals or enthusiasts within the vertical, get a platform to connect, share insights, and even forge collaborations. Publishers can monetize this aspect by offering premium networking features or exclusive expert sessions, or even facilitating industry partnerships.

The challenges facing the media industry are undeniable, but the potential of AI offers a silver lining here. By placing AI at the heart of their revenue models, publishers can not only navigate the current challenges but also chart a course toward a prosperous, innovative future. The key lies in harnessing AI's potential judiciously, ensuring that content remains at the core of all endeavors.

3.3.3 *Through the reader's lens*

The integration of AI into journalism and the world of information in general stands out as one of the most transformative shifts in the media landscape since Gutenberg. However, the success of this integration hinges not just on technological advancements but also on the acceptance and trust of the readership. After all, journalism, at its core, is a service to the public, and any change in its fabric will inevitably be scrutinized by its most ardent consumers.

Historically, readers have cherished the human element in journalism. The nuances of a journalist's voice, their unique perspectives, and even their inherent biases have added layers of depth and relatability to stories. This human touch, replete with emotions and imperfections, has been the cornerstone of traditional storytelling. Against this backdrop, the introduction of AI-generated content might be perceived as a sterile, mechanical intrusion into a deeply human domain. Such a shift can evoke feelings of unease and skepticism, with readers questioning the authenticity and soul of machine-crafted narratives.

A glance at other industries offers insights into this transitional phase. When ATMs were first introduced in 1967, many bank customers were wary, preferring human tellers for their banking needs. Over time, as people recognized the convenience and efficiency of ATMs, they became an integral part of our financial landscape. Fast-forward to the dawn of online shopping. Much like ATMs, e-commerce faced its share of skeptics initially. Consumers, wary of digital transactions and the impersonal nature of online shopping, took time to warm up to the idea. However, as they began to experience the myriad benefits – from the convenience of shopping from the comfort of their homes to the vast array of choices – online shopping became not just accepted, but preferred.

The Covid-19 pandemic further accelerated this shift. Interestingly, even sectors traditionally resistant to online purchases, such as grocery, underwent a transformation. The pandemic underscored the convenience and safety of online shopping, prompting even the most traditional shoppers to reconsider their habits.

Drawing parallels from these examples, the key to gaining reader acceptance for AI in journalism lies in transparency, education, and consistent value delivery. Let's take a deep dive into these three areas.

- *Transparent AI integration*
  The integration of AI into journalism and content creation is a groundbreaking development, but it also brings with it a host of ethical and practical considerations. Here's a more detailed exploration of what transparent AI integration entails.

  1. **Open algorithms**
     a) The need for clarity: In an age where misinformation is rampant, it's crucial for publishers to be transparent about the tools and methods they employ. When using AI algorithms, publishers have a responsibility to ensure their readers understand the basics of how these algorithms operate.

b) Demystifying AI for the masses: While the intricacies of AI might be complex, a simplified explanation can go a long way. For instance, explaining that AI might prioritize recent news events or trending topics can give readers a glimpse into its functioning.

c) Balancing transparency with propriety: It's important to note that being transparent doesn't equate to disclosing trade secrets. Publishers can maintain their competitive edge by keeping specific algorithmic details proprietary, but they should still offer a broad overview of AI's operations.

2. Clear labeling

a) Building trust through honesty: Readers place their trust in publishers to deliver accurate and unbiased news. By clearly labeling AI-generated content, publishers show that they respect their readers' right to know the origin of their news.

b) Differentiating content origins: Just as we differentiate between opinion pieces and factual reporting, there should be a clear distinction between human-authored and AI-generated content. This ensures that readers can approach the content with a clear understanding of its genesis.

c) Setting industry standards: As AI becomes more prevalent in journalism, there's a need for industry-wide standards on labeling. This can help create a uniform approach across different publications, ensuring that readers receive consistent cues regardless of where they consume their news.

- *Educational initiatives: Bridging the AI knowledge gap*
The rapid integration of AI into journalism underscores the need for educational initiatives that keep the public informed. As AI becomes a mainstay in content creation and curation, it's essential for readers to understand its influence and implications. Here's a deeper look into how educational initiatives can play a pivotal role in this.

1. AI workshops for readers

a) Interactive learning: Hosting workshops offers a hands-on approach to understanding AI. Through live demonstrations, readers can see AI in action, from content generation to data analysis. This demystifies the technology and makes it more accessible to the average person.

b) Q&A sessions: Workshops provide an invaluable opportunity for readers to ask questions directly to experts. Whether they're curious about the ethical considerations of AI or its technical aspects, these sessions can address concerns and clarify doubts.

c) Building a community: By attending these workshops, readers can connect with others who share similar interests. This fosters a community of informed individuals who can engage in meaningful discussions about the future of AI in journalism.

2. Informative articles and series

a) Staying updated: The world of AI is ever evolving. Periodic articles ensure that readers stay abreast of the latest developments, from new AI models in journalism to ethical debates surrounding their use.

b) Diverse perspectives: Articles can offer a range of viewpoints, from tech experts elucidating the intricacies of AI algorithms to journalists discussing their firsthand experiences with AI tools. This multifaceted approach provides readers with a holistic understanding.

c) Engaging visuals: Infographics, flowcharts, and other visual aids can make complex AI concepts more digestible. By breaking down information into easily understandable chunks, articles can cater to both AI novices and enthusiasts.

• *Consistent value delivery: Ensuring excellence in the AI age*
The integration of AI into journalism promises efficiency, scalability, and innovation. However, the heart of journalism lies in delivering value – accurate, relevant, and impactful stories that resonate with readers. As we tread this new path, ensuring consistent value delivery becomes paramount. Here's a deeper dive into the facets of this principle.

1. Quality assurance

a) Human touch in the machine age: While AI possesses the capability to generate content at unprecedented speeds, the human touch ensures that this content aligns with the ethos of journalism. Human oversight brings nuance, context, and depth, attributes that machines might overlook.

b) Guarding against bias: AI models, based on the data on which they're trained, can sometimes inadvertently introduce or perpetuate biases. Editors play a crucial role in identifying and rectifying these biases, ensuring that the content remains fair and balanced.

c) Continuous training: Just as journalists undergo training to hone their skills, AI models too need continuous training to improve. Human oversight, in this context, also involves identifying areas where the AI model might need further refinement.

2. Feedback mechanisms

a) Building a two-way street: Journalism isn't just about disseminating information; it's also about listening. By encouraging reader feedback, publishers establish a two-way communication channel, fostering a sense of community and engagement.

b) Refining the machine: Feedback isn't just valuable for human journalists. It's gold for AI models. Every piece of feedback can be used to train and refine AI models, making them more aligned with reader expectations.

c) Empowering readers: When readers know that their feedback is valued and acted upon, it empowers them. They become active participants in the journalistic process, not just passive consumers. This can enhance reader loyalty and trust.

As AI becomes more integrated into the content creation and distribution process, publishers must play an active role in shaping this evolution. Passive adoption of technology, without a clear understanding of its implications, can be detrimental. By championing transparency, prioritizing education, and delivering unwavering value, publishers can not only uphold but also elevate the noble profession of journalism. In doing so, they are ensuring that they continue to play a pivotal role in society, informing, enlightening, and empowering their readership. At the same time, these initiatives are paving the way for a future where journalists and editorial teams can harness the full potential of technology, evolving their roles and ensuring that the world of information thrives in the AI era, rather than being overshadowed by it.

Insight
Generative AI and Its Implications for Media and Journalism: From Threat to Opportunity

by *Mirja Cartia d'Asero**

In the past year, we have seen an explosion of articles, interviews, state-ments, events, and debates on AI. Generative AI and its implications in particular have become so prevalent in the discourse that even Zucker-berg's much-hyped Metaverse, heralding a new dimension of life, has been relegated to the attic. We know by now that AI is not a new phe-nomenon. Discussions began in 1950 with Alan Turing (the inspiration behind Apple's logo) asking, "Can the machine think?" Then, in 1955, more consciously, John McCarthy and others coined the term "artificial intelligence."

However, it was with the introduction of large language models and the advent of generative AI – an AI capable of conversing with humans to produce text, images, videos – that widespread alarm was triggered. Why? Algorithms, machine learning, and even AI have previously been incorporated into many jobs, especially those in "news factories," the ed-itorial offices of newspapers and information websites. But this kind of alarm had not been triggered before.

Aside from some resistance from people naturally resistant to change (as happens in every revolution, from the transition from movable type to offset printing or from the typewriter to the PC), technological innova-tions were positively received as their benefits in terms of time and work quality were immediately evident.

Generative AI, however, is now mostly perceived as a threat. The rea-son is simple: It's frightening that a robot or a computer can interact with us in such a familiar way, in "our" way of relating and speaking. In

---

* CEO Gruppo24Ore.

this case, AI is perceived not merely as an object, a "machine" capable of making rapid and highly reliable calculations, but rather as a subject capable of reasoning "like a human" and potentially replacing us in many sensitive activities, not just the most routine or heavy ones. There are countless studies confirming that we will lose millions of jobs … but we will gain new ones.

I personally find it inevitable that jobs will change and that we will need to acquire new skills for new types of professions that will be created. This primarily means cultivating those abilities that machines will never be able to replace.

Machines are not subjects; they process enormous amounts of data, can make decisions based on algorithms, and can even simulate "conscious" behaviors, but they do not feel emotions, have self-awareness, or possess consciousness. In other words, they do not "feel." Machines, at least for now, remain objects and do not become subjects: Siri, Cortana, and Alexa are perfect personal assistants capable of simplifying our lives but remain objects and not subjects. They lack what distinguishes humans today: creative intuition, empathy, and consciousness.

Federico Faggin, perhaps the greatest living Italian scientist, creator of the microprocessor and touch technology before Steve Jobs, after twenty years of study and research, has understood that there is something irreducible in human beings, something that no machine can ever replace. It is the consciousness that understands and feels emotions. Without this feeling, we would be robots.

Therefore, it is argued, and I fully agree, that with AI, a humanistic (interdisciplinary with science) and ethical approach is necessary that allows us to keep the human at the center of technological evolution.

In this context, we cannot but admire the breadth, the enormous computational capacity, the physical effort of AI in ways that humans cannot match. For this reason, I agree with Giuseppe Mayer when he argues that AI in journalism has amplified the human touch, without replacing it. I further agree with Reid Hoffman, the co-founder of LinkedIn, who speaks of human-centered AI, or AI as an amplifying intelligence that can give us cognitive superpowers.

What happens in the media? There is no shortage of fears that journalists will be replaced by AI. The publisher of the *New York Times* argues that "artificial intelligence will poison the information ecosystem." The *Washington Post* boasts of already using AI in the newsroom and even on social media. Others, such as the *Wall Street Journal*, threaten to sue for copyright infringement. Certainly, *de jure condendo*, it will be up to journalists and publishers to understand how to regulate this phenomenon while waiting for legislators to express themselves on the matter because the phenomenon certainly needs to be regulated to protect privacy, copyright, and algorithm transparency. The director of the *Financial Times*, Roula Khalaf, argues for the need to have a team in the newsroom that experiments with various AI tools but at the same time highlights the damage that can result from them. I go further and say that generative AI will evolve the profession of journalism in ways we cannot yet imagine.

It should also be reiterated that, especially in the media world, the quality of AI output strictly depends on the input. If we input verified, correct data, we will have reliable output; otherwise, we will have a picture of the Pope in a down jacket. I believe that in our sector, the real differential is represented by the quality and reliability of information and its sources: Being able to distinguish certain and authoritative information will be the key element for the professional and business market, the one in which we, Sole 24 Ore, are already recognized leaders.

Obviously, like other major players, we too have embarked on a process of identifying potentially more interesting areas of application in order to amplify our ability both to operate internally and to serve our readers and customers based on trust, on the credibility of information. I am convinced, for example, that a generative AI technology applied to our databases, to our ability to be a multimedia platform that already offers services to its customers, to the authority and quality of our work, will be elements of strength for the Gruppo24ORE to compete decisively in a market destined to transform radically.

4 Stakeholder and Reputation Management through AI

4.1 From handshakes to data points: The modern evolution of stakeholder relations

Stakeholder management, often perceived as a modern corporate strategy, is in fact an age-old practice deeply rooted in the annals of human history. At its core, it revolves around the intricate tension of building, nurturing, and maintaining relationships with a diverse group of individuals and entities that have a vested interest in an organization's actions, decisions, and overall trajectory. These stakeholders can range from investors, customers, and employees to suppliers, regulators, and even the local communities in which a business operates.

The practice of stakeholder management, while now formalized with frameworks, methodologies, and digital tools, has been a cornerstone of successful enterprises for millennia. Businesses, regardless of their size or nature, have always thrived or faltered based on the strength and quality of their relationships. Given this enduring significance, it becomes fascinating to trace the evolution of stakeholder management through the ages. The essence? Unchanged. The methods? Radically different. By charting this journey towards an AI-enriched world, we don't just glean lessons from different eras; we arm ourselves with the savvy to steer through the intricate maze of our modern, hyperconnected world.

4.1.1 Birthplaces of relationship management

In the sprawling marketplaces of the Roman Empire, from the Forum Romanum to the markets of Pompeii, the art of relationship-building was paramount. Merchants didn't just sell goods; they sold trust. They understood that a one-time sale could lead to lifelong patronage if the relationship was nurtured properly. Every interaction was an opportunity to understand needs, align expectations, and forge lasting partnerships. Trust was not just given; it was earned through consistent actions, mutual respect, and a genuine understanding of each party's aspirations and concerns.

Various tools facilitated stakeholder management in those days; the abacus, for instance, was used to keep track of transactions, ensuring transparency and trust in trade. Papyrus scrolls, clay tablets, and later, paper, served as mediums for written communication, the recording of agreements, and the maintenance of records. Face-to-face interactions were enhanced with the use of signet rings to seal agreements, ensuring authenticity and commitment. Our innate desire for connection, understanding, and trust has remained consistent through the ages. Recognizing and valuing these timeless human needs is essential. As we harness the technological tools of today and tomorrow, it's crucial to remember that genuine stakeholder management hinges on understanding these core human desires, ensuring that technology enhances, rather than replaces, the depth and authenticity of our relationships.

4.1.2 Digital dialogues: The modern dynamics of stakeholder interactions

Fast-forward to today, and while the settings have changed – from grand bazaars to sleek, glass-clad conference rooms of global corporations – the essence of stakeholder management remains the same.

Nevertheless, the advent of the digital age marked a paradigm shift in stakeholder interactions. The world, once vast and fragmented, suddenly became a global village. The introduction of email revolutionized communication, making it possible to send and receive messages in mere seconds, irrespective of distance. Whether stakeholders were situated in the same city or on opposite sides of the globe, messages could be exchanged in the blink of an eye. This immediacy not only expedited communication but also fostered a sense of closeness and accessibility between businesses and their stakeholders. Video conferencing tools bridged the gap further, enabling face-to-face interactions without the need for physical presence. The beauty of video conferencing lay in its ability to capture the nuances of communication – the facial expressions, the tone of voice, the gestures – elements that written communication sometimes missed. It brought back the personal touch, the warmth of face-to-face conversations, without the need for physical presence.

And the future looks even brighter; the latest marvel in this digital evolution is Apple's new "Apple Vision Pro."[1] This extended reality (XR) headset promises to redefine corporate meetings. Combining elements of virtual reality (VR), augmented reality (AR), and mixed reality (MR), the Apple Vision Pro offers immersive experiences that can transform how businesses interact with stakeholders. Imagine a world where physical presence is no longer a limitation, where meetings are not just about seeing and hearing but about truly experiencing. Eliminating the need for physical meetings with this new generation of devices leads to efficiency and sustainability, allowing for time savings, reduced travel costs, and minimized carbon footprints. Its advanced XR features foster real-time collaborative interactions in a shared virtual realm, significantly boosting team creativity and effectiveness. Furthermore, the immersive experience it provides ensures sustained attention, leading to more fruitful stakeholder discussions. Adding to its allure, companies have the ability to design bespoke virtual environments that align with their branding, offering a distinctive and memorable experience for all participants.

Reflecting on the digital media evolution in this realm, it's evident that the ascent of social media profoundly reshaped stakeholder communication dynamics. Platforms such as Facebook, X (formerly Twitter), LinkedIn, and Instagram emerged as the new town squares, where news traveled faster than light, and feedback, both positive and negative, could spread like wildfire. These platforms, with their user-friendly interfaces and vast networks, became the epicenters of global conversation.

One of the most profound impacts of social media was its democratizing effect. No longer were voices and opinions confined to boardrooms or limited to a select few. Every individual, regardless of their status or location, had the opportunity to voice their opinions, share their experiences, and engage in dialogues. This level playing field meant that businesses had to be more attentive, responsive, and genuine in their interactions. The casual consumer's feedback was as visible and valuable as that of the largest investor.

---

[1] https://www.entrepreneur.com/science-technology/the-apple-vision-pro-will-revolutionize-remote-work/453647.

Social media provided a space where businesses could engage direct-ly with their audience, fostering a sense of community and belonging. Moreover, the context of communication on social media is vastly dif-ferent. A single tweet or post can be interpreted in multiple ways, de-pending on the cultural, social, or personal context of the reader. This necessitates a deeper understanding of the audience, their values, and their expectations. Brands now had to craft messages that resonated with a diverse audience, ensuring clarity, authenticity, and relevance.

But the sheer volume of interactions, combined with the speed at which information traveled, made stakeholder management more complex. Companies were no longer just dealing with feedback from structured meetings or letters; they were navigating a sea of data points, tweets, comments, reviews, and more. The immediacy of social media meant that companies had to be ever vigilant, ready to respond to any crisis or feedback in real time.

The challenge of stakeholder management then evolved from simple communication to deciphering, managing, and making sense of this dig-ital cacophony. It became imperative for companies to invest in tools and strategies that could help them monitor, analyze, and engage with stake-holders effectively on these platforms. AI, sentiment analysis, and data analytics became crucial in sifting through the noise, identifying trends, and understanding stakeholder sentiments.

4.1.3 *Reputation: The currency of trust in a digital world*

The advent of the digital age, for all its merits in simplifying communi-cation and enhancing the potential efficacy of stakeholder engagement, has paradoxically multiplied the touchpoints of interaction. Where once businesses had a handful of channels to manage – personal meetings, let-ters, perhaps phone calls – they now find themselves navigating a sprawl-ing web of digital platforms, each with its own nuances and expectations.

In this intricate digital landscape, the task of ensuring a consistent and effective message across various platforms becomes key. It's no lon-ger sufficient to have a strong message; that message must be tailored, aligned, and optimized for each specific channel, be it a tweet, a Linke-dIn post, a newsletter, or a virtual conference. This systematic alignment of touchpoints ensures that stakeholders, regardless of where or how they interact with a business, receive a coherent and consistent experience. It's about ensuring that the brand's voice remains unambiguous and authentic, irrespective of the medium.

In this vast digital expanse, every tweet, every post, every comment, and every review – every single interaction – contributes to a larger narrative: the company's own reputation. This reputation, intangible yet immensely powerful, becomes the barometer by which stakeholders measure a company's credibility, trustworthiness, and overall value. In many ways, a company's reputation can be the deciding factor in its success or failure. At its core, reputation is the collective perception stakeholders hold about a company, which is shaped by its actions, communications, and the experiences it delivers. It's the sum of how a company is viewed, both in moments of triumph and in times of crisis. In essence, it's the digital age's currency of trust.

Reputation management, then, is about sculpting a digital persona that mirrors real-world values. Every element, from visual aesthetics to the words used in communications, plays a crucial role in shaping this digital persona. The ability to tell stories that resonate with the values and emotions of the target audience becomes an essential tool.

Strategic stakeholder and reputation management in this digitally enriched era offers unparalleled benefits, including:

- **Directing the digital narrative:** The digital age is defined by narratives. Stories shape perceptions, drive decisions, and create movements. Reputation management empowers brands to be not just passive participants in these narratives but active drivers. By understanding stakeholder sentiments, needs, and aspirations, companies can craft narratives that resonate, inspire, and mobilize.
- **Crafting a distinct digital image:** The digital realm is rife with noise. Every brand is vying for attention, and the competition is fierce. Proactively shaping perceptions isn't about drowning out competitors or masking flaws. It's about strategically highlighting what makes your company unique, valuable, and trustworthy. This positive image acts as a beacon, drawing stakeholders toward your brand amid the digital cacophony.
- **Resilience to crises:** The digital world is fast-paced. News, especially negative news, can spread globally within minutes. A robust reputation management strategy isn't just about preventing negative perceptions but also about having a plan in place to address them

when they arise. This resilience ensures that when crises occur, your brand can respond swiftly, transparently, and effectively, safeguarding its credibility.

- **Cultivating digital trust**: At the heart of any successful business relationship lies trust. In the digital age, where face-to-face interactions are often replaced by online exchanges, establishing trust can be challenging. Reputation management plays a pivotal role in this. By ensuring that a company's digital persona consistently reflects its values, promises, and deliverables, it fosters an environment where stakeholders feel secure in their interactions. This trust isn't just about making sales; it's about building long-term relationships that can weather challenges and evolve over time.
- **Fostering loyal digital advocates**: In an era where consumers have endless choices at their fingertips, loyalty is golden. A strong online presence, backed by positive feedback and consistent value delivery, creates a bond between brands and their customers. This bond isn't just transactional; it's emotional. Loyal customers become brand advocates, amplifying positive narratives and defending the brand in times of controversy.
- **Attracting the modern workforce**: The modern workforce, especially the younger generation, is discerning about where they work. They seek employers whose values align with theirs, who have a positive impact, and who are respected in their fields. A strong digital reputation signals to potential employees that your company is not just a place to work but also a place to grow, contribute, and make a difference.

In this new post-digital era, stakeholder and reputation management becomes both an art and a science. It's about understanding the nuances of each platform, the expectations of different stakeholder groups, and the broader cultural and social contexts in which these interactions occur. But it's also about data – tracking interactions, analyzing feedback, and using this information to refine and improve future engagements.

As we explore the complexities of reputation in the sections to come, we'll dive into the tools, strategies, and perspectives businesses require to traverse this evolving landscape of stakeholder management. We'll also uncover how AI is reshaping stakeholder interactions, transforming raw data into valuable insights, and ensuring that the personal connection, akin to a handshake, remains intact even in our digital era.

4.2   Leveraging AI in stakeholder management: A step-by-step approach

Generative AI, with its ability to create content, simulate scenarios, and predict stakeholder responses, offers unprecedented opportunities to enhance and streamline stakeholder engagement processes. As businesses seek innovative ways to engage with their relevant networks, integrating generative AI can provide deeper insights, automate personalized communication, and foster more meaningful relationships.

In this section, we'll guide you through a structured approach to weaving generative AI into your stakeholder management strategy. We'll break down each step of the process, highlighting its significance and illustrating it with real-world examples. Our aim is to offer a balanced blend of traditional stakeholder management practices and the innovative potential of generative AI.

4.2.1   *Identify all stakeholders*

To truly harness the potential of these relationships, businesses must first identify every stakeholder and understand the intricate web of relationships that exist among them. This is where modern tools and methodologies, powered by generative AI and advanced analytics, come into play.

One of the most effective ways to achieve clarity in stakeholder identification is through stakeholder mapping. This visual tool allows organizations to represent key players in a structured manner, highlighting their influence, interests, and potential impact on the company overall or on a specific project or strategy. By plotting stakeholders on a matrix based on their power and interest, businesses can prioritize their engagement efforts. This ensures that stakeholders with the highest potential impact are given due attention.

However, stakeholder mapping goes beyond mere identification. It provides a holistic view of the stakeholder ecosystem, revealing potential alliances, conflicts, and synergies. This clarity is invaluable, especially when navigating complex projects with multiple, sometimes conflicting, interests at play.

To enhance this mapping process, businesses can leverage data-driven stakeholder analysis. This approach processes vast amounts of data, offering insights into stakeholder behavior and patterns. For instance, companies such as HubSpot use advanced analytics to segment and understand their customer base, aiding in stakeholder identification.[2] Such detailed profiling ensures that businesses have a comprehensive understanding of each stakeholder's nuances.

Interactive stakeholder platforms, such as AI-powered chatbots, can also play a pivotal role in this process. They can gather real-time feedback, aiding in the identification and understanding of stakeholders. These platforms can engage stakeholders in real time, collecting valuable insights that can further refine the stakeholder map.

The benefits of such a comprehensive approach are manifold.

- **Prioritization**: By plotting stakeholders based on their power and interests, organizations can quickly identify which stakeholders require immediate attention and which can be engaged at later stages. Data-driven stakeholder analysis can be instrumental here. By investigating past interactions and feedback, this tool can assign scores to stakeholders, helping in plotting them on a matrix. Interactive stakeholder platforms, such as AI-powered chatbots, can gather real-time feedback, further aiding in determining the stakeholders' current interests and concerns. For instance, a stakeholder with high power and high interest, as identified through these tools, would be crucial to the project's success and would thus be a top priority.
- **Insight into stakeholder dynamics**: The mapping process often reveals insights that might not be immediately apparent. Stakeholder profiling and segmentation can provide a deeper understanding of these dynamics. By creating detailed profiles, businesses can understand the nuances of each stakeholder group. This can reveal why two stakeholders high interest have different motivations. Additionally, data-driven stakeholder analysis can uncover patterns in stakeholder behavior from historical data, offering further clarity.
- **Identification of potential risks and opportunities**: A comprehensive stakeholder map can highlight potential areas of conflict or synergy. Data-driven stakeholder analysis can highlight past instances of conflicts or collaborations, allowing businesses to antici-

---

[2] https://www.hubspot.com/.

pate potential future risks. At the same time, stakeholder profiling and segmentation can identify stakeholder groups that might have conflicting interests, providing an early warning system for potential challenges. Conversely, if multiple stakeholders share a common interest, there may be an opportunity for collaboration, which these tools can help identify.

- **Strategic engagement**: With a clear view of the stakeholder landscape, businesses can craft tailored engagement strategies. Interactive stakeholder platforms play a pivotal role here. By providing stakeholders with platforms to voice their opinions and concerns, businesses can ensure that their engagement is timely, relevant, and effective. Furthermore, stakeholder profiling and segmentation allows for targeted communication strategies for each stakeholder profile, ensuring that interactions not only are effective but also resonate with the stakeholders' specific interests and concerns.

By integrating these tools into the stakeholder management process, businesses can achieve a more nuanced, data-driven, and interactive approach to stakeholder identification, ensuring the success of their projects or strategies.

4.2.2 *Categorize stakeholders*

By categorizing stakeholders, organizations can tailor their engagement strategies, ensuring that each stakeholder group receives the right level of attention and the most relevant information. Their influence, interests, and potential impact on a project or strategy can vary widely. To navigate this complex landscape effectively, it's essential to categorize stakeholders, allowing for a more nuanced and tailored approach to engagement. The following four-tiered approach allows for more efficient allocation of resources, ensuring that high-impact stakeholders are prioritized.

- **Primary stakeholders**: These are the individuals or groups that stand to be directly affected, either positively or negatively, by the project or the company's actions. Their interests are deeply intertwined with the project's outcomes. Engaging with primary stakeholders is crucial as they often have the most significant influence on the project's success. Stakeholder profiling and segmentation can offer detailed insights into their behavior, preferences, and pain points, ensuring that engagement strategies are tailored to their specific needs.

Example: In the context of launching a new pharmaceutical drug, patients who will be using the drug and doctors who will be prescribing it are primary stakeholders. Their experiences, feedback, and advocacy can significantly shape the drug's market acceptance. Stakeholder sentiment analysis can gauge their perceptions and concerns, providing real-time feedback that can be invaluable in shaping the drug's marketing and distribution strategies.

- **Secondary stakeholders**: While they might not be directly impacted by the project, secondary stakeholders play a vital role in shaping its environment. They can influence primary stakeholders or even change the broader context in which the project operates. Trend analysis and forecasting can predict their behavior based on market trends, ensuring that their potential influence is anticipated and addressed.

  Example: Regulatory bodies, in the case of the pharmaceutical drug launch, are secondary stakeholders. While they don't use or prescribe the drug, their regulations, approvals, and guidelines can significantly impact its market presence.

- **Tertiary stakeholders**: These stakeholders have a more indirect or less immediate interest in the project. They might not engage with the project directly, but they influence or are influenced by the broader environment in which the project operates. Stakeholder profiling and segmentation can help in understanding their motivations and potential areas of interest, ensuring that their concerns are addressed proactively.

  Example: Shareholders or investors in the pharmaceutical company might be tertiary stakeholders. The success of the drug can influence the company's stock prices, impacting their investment.

- **Quaternary stakeholders**: This group is the most removed from the direct impacts of the project but can still have a role in shaping its broader context. Their engagement is more about understanding broader trends and contexts. Trend analysis and forecasting can provide insights into the broader market dynamics and potential areas of interest for these stakeholders.

  Example: Media outlets covering the healthcare sector might be quaternary stakeholders for the drug launch. Their reporting can shape public perceptions, even if they don't directly engage with the drug. Stakeholder sentiment analysis can gauge the media's perception of the drug, providing insights into potential areas of focus or concern.

Moreover, understanding the different categories of stakeholders can also help in anticipating potential challenges or opportunities. For instance, if a secondary stakeholder such as a regulatory body raises concerns, addressing those promptly can prevent potential challenges with primary stakeholders such as doctors or patients. Stakeholder sentiment analysis can provide real-time feedback on these concerns, ensuring that they are addressed promptly and effectively.

4.2.3 *Develop a communication plan*

Identifying and categorizing stakeholders is a foundational step, but the real challenge lies in establishing dynamic, meaningful communication with them. Beyond merely crafting content, it's about ensuring continuous alignment, enrichment, and adaptation to their unique needs and preferences. In this digital age, where data-driven insights reign supreme, leveraging AI tools can significantly enhance the effectiveness of a communication plan. Platforms such as MailChimp have already demonstrated the power of AI in tailoring communications to ensure optimal stakeholder engagement.[3]

A meticulously designed communication plan, tailored to the unique needs and preferences of each stakeholder group, is pivotal. Here's how AI can be integrated into the communication plan.

- **Message content**: AI can support the crafting of messages specific to stakeholder groups. For instance, while investors might be keen on financial metrics, employees might be more attuned to organizational culture and growth opportunities. AI-driven enhanced communication can analyze past interactions and feedback to craft messages that resonate with each group's interests and concerns.

---

[3] https://mailchimp.com/.

- **Communication channel**: AI can suggest tailored engagement methods based on stakeholder behavior. For example, while top-tier executives might prefer formal reports, younger consumers might be more receptive to interactive webinars or social media campaigns. Predictive engagement strategies can analyze past engagement metrics to suggest the most effective communication channels for each group.
- **Frequency**: Automated reporting can offer real-time insights into stakeholder interactions, helping organizations determine the optimal frequency of communication. High-power, high-interest stakeholders might require regular updates, while others might be content with less frequent touchpoints. AI can analyze engagement rates to suggest the best communication frequency for each group.
- **Tone and style**: AI can analyze feedback and engagement metrics to determine the most effective tone and style for each stakeholder group. For instance, a technical group might appreciate data-driven communications, while a general consumer base might resonate more with emotive, story-driven content.

A tailored communication plan offers a multitude of advantages for organizations. Firstly, it paves the way for enhanced engagement. When stakeholders receive messages that resonate with their perspectives and needs, they are more likely to engage deeply, leading to interactions that are not just frequent but also more fruitful. Secondly, the importance of risk mitigation cannot be overstated. By ensuring that communications are clear, consistent, and timely, organizations can nip potential misunderstandings in the bud, preventing them from escalating into conflicts. This proactive approach can save both time and resources in the long run. Tailored communications play a pivotal role in reputation management. By addressing stakeholder concerns head-on and proactively highlighting organizational achievements, companies can bolster their reputation and enhance their brand image in the eyes of their stakeholders and the broader public.

Lastly, a well-structured communication plan isn't just about broadcasting messages; it's also about listening. By establishing regular communication channels, organizations create a feedback loop. This offers stakeholders a platform to voice their feedback, raise concerns, or make suggestions. Such insights, coming directly from those who have a stake in the organization's success, can prove invaluable in refining strategies and operations.

4.2.4 *Engage stakeholders early and often*

Engaging stakeholders early and consistently is not just a best practice; it's a strategic imperative. In taking such an approach, organizations can secure stakeholder buy-in, build trust, and set the stage for smoother project execution. Engaging stakeholders at the outset, even before major decisions are made, offers several advantages. Early engagement provides organizations with a wealth of insights, perspectives, and feedback. This enables them to make decisions that are not only better informed but also more holistic. With the rise of interactive stakeholder platforms such as HubSpot and MailChimp, which we already mentioned, as well as others such as Insightly and Totango, organizations can facilitate real-time interactions, gathering immediate feedback and insights. These platforms, powered by generative AI, can simulate various stakeholder responses, helping organizations anticipate reactions and tailor their strategies accordingly.

When stakeholders feel they are part of the decision-making process, it fosters a deeper sense of trust. They are more likely to support initiatives when they've had a say in shaping them. Innovation and co-creation strategies, underpinned by AI, involve stakeholders directly in the innovation process. This collaborative approach ensures that solutions are co-designed, leveraging the collective intelligence of both the organization and its stakeholders.

While early engagement lays the foundation, continuous engagement ensures that the momentum is maintained. Regular interactions with stakeholders serve multiple purposes.

- **Adaptive strategies**: As projects evolve, continuous engagement allows organizations to adapt their strategies based on real-time feedback from stakeholders. Companies such as Adobe, for instance, use interactive platforms to gather user feedback, ensuring continuous engagement. These platforms, often integrated with generative AI, allow for dynamic adjustments based on user interactions.
- **Strengthening relationships**: Regular touchpoints, facilitated by AI-driven platforms, reinforce relationships. They ensure that stake-

holders feel not only valued but also heard. This continuous dialogue fosters a deeper sense of partnership, with stakeholders becoming active participants rather than passive observers.

- **Feedback loop:** Establishing a two-way communication channel is pivotal. It allows organizations to both disseminate information and gather feedback.

In an age where business dynamics are constantly shifting, stakeholder engagement remains a constant imperative. Leveraging the power of generative AI and innovative engagement strategies can ensure that organizations remain agile, responsive, and always in tune with their stakeholders' needs and concerns.

4.2.5 *Monitor and manage stakeholder sentiments*

Today the ebb and flow of public sentiment can change direction in the blink of an eye. For organizations navigating this tumultuous sea of opinions, staying attuned to stakeholder sentiments is not just a luxury – it's a necessity.

Historically, the realm of sentiment analysis was dominated by traditional machine learning techniques. These methods, while effective, often involved laborious processes: collecting vast amounts of data, manually annotating them for sentiment, engineering features to make the data understandable to machines, and then training models to recognize patterns. The end goal? To predict sentiments of new, unseen data.

Enter the era of generative AI, particularly LLMs: these tools, trained on vast swathes of the internet, have fundamentally transformed the sentiment analysis game. No longer do developers need to wade through the tedious steps of data collection, annotation, and model training. With generative AI, the power of sentiment analysis is unlocked with a simple, well-crafted prompt. This shift signifies a move toward more accessible and efficient sentiment analysis methods, democratizing the power of AI for businesses of all sizes.

The magic lies in LLMs' capability for in-context learning. By providing a series of text and sentiment pairs as examples, or even a single example, these models can be conditioned to evaluate the sentiment of new text. This dynamic conditioning allows LLMs to adapt on the fly, making them versatile tools for various sentiment analysis applications.

It's important to recognize that their outputs, while often impressive, can sometimes be unpredictable. This unpredictability underscores the importance of rigorous evaluation and iterative refinement. Developers must remain vigilant, ensuring that the insights derived are accurate, relevant, and aligned with the organization's objectives.

Understanding stakeholder sentiments offers a plethora of benefits. For example, monitoring tools provide real-time insights into how stakeholders perceive initiatives, products, or decisions, allowing for immediate course corrections if needed. By tracking sentiment trends, organizations can anticipate potential challenges or opportunities, crafting strategies that are proactive rather than reactive.

But merely monitoring sentiments is not enough. Organizations need to actively manage them, ensuring that positive perceptions are amplified while addressing negative ones. Some strategies include:

- **Active listening:** Go beyond mere tracking and genuinely engage with stakeholder feedback to understand their underlying concerns or aspirations.
- **Responsive communication:** Address negative sentiments promptly and transparently, assuring stakeholders that their concerns are being addressed.
- **Feedback integration:** Use the feedback from sentiment analysis to refine strategies, products, or initiatives, showcasing to stakeholders that their opinions drive organizational decisions.

Nike, a global sportswear giant, exemplifies the power of sentiment monitoring. With each product launch or marketing campaign, Nike is acutely aware of the real-time reactions of its vast consumer base. Leveraging tools that monitor social media, blogs, and forums, Nike captures the pulse of consumer sentiments. But what sets Nike apart is its agile approach to sentiment management, powered in part by the capabilities of generative AI.

When a particular shoe design receives mixed reviews, Nike's design team might take that feedback into account for future iterations. If a marketing campaign sparks controversy, Nike is quick to respond, either standing by its message or making amends based on the feedback. This agility is further enhanced by generative AI's ability to simulate various scenarios, helping Nike anticipate stakeholder reactions and craft responsive communication strategies.

By involving local communities, suppliers, and consumers, and by leveraging the power of generative AI for real-time sentiment analysis and simulation, Nike ensures that its initiatives are in harmony with global sentiments. This approach not only enhances the success rate of its projects but also bolsters Nike's reputation as a brand that listens, adapts, and evolves based on stakeholder feedback.

4.2.6 *Address conflicts proactively*

In the intricate business of stakeholder management, conflicts are inevitable. Different stakeholders come with varying interests, perspectives, and expectations. While these differences can be a source of rich insights and diverse viewpoints, they can also lead to conflicts. Addressing these conflicts proactively, rather than letting them fester, is pivotal in maintaining trust, ensuring alignment, and driving the organization's objectives forward. With generative AI tools and strategies, conflicts are not only addressed but also anticipated and mitigated.

By directly addressing conflicts, organizations convey a clear message that they value stakeholder opinions and are committed to resolving differences. AI-driven sentiment analysis can gauge stakeholder sentiments in real time, allowing organizations to address concerns promptly.

Proactively addressing conflicts can prevent them from escalating, mitigating potential risks to the project or the organization's reputation. Generative AI can simulate various scenarios, helping organizations anticipate potential conflicts and craft responsive strategies. Resolving conflicts paves the way for more collaborative stakeholder engagement, harnessing the collective strengths of diverse stakeholder groups. AI-powered collaboration tools can facilitate seamless communication and co-creation, ensuring that all voices are heard.

Organizations need to have robust strategies in place to address and resolve potential conflicts. Some strategies might include:

- **Open dialogue:** Create platforms where stakeholders can voice their concerns, ensuring that they feel heard and valued. In this area AI-driven platforms can analyze feedback in real time, highlighting areas of concern.
- **Empathy and understanding:** Approach conflicts with an empathetic mindset, seeking to understand the underlying concerns or motivations of conflicting stakeholders. Generative AI can offer in-

sights into stakeholder behavior and motivations, ensuring a more empathetic approach.

- **Transparent communication:** Clearly communicate the organization's stance, decisions, and the rationale behind them, ensuring that stakeholders understand the bigger picture.
- **Collaborative problem-solving:** Engage conflicting stakeholders in the problem-solving process, ensuring that solutions are co-created and mutually beneficial. Generative AI can simulate potential solutions, offering a range of options to consider.

4.2.7 *Evaluate and refine the strategy*

Stakeholder dynamics are continually evolving since these dynamics are influenced by a myriad of factors, including societal shifts, market trends, and rapid technological advancements. Given this ever-changing landscape, it's imperative for organizations to adopt a mindset of continuous evaluation and refinement. This ensures that their stakeholder engagement strategies are not only up to date but also effective, relevant, and in alignment with both the organization's objectives and the evolving expectations of stakeholders.

By consistently evaluating their strategy, organizations can ensure it remains attuned to the current expectations and concerns of stakeholders. This is where the power of generative AI can be harnessed. For instance, data-driven stakeholder analysis, powered by AI, can provide comprehensive insights into stakeholders, ensuring a more tailored and effective engagement strategy.

Proactively identifying and addressing emerging stakeholder concerns can help organizations pre-empt potential risks, ensuring smoother operations. Generative AI's scenario modeling can assess potential impacts of changes in strategy, allowing businesses to make informed decisions and mitigate risks effectively. An effective and relevant stakeholder management strategy can significantly accelerate the achievement of organizational objectives by harnessing the support and collaboration of stakeholders.

Recognizing the need for strategy refinement is just the first step. To truly make a difference, organizations must adopt structured approaches.

- **Feedback mechanisms:** It's crucial to establish structured feedback mechanisms, such as surveys or focus groups. These tools can provide invaluable insights by gathering stakeholder feedback directly related to the engagement strategy.

- **Performance metrics**: Organizations should define and consistently track key performance metrics related to stakeholder engagement. Metrics such as stakeholder satisfaction levels or the effectiveness of communication strategies can offer a clear picture of the strategy's impact.
- **Regular reviews**: It's beneficial to schedule regular strategy review sessions. These sessions can bring together key internal stakeholders to evaluate the strategy's current effectiveness and pinpoint areas that might benefit from improvement.
- **Stakeholder inclusion**: Including stakeholders in the strategy refinement process can be a game changer. Their unique insights and perspectives can provide a more comprehensive view, ensuring a well-rounded and effective revised strategy.

As the business landscape continues to evolve, so too must stakeholder management strategies. By seamlessly integrating generative AI into the strategy refinement process, organizations can ensure they remain at the forefront of stakeholder engagement, driving success in their specific area.

4.3   Machines as stakeholders: Navigating the algorithmic paradox

Artificial intelligence and digital transformation are no longer mere buzzwords; they've seamlessly woven themselves into the very fabric of our daily lives. Consider the simplicity of our mornings: a virtual assistant such as Alexa briefs us on the day's weather, while Spotify curates the perfect playlist to kickstart our day. These devices, once seen as mere luxuries, have now become indispensable companions, influencing our daily routines, purchasing decisions, and even our social interactions.

Yet there's more beneath the surface. These devices, powered by intricate algorithms, aren't just passively responding to our commands; they're actively guiding our choices. Whether it's suggesting a new track, recommending a product, or even shaping our opinions, these algorithms are emerging as leading players in the theater of modern consumption. For instance, when you ask Alexa for a product recommendation, there's a likelihood that it will prioritize Amazon-branded products over bet-ter-rated alternatives.[4]

This brings forth a pivotal challenge for businesses: how to navigate this new landscape where algorithms aren't just tools but genuine stake-holders? They dictate what content we see on our social media feeds, recommend products on e-commerce platforms, and even influence our music and movie choices on streaming services. Their decisions, based on big datasets and intricate programming, can guide a user toward one choice over another, often without the user even realizing it.

For businesses, this means that the battleground for consumer atten-tion and loyalty has expanded. It's no longer just about outdoing com-petitors in terms of product quality, pricing, or marketing. Now, there's an added layer: understanding and influencing the algorithms that stand between businesses and their customers. If an algorithm can sway a con-sumer's choice, then businesses must figure out how to ensure that sway is in their favor.

But how does a business engage with an entity that doesn't have emo-tions, biases, or personal preferences? How does one negotiate with or influence something that operates based on data and logic? These are the challenges that businesses face in this new landscape.

The first step is understanding. Businesses must invest in understand-ing how these algorithms work, the data they use, and the logic that drives their decisions. This might involve hiring experts, collaborating with tech companies, or investing in research and development.

Next, businesses must align their strategies with the digital logic of these algorithms. This could mean optimizing content for search en-gines, tailoring products based on data-driven insights, or even collabo-rating directly with tech platforms to ensure favorable algorithmic treat-ment.

Lastly, there's an ethical dimension to consider. As businesses seek to influence algorithms, they must ensure that their efforts are transparent, ethical, and in the best interests of their consumers. After all, trust is still a valuable commodity, and in the age of digital scrutiny, it's one that can be easily lost.

---

[4]   https://themarkup.org/amazons-advantage/2021/10/14/amazon-puts-its-own-brands-first-above-better-rated-products.

As algorithms transition from tools to real and concrete stakeholders, businesses are presented with both challenges and opportunities. Those willing to adapt, learn, and innovate in this new landscape will not only survive but also thrive, shaping the future of commerce in an algorithm-driven world.

Insight
Leveraging Generative AI for Stakeholder Analysis and Reputation Management

by *Matteo Flora*[*]

The concept of stakeholders from a reputational point of view is deeply rooted in management and communication theories. A stakeholder can be broadly defined as any entity – an individual, a group, or an organization – with a legitimate interest in an organization. They can impact, or be impacted by, the organization's decisions and actions. Freeman's seminal work on stakeholder theory proposes that stakeholders are not just shareholders or investors but also include employees, customers, suppliers, government bodies, and even the communities the organization serves or may impact.[1] Therefore, the landscape of stakeholders is a complex ecosystem that requires careful examination.

Stakeholder analysis is a systematic process used to identify an organization's stakeholders and understand their interests, influence, interrelationships, and implications for the company. The objective is to map the field of entities with stakes in the organization's functioning and outcomes, to identify potential risks and opportunities, and to inform the development of strategies for stakeholder management.

Generative AI, a subset of artificial intelligence, uses algorithms to generate data similar to input.[2] AI is increasingly being leveraged to map and define stakeholders: traditional stakeholder analysis methods often result in a time-consuming process, while AI-enabled analysis can auto-

---

[*] Entrepreneur at The Fool, LT42, 42LawFirm.
[1] Freeman, R. E. (1984), *Strategic Management: A Stakeholder Approach*, Pitman.
[2] Goodfellow, I., Bengio, Y., Courville, A., & Bengio, Y. (2016), *Deep Learning* (Vol. 1), MA: MIT Press.

mate these tasks, offering efficient, objective, comprehensive mappings of stakeholders.

Beyond identifying and analyzing stakeholders, AI can also be used to create comprehensive profiles of stakeholders. AI can provide a holistic picture of each stakeholder by integrating and analyzing various data sources, from demographic to behavioral and interaction data. For instance, it can reveal a stakeholder's preferences, motivations, and concerns, thus enabling more targeted and personalized engagement strategies.

Consider a hypothetical prompt for an LLM: "Describe a stakeholder profile for a young, tech-savvy customer of a tech company." The LLM might generate a response that outlines the stakeholder's demographic attributes and likely values, preferences, behaviors, and influencers. Such detailed profiles can greatly inform an organization's stakeholder engagement strategies, allowing them to tailor their messages and initiatives in a way that resonates with each stakeholder category.

The utility of generative AI and LLMs is particularly noteworthy in personalizing stakeholder messages: AI can create customized messages for each stakeholder category, starting from a standard message. For example, an LLM such as GPT can generate various versions of a statement or notice based on the context or the intended recipient.

AI's prowess in personalizing messages is not limited to developing different messages for different stakeholder groups. It extends to generating variations of the same message to cater to individual stakeholders within a group based on their unique characteristics. The ability of AI to transform generic communication into personalized messages is reshaping stakeholder communication.

LLMs, for example OpenAI's GPT, can not only generate human-like texts but, to some extent, also comprehend the context, tone, and messages within them. This characteristic makes them an invaluable tool in examining and deciphering the vast amount of text data generated by stakeholders across various platforms.

Creating a reputation analysis system using LLMs gives organizations a granular view of stakeholder sentiment. Such systems capture stakeholders' thoughts, opinions, and attitudes and provide a clear, quantifiable measure of an organization's reputation among different stakeholder groups. This helps the brand not only to understand the single points of view better but also to determine and plan messages to be delivered to each and every one of the recipients.

Generative AI and LLMs can also conduct proactive reputation management: by constantly monitoring and analyzing stakeholder sentiments and interactions, AI can provide early warnings of potential reputation risks. AI's predictive capabilities can be used to forecast possible shifts in stakeholder sentiment, giving organizations an opportunity to address issues before they escalate.

While AI and LLMs offer immense potential for enhancing stakeholder analysis and management, it is important to remember that these technologies should not replace human judgment and engagement. Rather, they should serve as valuable tools that augment human capabilities, providing insights, efficiency, and scale that were previously unattainable.

5 AI and Applications for Marketing

5.1 The Renaissance of marketing in the AI era

Nestled amid the rolling hills of Costigliole d'Asti, at his serene resort Le Marne, Guido Martinetti, co-founder of the renowned gelato brand Grom and a passionate wine producer, has a unique perspective on what marketing is all about. For many, marketing is a tool, a means to an end, often driven by numbers and profit margins. In the wrong hands, it can become a sterile and impersonal tool, especially when the primary goal is sheer profit maximization.

But for Guido, marketing is an art, a way of life, and a means of genuine connection. His approach to marketing is a testament to the power of authenticity. For him, marketing is not just about selling a product; it's about telling a story, sharing a passion, and connecting with people on a profound level. The same love and dedication he poured into crafting the perfect scoop of gelato, he now infuses into every bottle of wine he produces. It's not just about taste or quality; it's about the experience, the memories, and the emotions these products evoke.

In an era where many view customers as mere data points, Guido sees them as individuals with their own stories, dreams, and desires. He understands that behind every purchase there's a person seeking an experience, a moment of joy, or a taste of nostalgia. By viewing marketing as an art form, he creates sincere and deep connections, transcending the traditional consumer–brand relationship.

This perspective is a refreshing reminder in our AI-driven world. While technology can provide tools to optimize and streamline, it's the human touch, the genuine love for the craft, and the respect for the customer that truly make a brand stand out. For Guido, customers are not just consumers; they are individuals to be loved and respected. After all, they are the backbone of any enterprise, providing the support and nourishment businesses need to flourish. As we delve deeper into the applications of AI in marketing, let's keep Guido's philosophy in mind. Technology is a tool, but it's the human touch, the genuine connections, and the authentic stories that truly make marketing resonate.

5.1.1 *A Brief evolutionary history of marketing*

Long before the concept of "marketing" became a buzzword in the business world, its essence was already pulsating in bustling marketplaces of ancient civilizations. For instance, the Romans, known for their meticulous attention to detail, crafted distinct amphora shapes and markings, a primitive form of branding, to provide information about the contents they held.

The emergence of mass media platforms, such as radio, television, and newspapers, offered marketers a broader canvas to showcase their products. These platforms were powerful mediums that could craft narratives, create iconic brand mascots, and even influence public opinion.

However, as the 20th century neared its end, the winds of change began to blow again. The dawn of the digital age signaled a paradigm shift in marketing strategies. The internet, with its vast expanse and limitless potential, began to reshape the marketing landscape. Traditional advertising methods started to intertwine with digital techniques. Suddenly, terms such as email marketing, banner ads, and SEO became the buzzwords of the industry. One of the most transformative aspects of digital marketing was its democratizing effect. No longer were massive advertising budgets a prerequisite for global reach. Even a small startup could craft a compelling online presence and engage with audiences from different corners of the world. This digital revolution also gave birth to a new breed of professionals: digital marketing experts, who understood the intricacies of online branding and promotion.

Fast-forward to today, and the marketing landscape is more dynamic than ever. Modern consumers expect a seamless and personalized experience across all touchpoints. To cater to these evolving demands, businesses are harnessing cutting-edge technologies, with generative AI being at the forefront. Whether it's crafting content tailored to individual customer behaviors, optimizing performance, or automating routine sales tasks, AI is redefining the boundaries of what's possible.

A study by Gartner reveals that consumers are more at ease with generative AI's magic unfolding in marketing than in any other sector.[1] In fact, 38 percent of consumers expressed comfort with the use of generative AI in marketing, with another 27 percent remaining neutral. This sentiment starkly contrasts with other sectors such as manufacturing, healthcare, and legal services, where discomfort with generative AI often overshadows its acceptance. This proactive stance is further evidenced by the fact that over 64 percent of marketers are already deploying or piloting AI or machine learning projects.

Beyond mere statistics, the real-world applications of AI in marketing are manifold and growing. Copywriters, for instance, are turning to advanced tools such as Jasper to refine their craft.[2] The realm of email marketing has seen a surge in the use of platforms such as copy.ai, optimizing outreach and engagement.[3] Creative strategists, always on the lookout for innovative approaches, are leveraging AI-driven tools such as GPT, not just for mundane tasks, but also for critical activities such as drafting positioning papers and fine-tuning headlines or crafting user personas. The design world isn't far behind, with professionals experimenting with groundbreaking tools such as DALL-E2 and Midjourney.[4] Even established software such as Adobe's Photoshop and Premiere Pro are integrating AI-powered features, pushing the boundaries of creativity.

In essence, the marketing world is not just tiptoeing around AI; it's embracing it with open arms, setting a precedent for other industries to follow.

5.1.2 The benefits of AI marketing

As we witness the accelerated evolution and embrace of predictive and generative AI technologies, the realm of AI marketing has moved beyond mere speculation, firmly establishing its transformative impact on

---

[1] https://blogs.gartner.com/nicole-greene/2023/07/19/cmos-need-to-give-generative-ai-a-chance-before-its-too-late/.

[2] https://www.jasper.ai/?fpr=p2p.

[3] https://www.copy.ai/.

[4] https://openai.com/dall-e-2; https://www.midjourney.com/.

traditional tactics. According to a study from MailChimp, 88 percent of marketers have already incorporated AI to bolster their initiatives, and they believe that amplifying their AI and automation usage is crucial not only to meet evolving customer expectations but also to secure a distinct competitive edge.[5] AI and automation in general are not just about staying current; they are pivotal in meeting ever-changing customer expectations and carving out a unique competitive position. The integration of AI into the marketing domain has unlocked a plethora of benefits, revolutionizing how brands engage with their consumers. Here are a few examples:

- **Precision in data collection:** One of the standout capabilities of generative AI is its ability to meticulously simulate customer behaviors and preferences, thereby crafting comprehensive customer profiles. Traditional data collection methods often rely on historical data, which, while valuable, only provides a retrospective view. Generative AI goes a step further. By analyzing data points such as past purchase histories, browsing patterns, and even social media interactions, it can generate projections of potential future buying patterns. This predictive capability allows brands to not only respond to but also anticipate customer needs, ensuring that marketing strategies are always one step ahead.

  Example: Consider a fashion e-commerce platform in a world where trends change at the blink of an eye. By employing generative AI, this platform can predict upcoming fashion trends based on a combination of user searches, purchases, and even global fashion influencers' activities. This foresight ensures that they not only stock up on in-demand items but also can strategize their marketing campaigns around these trends, offering personalized recommendations to users. Imagine a scenario where a user has been searching for sustainable fashion options; the AI can predict that they might be interested in an upcoming eco-friendly collection, prompting the platform to send a tailored notification or offer. Such precision in data-driven decision-making can significantly enhance user experience and boost sales.

---

[5] https://mailchimp.com/intuit-mailchimp-finds-vast-majority-of-smb-marketers-are-bought-into-ai/.

- **Scaling marketing personalization**: Today consumers are inundated with a deluge of content, making it imperative for brands to stand out by offering uniquely tailored experiences. Generative AI emerges as a lighthouse in this challenge. It possesses the capability to craft personalized content for individual users at a scale previously deemed unattainable. By delving deep into a user's interaction history, which includes their clicks, searches, likes, and even time spent on particular content, generative AI can curate product recommendations or mold content that aligns seamlessly with specific user preferences.

Example: Consider the world of streaming platforms, where the sheer volume of available content can be overwhelming for users. Platforms such as Netflix or Spotify have turned this challenge into an opportunity. By leveraging the power of AI, they can analyze a user's viewing or listening history, down to the genres they prefer, the time they typically watch or listen, and even the moods they often resonate with. Using this data, generative AI can then craft personalized playlists or show recommendations. For instance, if a user frequently listens to upbeat 80s music on Spotify, the AI might generate a 'Feel-Good Retro Hits' playlist for them. Similarly, Netflix has ingeniously harnessed the capabilities of AI to enhance user experience. Recognizing that they have a mere ninety seconds to capture a viewer's attention, Netflix employs a unique method to personalize thumbnails for each user. They utilize an algorithm called Aesthetic Visual Analysis (AVA) to sift through countless frames of a show or movie, selecting the most captivating ones.[6] After annotating each frame with metadata, they categorize them based on composition, characters, and image quality. But the personalization doesn't stop there. Netflix then examines your interaction with their platform, considering factors including your preferred genres, viewing duration, and even your geographical location. By comparing your data with that of similar users, they can tailor thumbnails to your taste. For instance, if you've recently watched a movie starring Uma Thurman, the thumbnail for "Pulp Fiction" might prominently feature her, rather than another actor

---

[6]   https://blogs.cornell.edu/info2040/2022/09/28/how-netflix-uses-matching-to-pick-the-best-thumbnail-for-you/.

such as Samuel L. Jackson. Additionally, Netflix has incorporated a machine learning algorithm named Contextual Bandits that refines thumbnail choices in real time based on your ongoing interactions. So, the thumbnails you see today might be different from those you see tomorrow, all thanks to the continuous learning process of this algorithm.

- **Reducing marketing costs**: In an era where every dollar counts, optimizing the allocation of marketing budgets is essential for businesses, especially for startups and small and medium-sized enterprises with limited resources. Generative AI offers a transformative solution to this challenge. By automating intricate processes such as content creation, ad placements, and even audience targeting, generative AI ensures that every cent spent is directed toward maximum impact. This not only streamlines operations but also significantly reduces overheads, especially when compared with traditional methods that often involve multiple intermediaries and manual interventions.

  Example: Consider a budding startup that's launching a groundbreaking app. In the traditional marketing landscape, they might have to engage with expensive marketing agencies, graphic designers for promotional content, and media planners for ad placements. However, with generative AI, this startup can automate a significant portion of these tasks. The AI can generate compelling promotional content tailored to their target audience, from catchy taglines to engaging visuals. Furthermore, it can analyze vast datasets to determine the most effective ad placements, ensuring the startup's advertisements reach their intended audience at the optimal time. This, of course, reduces the startup's reliance on costly external agencies but also ensures that their marketing budget delivers the highest possible return on investment.

- **Deepening customer engagement**: In today's digital age, merely attracting customers isn't enough; brands must engage them deeply, offering value at every touchpoint. Generative AI provides support in this area by transforming passive content into interactive experiences. By leveraging the capabilities of generative AI, brands can create dynamic content elements such as chatbots, virtual shopping assistants, or even personalized virtual showrooms. These tools don't just serve up information; they interact, learn, and adapt to

each user's unique needs, ensuring a tailored experience that resonates.

Example: Picture a leading tech store aiming to elevate its online
shopping experience. Instead of relying on static product listings
and generic FAQs, they introduce an AI-powered virtual assistant.
When customers visit the site, this assistant proactively engages
with them, asking about their specific tech needs, preferences, or
problems they're trying to solve. Based on the conversation, the
AI assistant can then generate product recommendations, offer insights, or even simulate how a particular tech product might fit into
the customer's life. Such an interactive approach not only simplifies
the shopping process but also makes customers feel valued and understood, fostering loyalty and deepening their engagement with
the brand.

- **Predictive modeling and reducing customer churn:** In every business, retaining existing customers is as crucial as acquiring new
  ones. Generative AI delves deep into the intricacies of customer
  behavior, identifying subtle patterns and signals that might indicate dissatisfaction or intent to leave. By predicting potential churn,
  brands can move from reactive problem-solving to proactive customer engagement. This foresight allows them to tailor retention
  strategies, ensuring that customers feel valued and understood.

  Example: Consider a popular online magazine subscription service.
  They notice a trend of subscribers dropping off after a few months.
  Using generative AI, they analyze reading habits, article interactions, and feedback. The AI identifies a segment of users who tend
  to lose interest after not finding content in their niche interests. Before these users cancel their subscriptions, the service reaches out,
  offering curated content lists or even exclusive articles tailored to
  their preferences, effectively reducing churn.

- **Boosting revenue:** Static pricing models can be a hindrance to maximizing profits. Generative AI, with its ability to simulate countless
  sales scenarios, offers brands a dynamic approach to pricing. By analyzing factors including demand, competitor pricing, and seasonal
  trends, AI can optimize pricing strategies in real time, ensuring
  that brands capitalize on every revenue opportunity.

  Example: An online fashion e-commerce platform, during the fes-
  tive season, witnesses a surge in traffic. Their generative AI system,

recognizing the increased demand and analyzing competitor pricing, dynamically adjusts the prices of hot-selling items, ensuring they strike a balance between demand and profitability, leading to maximized revenue.

- **Enhancing marketing productivity and agility**: The modern marketing landscape is vast, with myriad data points to analyze and strategies to consider. Generative AI acts as a force multiplier in this domain. By automating routine and often time-consuming tasks, AI ensures that marketing teams aren't bogged down with operational intricacies. This automation ensures timely insights, accurate forecasting, and more, allowing marketing professionals to channel their energies toward innovation and strategic planning.

  Example: A digital marketing agency, handling multiple clients across sectors, faces the challenge of timely report generation. Each client's data is unique, with different KPIs and metrics to consider. Instead of dedicating countless hours to manually creating these reports, the agency employs a generative AI system. This AI analyzes data from various campaigns, generating comprehensive monthly performance reports tailored to each client's needs. Not only are these reports timely, but they also offer deep insights, allowing the agency to suggest data-driven strategies, enhancing their value proposition.

5.1.3 *Essential factors for achieving success*

While the temptation to let AI take the reins entirely is strong, especially given the pressures of modern marketing demands, this approach can be dangerous from a company reputation perspective. Relying solely on AI's foundational models, without thoughtful enrichment and alignment with business goals, can lead to generic outputs that might be out of touch with the brand's essence and its audience's expectations. To navigate these complexities and truly harness the potential of AI in marketing, it's imperative to consider the following success factors.

- **Quality data and context**: The foundation of any successful AI endeavor lies in the data it's built upon. Think of AI as an artist, and data as its canvas and paints. Just as an artist's work is influenced by the quality of their materials, AI's efficacy is determined by the caliber of the data it processes. The phrase "garbage in, garbage out" is particularly apt here. If an AI system is fed with skewed, outdated, or irrelevant data, the output will inevitably be flawed, no matter how advanced the algorithm is. It's about not just quantity but also quality. Data must be meticulously curated, cleaned, and contextualized. Without this, even the most sophisticated AI models can produce misleading or downright erroneous results.

Moreover, understanding the context in which data is collected and used is crucial. Just as an artist needs to understand the nuances of their subject and the emotions they wish to convey, businesses must grasp the broader context of their data. This ensures that AI-driven insights align with real-world scenarios and are genuinely beneficial in shaping marketing strategies.

Companies must invest time and resources in ensuring their data is pristine, relevant, and contextual. Only then can they truly unlock the transformative potential of AI in marketing.

- **Clear KPIs to drive better outcomes**: Without a compass, even the most advanced ship can lose its way. That compass, in the realm of AI-driven business strategies, is embodied by well-defined KPIs. Consider the vastness of possibilities that AI presents. From optimizing supply chains to personalizing customer experiences, the applications are myriad. But how does a company discern whether its AI-driven chatbot is genuinely enhancing customer satisfaction? Or if its AI-optimized supply chain is delivering tangible cost savings? The answer lies in setting clear, measurable KPIs. These indicators serve as guidelines, shedding light on the efficacy of AI implementations and illuminating areas of success or needed refinement.

For instance, an e-commerce platform might deploy an AI tool to enhance product recommendations for users. A vague goal might be to "improve user engagement." But what does that truly entail? Instead, a clear KPI would be "increase the click-through rate on product recommendations by 15 percent in the next quarter." This specificity not only provides a tangible target but also offers a metric against which success can be measured.

Furthermore, KPIs instill a sense of accountability. They ensure that AI isn't adopted merely for the sake of being on the cutting edge but is instead harnessed with purpose and intent. They transform AI from a nebulous concept into a tool with clear benchmarks for success.

- **Experimentation and broad perspectives:** A company's approach to AI cannot be rigid or linear; it must be fluid, adaptive, and, above all, experimental. The essence of experimentation lies in the willingness to take calculated risks. Traditional marketing methods, while tried and tested, may not always align with the dynamic capabilities of AI. Hence, companies must be prepared to challenge their own conventions, to pivot when necessary, and to embrace failures as learning opportunities. After all, every misstep in the AI landscape is a lesson that brings clarity to the next endeavor. Here a broad perspective is crucial. AI, with its vast computational abilities, can process and analyze data at scales and depths beyond human capacity. But its true potential is unlocked when it's guided by diverse, out-of-the-box thinking. It's not just about feeding the AI data but also about posing the right questions, framing problems in novel ways, and seeking insights from angles previously unconsidered. Sometimes, it's the questions we haven't thought to ask that lead to the most groundbreaking discoveries.
- **Orchestrating different tools:** Imagine trying to convey the content of an opera using only the strings section of an orchestra. While the violins and cellos produce beautiful melodies, the overall sound might lack the depth and richness that the brass or percussion sections could bring. Similarly, relying on a single AI tool to drive marketing efforts might yield results, but integrating multiple tools can elevate the campaign to new heights. For instance, while one AI tool might excel at generating text-based content, another might be adept at creating visually appealing graphics. Yet another might specialize in video production or audio synthesis. By leveraging the strengths of each tool, marketers can craft content that resonates on multiple levels, engaging the audience's visual, auditory, and cognitive senses. Consider a brand launching a new product. An AI tool specializing in text might generate a compelling product description, while another focused on imagery might produce eye-catching graphics. A third tool could then weave these elements into a captivating video advertisement. The result? A multidimensional campaign that tells a consistent and engaging story across various mediums. But composability is not just about using multiple tools; it's about ensuring they work in tandem, complementing each other's strengths. It's akin to a conductor ensuring that the flute doesn't

overpower the trumpet or that the drums play in sync with the piano. In the AI realm, this means ensuring that the output of one tool seamlessly integrates with that of another, creating a fluid and unified user experience.

- **Interpreting and applying AI results:** The outputs generated by AI systems, often vast and intricate, are not self-executing mandates. They are, instead, intricate puzzles that require a discerning human eye to piece them together meaningfully.

  Let's try another music metaphor. Imagine AI as a prodigious musician, playing a symphony of data. While the notes (or data points) it produces are technically flawless, it requires a skilled conductor (or interpreter) to ensure that the orchestra (or business) follows the rhythm and harmony to create a cohesive, impactful performance. Without this human element, the music, no matter how perfect, may lack soul and resonance. This is where the role of the interpreter becomes paramount. These are individuals who not only possess a deep understanding of AI and its intricacies but also have the business acumen to contextualize its outputs within the broader organizational landscape. They bridge the gap between raw data and actionable insights, ensuring that AI's recommendations align with the company's goals, values, and market realities.

  An AI system might analyze consumer behavior and suggest that a particular demographic segment is likely to respond positively to a new product line. However, it's the human interpreter who will consider factors such as brand positioning, market competition, and logistical challenges to determine the best way to launch and promote the product. These interpreters play a crucial role in mitigating the potential pitfalls of AI. While these technologies can process big data at lightning speed, they can sometimes miss the nuances, cultural contexts, or emerging trends that a human eye can catch. By combining the computational strengths of AI with the intuitive, experiential knowledge of humans, companies can harness the best of both worlds.

- **Breaking down silos:** Silos refer to isolated departments or teams within an organization that operate independently of others, often leading to a lack of communication and collaboration. In the context of media channels, silos can manifest as separate teams handling different marketing channels, such as social media, email marketing, and paid search, with little or no interaction between them. This separation can result in disjointed marketing efforts, missed opportunities, and inefficient allocation of resources. When marketing channels operate in silos, AI systems may only have access to fragmented data, limiting their ability to provide holistic insights and recommendations. For instance, if the social media team operates independently of the email marketing team, an AI system might not be able to correlate data between these channels effectively, leading to missed opportunities for cross-channel campaigns or promotions. So, how can organizations tackle this pervasive issue? By ensuring data accessibility, championing a data-first mindset, and empowering employees through education, organizations can overcome these obstacles to foster integrated and data-driven marketing.

5.2   Augmented customer experience

In the contemporary digital era, the dynamics of customer journeys have undergone a profound transformation. The digital revolution has not only expanded the avenues through which customers interact with brands but also layered these pathways with intricate nuances. Their decisions are shaped by a myriad of influences, from past purchases and personalized recommendations to the impact of referral campaigns and peer reviews.

The term "omnichannel" has transitioned from being a buzzword to an essential business strategy – a table stake. Modern consumers, empowered by technology with smartphones and wearables, expect a unified experience, irrespective of the channel they engage with. Whether they're shopping in a brick-and-mortar store, browsing an e-commerce website, or interacting with a brand on social media, they anticipate a seamless transition between these touchpoints. The challenge for businesses, therefore, is to weave these disparate interactions into a cohesive, personalized narrative for each customer.

AI's unparalleled prowess in data analytics allows businesses to delve deep into the intricacies of customer behaviors. It can identify subtle patterns, anticipate future interactions, and furnish businesses with actionable insights that were previously unattainable. No longer do businesses have to adopt a reactive stance; with AI, they can proactively tailor their strategies to align with individual customer preferences.

Consider a customer who frequently browses eco-friendly products online but never completes a purchase. AI can identify this behavior and, in real time, offer them incentives or information that might nudge them toward a purchase.

The integration of AI doesn't stop at online interactions. With the rise of AI-powered chatbots and virtual assistants, even offline touchpoints such as in-store queries can be enhanced. These AI solutions can provide instant, personalized responses, bridging the gap between online and offline experiences; seamlessness and personalization are now two of the key competitive "moats."

The amalgamation of AI-driven insights and a robust omnichannel approach is setting new benchmarks in customer experience. Businesses that harness this synergy are not only poised to meet the evolving expectations of their customers but are also well equipped to anticipate and shape these expectations in the future.

5.2.1 Mapping the customer journey with AI

Every click, scroll, and interaction leaves a trace. These seemingly inconspicuous actions, when pieced together, form the intricate tapestry of a customer's journey. But understanding this journey isn't merely about tracing a path; it's about delving deep into the psyche of the consumer, discerning their motivations, preferences, and pain points. Only by truly understanding them can businesses act in a manner that resonates.

The digital age has ushered in an era of unprecedented customer interactions. Every day, billions of online actions are recorded, from simple website visits to complex purchase behaviors. Traditional models, even the most sophisticated econometric ones, are ill-equipped to handle this sheer volume of data. While they might capture a snapshot, a static image of customer behavior, they falter when it comes to understanding the dynamic nature of these interactions. The direction, momentum, and underlying motivations behind customer actions remain elusive in these models. It's akin to trying to understand the plot of a movie by looking at a single still frame. To truly connect with customers, businesses must map out these stages meticulously. But it's not just about plotting points; it's about understanding the flow, the transitions, and the nuances. This is the essence of customer journey mapping – a continuous process of understanding, adapting, and enhancing the customer's journey through your brand's world.

1. **Set a clear objective for the map**: Journey mapping serves as a visual representation of every experience your customers have with you. It's a holistic view of the customer's experience, from initial contact to long-term engagement. However, without a clear objective, this map can become directionless, failing to provide actionable insights. Generative AI can help businesses define clear objectives by analyzing past customer interactions and predicting future trends. This ensures that the map is aligned with business goals and customer expectations.

   Example: A retail company wants to increase its online sales. Using generative AI, the company analyzes past customer interactions on its e-commerce platform. The AI identifies that many customers abandon their carts before completing a purchase. With this insight, the company sets a clear objective for its customer journey map: to reduce cart abandonment rates.

2. **Define your personas and highlight target customers**: Personas represent fictional, generalized characters that encompass the various needs, goals, and observed behavior patterns of your potential and existing customers. They help businesses understand their customers better and tailor their offerings accordingly. By defining personas, businesses can visualize their audience's needs, aspirations, and potential barriers, ensuring that marketing and service strategies are aligned with customer expectations. AI can analyze vast datasets to segment customers based on behavior, preferences, demographics, and past interactions. This results in more accurate and detailed personas. AI can also predict future behavior trends of different personas, allowing businesses to proactively tailor their strategies. As customer behaviors and market dynamics change, AI can adapt and evolve personas in real time, ensuring they always reflect the current customer landscape.

   Example: An online streaming service uses AI to analyze viewing habits. It identifies that a segment of users frequently watches romantic comedies and another segment prefers action thrillers. Using this data, the service creates two distinct personas, "Rom-Com

Rachel" and "Action Andy," tailoring content recommendations accordingly.

3. **Define stages and identify goals for each:** Every customer journey can be broken down into distinct stages, from the initial awareness of a brand to the final purchase and even post-purchase interactions. By defining these stages, businesses can better understand the progression of a customer's relationship with their brand. Identifying goals for each stage ensures that there's a clear understanding of what needs to be achieved to move the customer to the next stage. AI can analyze customer behaviors and patterns to help businesses more accurately define the stages of the journey. Based on past data and predictive analytics, AI can suggest optimal goals for each stage, ensuring higher conversion rates and customer satisfaction. As market dynamics and customer behaviors change, AI can adapt and redefine stages in real time, ensuring the journey map remains relevant.

   Example: A travel agency wants to improve its holiday package sales. Using AI, it analyzes the stages customers go through: discovery, consideration, booking, and post-trip feedback. The AI identifies that many customers drop off during the consideration stage. The agency sets a goal to enhance content during this stage to improve conversions.

4. **List out touchpoints:** Touchpoints are the various interactions customers have with a business. They can range from visiting a website, to reading a blog post, to speaking with customer service. Identifying these touchpoints is crucial as it helps businesses understand where their customers are interacting with them and where potential pain points or opportunities might exist. AI can automatically track and identify new touchpoints, especially in digital landscapes where new interaction points can emerge rapidly. For each touchpoint, AI can analyze customer feedback, reviews, and social media mentions to gauge sentiment, helping businesses understand how customers feel about each interaction. AI can rank touchpoints based on importance or influence on the customer's decision-making process, allowing businesses to focus their efforts more effectively.

   Example: A fashion e-commerce platform uses AI to track customer interactions. The AI identifies touchpoints such as social media ads, email newsletters, product pages, and checkout pages. By listing these touchpoints, the platform can ensure a cohesive marketing strategy across all channels.

5. **Gather data and customer feedback**: Collecting data and feedback is crucial to understanding how customers feel about their interactions with a business. This feedback provides invaluable insights into what's working, what's not, and where improvements can be made. AI can automate the process of gathering data from various sources, ensuring a comprehensive view of customer feedback. AI can also identify emerging trends in feedback, allowing businesses to anticipate and address issues before they become widespread.

   Example: A restaurant chain uses generative AI to analyze feedback from multiple sources, including online reviews, social media mentions, and in-store feedback forms. The AI provides a comprehensive view of customer sentiments, highlighting areas of praise and criticism.

6. **Determine pain points and points of friction**: Identifying pain points is crucial as they represent barriers or negative experiences that customers face. By addressing these pain points, businesses can enhance customer satisfaction and loyalty. Before a pain point becomes a significant issue, AI can predict potential problems by analyzing patterns in customer behavior and feedback. AI can sift through vast amounts of data to identify the root cause of a pain point, allowing businesses to address the underlying issue rather than just the symptom. These systems can also be trained to send real-time alerts to relevant teams when a new pain point emerges, ensuring swift action.

   Example: An online bookstore uses AI's predictive analytics to analyze the browsing behavior of its users. The AI identifies that many users struggle to find books in specific genres due to a lack of clear categorization. This insight points to a pain point in the user journey that the bookstore can address.

7. **Identify areas for improvement**: The goal of mapping the customer journey is to enhance the customer experience. Identifying areas of improvement is a critical step toward achieving this, as it pinpoints where efforts should be focused to make the most significant impact. AI can predict potential future pain points or areas of friction, allowing businesses to proactively address them. Beyond just pinpointing areas of improvement, AI can delve deeper to identify the root causes of issues, ensuring that solutions address the core

problem. AI can suggest actionable strategies or tools to address identified areas of improvement, based on past data and successful interventions.

Example: A fitness app uses AI to analyze user engagement with its workout routines. The AI predicts that users are likely to disengage after three weeks of usage. To counter this, the app introduces new, personalized workout challenges at the three-week mark, ensuring continuous user engagement.

5.2.2 *Humanizing customer interactions with AI*

In today's digital age, businesses are increasingly reliant on technology to streamline operations and enhance customer interactions. However, amid this technological boom, there's a burgeoning understanding that the most impactful customer experiences are rooted in human-centric approaches. This sentiment echoes Guido Martinetti's perspective on marketing, emphasizing the irreplaceable value of genuine human connections.

Surprisingly, AI, which many initially perceived as the epitome of cold, impersonal automation, is emerging as a crucial tool in humanizing digital interactions. Rather than distancing customers, AI is acting as a bridge, seamlessly melding the efficiency of digital processes with the warmth and understanding of the human touch.

A truly humanized customer experience goes beyond mere transactional interactions. It's rooted in understanding and empathy, recognizing each customer as a unique individual with distinct needs and desires.

In essence, AI empowers businesses to see their customers not as mere data points, but as real people with real emotions, aspirations, and expectations. Numerous tools have emerged that harness the power of generative AI to infuse a human touch in digital customer experiences. However, before delving into these examples, it's crucial to emphasize that these are, at their core, tools. They are tailored solutions to specific challenges, not universal panaceas. Their integration into a strategy aimed at elevating the customer experience should always be preceded by a thorough evaluation of the associated business factors.

- **Chatbots and customer service augmentation**: Advanced chatbots, powered by AI, are at the forefront of revolutionizing customer service. They are not mere digital tools that respond to queries like traditional interactive voice response (IVR) systems; they are evolving into entities that understand context, gauge the mood of the customer, and tailor their responses accordingly, ensuring a more personalized and empathetic interaction. When grounded in a company's knowledge base, these chatbots possess the capability to adapt, learn, and evolve. Their learning isn't confined to static information; they dynamically assimilate new data from ongoing interactions, refining their responses over time. This ability to learn allows them to not only answer queries but also propose solutions, test alternative approaches, and even pre-emptively address concerns before they arise. Chatbots powered by generative AI can grasp the context of a customer's request, allowing them to provide more relevant and helpful responses. This not only reduces the dependency on human agents but also ensures that these chatbots can handle more complex requests autonomously. Moreover, they can analyze datasets and learn from past interactions to refine their responses over time.

Take, for example, the realm of financial services. In an environment where security and precision are of utmost importance, such as with banking applications, chatbots can do more than just relay account balances or recent transactions. By analyzing a user's transaction history and discerning patterns in their financial behavior, these chatbots can offer a level of personalized service previously thought to be the exclusive domain of human financial advisors.

Now, continuing to delve into the topic of using AI for customer management, let's try to take a look from the other side of the table. What about the agents? While the initial fear surrounding AI was that it might replace human jobs, especially in sectors requiring repetitive tasks, the reality is proving to be quite different. A recent study conducted by Stanford and MIT sheds light on this very issue.[7] The research found that chatbots can boost the productivity of low-skilled and entry-level employees in customer service by up to 14 percent. This is a significant revelation, challenging the prevailing notion that automation would primarily benefit highly skilled workers while sidelining those at entry level. One of the most striking findings of

---

[7] https://www.nber.org/papers/w31161.

the study was the potential of AI to narrow the gap between high-ly skilled and lower-skilled staff. This is particularly relevant in the customer support domain, where differences in experience and skills can lead to varied levels of customer satisfaction. Generative AI, with its ability to provide real-time insights, suggestions, and data-driven responses, acts as a valuable assistant to less experienced agents. It equips them with the tools and knowledge that might typically be associated with their more experienced counterparts.

For instance, when faced with a complex customer query, a less experienced agent might take longer to respond or might need to consult with a colleague. However, with the support of a generative AI system, the agent can receive real-time suggestions based on the company's knowledge base, past interactions, and even potential solutions to similar problems encountered by other agents.

The implications of these findings extend beyond just improved productivity. As the study suggests, the integration of AI tools could eventually influence how organizations compensate their employees and the dynamics between managers and their teams. If AI tools can elevate the performance of less experienced workers to match that of their seasoned colleagues, it could lead to a more equitable distribution of rewards, bonuses, and even promotions.

The integration of generative AI in customer support is then not just about automation or efficiency; it's about providing every agent, regardless of their experience level, with the tools and insights they need to deliver exceptional customer service.

- **Yield optimization platforms**

  Here we offer another musical metaphor. Generative AI, like a mu-sical composer, draws inspiration from vast datasets, learning pat-terns and structures. In the realm of web design, this means AI can understand user preferences, behaviors, and interactions, using this knowledge to create or suggest design elements that resonate with the target audience. Moreover, generative AI's ability to create content means that websites can have dynamic content that changes based on user behavior. Think of a home page that alters its lay-out, featured products, or even color scheme based on the user's past interactions or preferences. Such a level of personalization was unthinkable a few years ago but is now a reality thanks to advance-ments in AI.

By understanding how users interact with a site, AI can suggest design changes that enhance usability and functionality. This ensures that the user experience is not just good but exceptional, tailored specifically to individual preferences.

For example, Dynamic Yield's platform leverages AI to provide personalized experiences across various channels, including websites and mobile apps.[8] By analyzing user behavior, it can recommend design modifications or content adjustments or even introduce entirely new features tailored to user preferences. Such personalization ensures users feel appreciated, recognized, and specifically catered to, fostering greater engagement and loyalty.

To truly grasp the potential of these platforms, consider the collaboration between McDonald's and Dynamic Yield. As part of their growth plan, called "Accelerating the Arches," McDonald's introduced new digital tools including a mobile app, digital menus, and self-service ordering stations. But they realized something was missing: a way to make these digital tools feel more personal for each customer.

With Dynamic Yield's expertise, McDonald's started suggesting products to customers in over 12,000 of their drive-throughs in the United States in just half a year. But Dynamic Yield's system did more than just suggest products. It got to know each customer's likes and dislikes. Using advanced technology, it fine-tuned its product suggestions on McDonald's digital menus. This meant customers were more likely to buy additional items, increasing McDonald's sales.

Now, McDonald's uses Dynamic Yield's system not just in the United States but also in many other places worldwide. They constantly test and refine the product suggestions on their digital screens to make sure they're offering the best to their customers.

- **Virtual try-ons and augmented reality**
  Brands have been leveraging this technology for years to allow customers to virtually "try on" products, bridging the gap between the digital and physical realms. Take Sephora, for instance. The beauty giant has been using AI-driven augmented reality (AR) tools since

---

[8] https://www.dynamicyield.com/.

2018, enabling customers to test makeup products on their skin virtually.[9] This approach ensures that customers can visualize how a particular shade or product looks on them, leading to more confident purchase decisions.

But now, with generative AI, the innovation doesn't stop at visualization. The combination of AI with AR is pushing the boundaries of virtual try-ons. These technologies can work in tandem to create more immersive and personalized experiences. Generative AI can produce new, unique virtual items based on user preferences, which can then be visualized using AR tools. This synergy allows for a dynamic and tailored shopping experience, where the virtual world adapts to the user's desires. Google, in its continuous endeavor to enhance online shopping experiences, has introduced a state-of-the-art virtual try-on tool powered by generative AI.[10] This tool is seamlessly integrated into its search engine and, as of its initial release, focuses on women's tops. What sets this tool apart is its ability to allow shoppers to select a model to virtually try on tops from renowned brands such as H&M, Loft, and Anthropologie. The technology is designed to cater to a diverse audience, enabling consumers to visualize how garments might appear on individuals ranging from size XXS to 4XL, encompassing various skin tones, body shapes, and hair types. This new generative AI model can take just one clothing image and accurately reflect how it would drape, fold, cling, stretch, and form wrinkles and shadows on a diverse set of real models in various poses.

- **Optimizing content for voice search**
  With the widespread adoption of voice-activated assistants such as Siri, Alexa, and Google Assistant, an increasing number of users are turning to voice commands for their online searches. The essence of voice search is inherently human – it's about conversation, dialogue, and natural expression. Generative AI plays a pivotal role in this landscape. It can understand and process the nuances of spoken language, ensuring that voice search results are not only accurate but also contextually relevant. This is crucial for businesses aiming

---

[9] https://medium.com/marketing-in-the-age-of-digital/sephora-leading-the-way-with-augmented-reality-c117eed0faa0.

[10] https://blog.google/products/shopping/ai-virtual-try-on-google-shopping/.

to humanize their digital interactions, as voice search inherently mirrors natural human conversation.

Voice search is fundamentally different from traditional text-based search. Users typically employ natural language, longer queries, and more specific phrases when speaking to voice assistants. For instance, while a user might type "weather New York" in a search bar, they're more likely to ask, "What's the weather like in New York today?" when using voice search. This distinction underscores the importance of optimizing content for conversational queries and long-tail keywords.

This finesse extends to the inherently conversational nature of voice search queries. When users frame their searches as questions or statements, they anticipate responses that echo human conversation. Generative AI is adept at crafting content that resonates with this conversational essence, fostering interactions that feel authentic and genuine.

Voice search optimization, powered by AI, is no longer a mere trend but has become a cornerstone of modern SEO strategies (more on content production through AI later in this book). By aligning content with natural language and conversational patterns, companies including Starbucks, Tripadvisor, and Domino's have already tapped into the vast potential of voice search, reaching broader audiences and ensuring they remain at the forefront of digital evolution.[11]

As we've explored in this chapter, the ultimate goal of AI in customer interactions is to bridge the gap between the efficiency of digital platforms and the warmth of the human touch. Voice search epitomizes this objective. By allowing users to engage with technology in the most human way possible – through speech – it fosters a sense of connection and intimacy that traditional text-based searches can't replicate.

With advancements in natural language processing and machine learning, AI systems will better understand context, history, and even cultural nuances. The challenge for businesses will be to ensure that as

---

[11] https://www.retaildive.com/ex/mobilecommercedaily/starbucks-ai-barista-further-reduces-human-interaction-shifts-mobile-ordering; https://www.clickz.com/alexa-show-me-tripadvisors-voice-activated-marketing-strategy/; https://www.silicon.co.uk/software/dominos-alexa-voice-commands-218265.

they integrate more AI into their operations, they remain committed to delivering genuine, human-centric experiences.

5.3   AI-Driven advertising strategies

The journey from a company's brief to the final execution of an ad campaign is a complex tapestry of strategic planning, creative ideation, and precise execution. It all begins with the client's brief, a foundational document that encapsulates their objectives, target audience, and envisioned outcomes. This brief serves as a roadmap for the strategy team within an advertising agency. These strategists immerse themselves in comprehensive market research, dissecting the intricacies of the target audience and gauging the competitive landscape to identify potential opportunities and threats.

Following this in-depth analysis, the baton is passed to the creative team. This ensemble of thinkers and visionaries brainstorm and conceptualize ideas, ensuring that their creative sparks align seamlessly with the strategic insights gleaned earlier. Their mission is to craft an engaging narrative that resonates with the target audience, compelling them to engage with the brand.

Once a concept is solidified, the next challenge is to mold it into various formats suitable for diverse platforms, whether it's print, digital, or broadcast. But the journey doesn't end here. After crafting these creative assets, the pivotal phase of distribution commences.

Distribution is not merely about broadcasting a message; it's about ensuring that the right message reaches the right audience through the optimal channel at the right time. This is where understanding the nuances of media planning becomes crucial. Agencies must determine which channels – be it television, radio, online platforms, or outdoor mediums – are most frequented by their target demographic. Moreover, they must ascertain the frequency of the message: How often should an ad be displayed to strike a balance between awareness and overexposure? Additionally, with multiple creative assets at their disposal, agencies must decide which version of the ad aligns best with each channel, ensuring consistency in messaging while tailoring the content to the platform's unique characteristics.

In essence, the last stage of an ad campaign is a meticulous exercise in optimization and adaptation. It's about ensuring that every creative asset is leveraged to its fullest potential, and that the brand's message is disseminated effectively and efficiently.

This journey from a company's brief to the final execution of an ad campaign, as described, is a human-intensive process, deeply rooted in human intuition, creativity, and expertise. However, as we stand on the cusp of a technological revolution, the integration of generative AI into this process presents a tantalizing prospect. Generative AI can complement and enhance the human-centric aspects of advertising. For instance, in the strategic planning phase, AI can process and analyze market data from different sources at speeds incomprehensible to humans, identifying patterns and insights that might be overlooked by even the most experienced strategists. This can lead to more informed and precise strategic decisions.

In the realm of creative ideation, while the human touch is irreplaceable in crafting compelling narratives, AI can assist in refining and tailoring these narratives for diverse audiences and, why not, it can support in the ideation phase by challenging the team assumptions. It can generate multiple variations of ad copies, suggest design elements, and even predict audience reactions to different creative concepts, ensuring that the final creative output is both innovative and effective.

When it comes to distribution, generative AI can play a pivotal role in media planning. By analyzing historical but also real-time data, AI can predict the optimal channels, times, and frequencies for ad placements. It can also assist in real-time campaign optimization, adjusting strategies based on live audience reactions, ensuring that ads are always placed in the most impactful manner.

However, while the potential benefits of integrating generative AI into advertising are immense, it also raises pertinent questions. How do we strike a balance between human creativity and AI efficiency? To what extent can we rely on AI without compromising the unique human touch that defines great advertising? And as AI continues to evolve, how will the roles of human advertisers transform? My personal view is that it's likely that the advertising realm will witness a harmonious blend of human expertise and AI capabilities. The challenge lies in ensuring that this blend leverages the strengths of both, creating advertising campaigns that not only are efficient and data-inspired but also resonate deeply with human emotions and experiences.

5.3.1 *Precision in campaign optimization*

The value of generative AI in advertising isn't confined to the data an enterprise possesses at the onset of a campaign. Instead, its true strength lies in its ability to continuously harness fresh and contextual information, even as the campaign unfolds. This dynamic data assimilation allows businesses to pivot and adapt, making strategies such as remarketing and retargeting exceptionally responsive and effective.

Remarketing and retargeting, while buzzwords in the digital marketing realm, aren't innovations birthed in the AI era. They've been foundational strategies for over a decade, designed to recapture the attention of potential customers who've shown interest but haven't converted. However, the infusion of generative AI has rejuvenated these strategies, giving them a fresh dynamism. In the days before AI, "one-time visitors" to a website often became missed opportunities. Businesses had limited tools to re-engage them effectively.

Yet with the capabilities of generative AI, our approach to these visitors has evolved profoundly. Instead of merely tracking their digital footprints, AI enables a deep dive into discerning patterns, preferences, and potential triggers for conversion for each visitor. Businesses can now craft hyper-personalized campaigns, presenting users with tailored offers and content that align with their unique journey and interests. This level of personalization, driven by generative AI, significantly boosts the likelihood of conversion.

Let's draft a use case for these technologies applied to campaign optimization. Imagine a global e-commerce platform that sells a wide range of products, from electronics to fashion. The platform has recently launched a new line of sustainable activewear. Using generative AI, the platform quickly crafts multiple ad copies tailored to different audience segments, from eco-conscious millennials to fitness enthusiasts. Each ad is not only designed to appeal to the specific interests of these segments but also to highlight the unique selling points of the sustainable activewear line.

As the campaign rolls out, the platform uses AI to continuously monitor user interactions. It identifies that while eco-conscious millennials are engaging well with ads that emphasize the sustainable aspect of the activewear, fitness enthusiasts are more responsive to ads that highlight the performance and comfort of the products.

Now, here's where the power of remarketing and retargeting, super-charged by AI, comes into play. The platform notices that a significant number of users, especially from the fitness enthusiasts segment, are adding products to their cart but not completing the purchase. Using generative AI, the platform crafts personalized retargeting ads for these users. For instance, a user who added a pair of sustainable running shoes to their cart but didn't purchase them might receive a retargeting ad highlighting the shoe's performance benefits, along with a limited-time discount.

Furthermore, the platform uses AI-powered lead scoring to identify high-value customers who have shown interest in similar products in the past but haven't engaged with the new activewear line. These leads are then targeted with bespoke remarketing campaigns, offering them exclusive previews or early-bird discounts.

The result? A significant uptick in conversions, with the platform not only recapturing potential lost sales but also deepening its engagement with high-value customers. This scenario underscores the profound impact of generative AI in making advertising campaigns more adaptive, precise, and result-driven – in a word: optimized.

5.3.2 *Personalized direct marketing*

Businesses are constantly evolving to stay ahead of the curve, especially when it comes to forging meaningful connections with their audience. Traditional marketing strategies, while valuable, sometimes lack the nimbleness and precision needed to cater to the ever-changing consumer landscape. By harnessing the power of customer data, generative AI, integrated with customer relationship management (CRM) systems, can predict future behaviors, preferences, and purchase intentions, allowing businesses to craft marketing strategies that are not just broad-brush but are meticulously tailored to individual customer journeys. A shining example of this innovation is the personal CRM app Clay.[12] Launched in 2021, Clay began as a platform that amalgamated information from your address book and various social networks, such as Facebook, Twitter, and LinkedIn. This integration aimed to create a system more potent than

---

[12] https://clay.earth/.

a mere address book but without the sales-centric focus of traditional CRM systems. Instead, Clay described its product as a "home for your people," carving a niche for a personal relationship-focused database and contact system.

With Clay, users could stay updated with their peers' latest achievements, posts, and even birthdays. It also allowed users to jot down essential notes about their interactions, such as the context of their last meeting or topics of discussion. These features were designed to help users nurture and manage their relationships more thoughtfully, aiding in everything from network expansion to simply being a better friend or colleague.

However, the real game changer was the introduction of Clay's AI assistant, Nexus. This feature was designed to help users derive more insights from their network of contacts. Nexus, powered by a combination of technologies from OpenAI, Anthropic, and other open-source platforms, allows users to query their network for insights. For instance, users could ask Nexus for recommendations on whom to invite to an upcoming dinner party or seek advice on contacts knowledgeable about specific topics. This AI-driven approach not only simplifies relationship management but also offers insights and recommendations, enhancing the user experience.

While tools such as Clay provide businesses with a deeper understanding of their potential customers, it's the application of this knowledge that truly makes a difference. Knowing intricate details about potential clients or leads can supercharge any campaign aiming to communicate a brand's offerings. Among the myriad of communication tools available, one stands out for its longevity and effectiveness: email marketing.

With the integration of generative AI, email campaigns can be meticulously crafted, resonating with individual user preferences and ensuring heightened engagement. From segmenting email lists based on user behavior to predicting the best times to send emails for optimal open rates, AI is redefining how businesses approach their email strategies.

One of the most impactful applications of generative AI in email marketing is content personalization. For instance, if a user has been browsing a website and showing interest in specific products or services, AI can curate personalized product recommendations in subsequent emails. Such recommendations are not based on mere guesswork but are derived from the user's browsing history, past purchases, and other online behaviors. This level of personalization, as simple as it may sound, can be the difference between a user dismissing an email and making a purchase. By presenting users with content that aligns with their interests, businesses can entice them to take desired actions, be it making a purchase, signing up for a webinar, or any other conversion goal.

Once you've engaged a potential customer with tailored content, the next step is to nurture them and convert them into a loyal client. The capabilities of AI in lead generation don't stop at mere identification. One of the most significant advantages of using this technology in this domain is its predictive analytics capability. For instance, AI can evaluate and rank these potential leads based on a myriad of factors, predicting their propensity to convert into actual clients. Such predictive lead scoring ensures that marketing and sales teams are not shooting in the dark.[13] Instead of spreading their efforts thinly across a vast pool of leads, they can aim a laser-focus on those that show the highest promise.

This not only drives optimal resource utilization but also significantly boosts conversion rates. In essence, with generative AI, advertising becomes less of a broad stroke and more of a precision tool, tailored to resonate and engage with the most receptive audience segments.

5.3.3 *The digital advertising evolution*

Generative AI is also redefining in many ways the media buying landscape. By predicting the optimal platforms and timings for ad placements, it ensures maximum visibility and engagement with precision and efficiency. But the benefits don't stop there. The advent of real-time autonomous ad purchasing algorithms has added another dimension to this revolution. These algorithms, driven by AI, can instantaneously purchase ad slots, ensuring that advertisements are positioned in contexts that deeply resonate with the target demographic. This real-time decision-making capability ensures that ads are always placed in the most relevant and impactful environments.[14] A prime beneficiary of this AI-driven revo-

---

[13] https://www.techtarget.com/searchcustomerexperience/definition/lead-scoring.

[14] For more on what is called "programmatic advertising," please see https://iabeurope.eu/programmatic-advertising/.

lution is the so-called native advertising. This ad format has long been celebrated for its ability to offer audiences a seamless and non-disruptive experience. Unlike traditional ads that can sometimes feel jarring or out of place, native ads are designed to blend harmoniously with the content they accompany. Generative AI doesn't just ensure seamless integration for this advertorial content; it takes the concept to a whole new level. By analyzing data, including user behavior, content themes, and engagement patterns, generative AI can craft ads that are native not only by design but also by context.

Any comprehensive discussion on this topic would be incomplete without addressing the profound impact of AI on search engines. While the integration of generative AI into search engines seems to promise a more personalized and dynamic user experience, there's an underlying narrative that's equally compelling: the potential obsolescence of traditional search engines in the not-so-distant future. To grasp the magnitude of this potential paradigm shift, let's delve into the evolution of Google, which has dominated the digital landscape for over two decades. If we rewind to the early days of Google, it's evident that the platform's primary objective was to provide users with the most relevant and accurate search results. Those who have been on the internet long enough might recall that sponsored results were clearly demarcated, ensuring transparency for users. Fast-forward to today, and the landscape has shifted dramatically. A significant portion of Google's search results, estimated at 60–70 percent, don't necessarily represent the best answer to our queries. Instead, these results are often cluttered with ads, making the distinction between organic and sponsored content increasingly blurred.

Why is this the case? The answer lies in monetization. Google, despite its massive investments in research, development, and AI, continues to prioritize ad revenues over user experience. The platform's current model capitalizes on its inefficiencies, leveraging ads to generate revenue. This approach, while profitable, has led to a dilution in the quality and relevance of search results. Now imagine a search engine powered by advanced AI, providing search results with an 80 percent relevance rate, thereby eliminating the need to sift through dozens of irrelevant links. Such a model would streamline the search process, offering users precise and contextually relevant information without the distractions of superfluous ads.

This brings us to a critical juncture: the innovator's dilemma. Google, a titan of the digital revolution, finds itself at a crossroads. Its vast size and established business model might hinder its ability to adapt swiftly to the rapid advancements of generative AI. As history has shown, even industry leaders are not immune to disruption. The search industry, once thought to be invincible, might be the first major casualty of the AI revolution in the digital advertising area.

Insight
The AI Marketing Era

by *Aldo Agostinelli**

In the diverse world of marketing, generative AI emerges as a catalyst for innovation. This technology not only redefines the company–customer interaction but also revolutionizes business strategies, opening new perspectives of efficiency and precision. Solutions such as Tableau and Power BI allow the creation of advanced visualizations to monitor and analyze campaign performance, identifying trends and providing valuable insights. Cutting-edge platforms such as Marketo leverage AI to automate key processes including email sending, social media management, and lead nurturing, improving the efficiency of company interactions with customers. Predictive analysis, essential for anticipating market trends, finds support in powerful tools such as IBM Watson and Google Cloud AI, which analyze customer purchasing habits and guide real-time strategic adaptations.

But these new technologies are also revolutionizing the creation of quality content thanks to tools such as Jasper and Diaspro, which are capable of quickly generating posts, articles, copy, and all kinds of text suited to marketing needs. As for long-term content, such as landing pages, emails, and articles, platforms such as MarketMuse prove to be valuable allies.

Intelligent chatbots powered by AI, including Dialogflow and IBM Watson Assistant, optimize the customer experience by responding to questions in a timely and available manner 24/7.

---

* Chief Sales Marketing Officer at Telepass.

Search engine optimization, which is crucial in digital marketing, is facilitated by AI solutions such as SEMrush and Moz, which analyze the competition, track keywords, and suggest improvements for better search engine ranking.

In the field of email marketing, platforms such as MailChimp leverage AI to segment the audience and deliver highly personalized emails, greatly improving campaign effectiveness. Seventh Sense, meanwhile, determines the optimal time to send emails based on the behavioral profiling of recipients.

Sentiment analysis on social media, also necessary for brand reputation assessment, is made possible by a whole series of AI tools such as Brandwatch and Hootsuite Insights.

Finally, predictive marketing benefits from solutions such as Infer and InsideSales, which use AI to identify the most promising leads and guide sales strategies.

These examples represent just a small selection of the hundreds of AI tools available on the market. The landscape is dynamic and constantly evolving, with new solutions emerging all the time. It is up to each company to decide which marketing sectors to implement and then select the most suitable tools to achieve the set strategic objectives.

As stated by Chris Anderson in 2006, "One size doesn't fit all." In the current context, generative AI presents itself as the ideal solution for the growing demand for customization by consumers, which extends to multiple sectors, from fashion to cosmetics, from furniture to food and beverage.

By aggregating market data from different sources, generative AI is also able to conduct advanced analysis for target segmentation and provide a detailed assessment of consumer preferences, choices, and information, both online and offline, with unprecedented speed and accuracy. This advanced analytical capability allows not only a thorough understanding of consumer behavior, but also efficient testing of innovative concepts, ideas, and models, thus contributing significantly to improving the search and purchasing experience for a wide range of products.

In this sense, Stitch Fix represents a paradigmatic example of the progress enabled by AI. The brand uses advanced algorithms to develop tailored recommendations for its customers and suggest personalized style choices. For this purpose, the company introduced DALL·E in order to create visual representations of products based on customer preferences in terms of color, fabric, and style. Thanks to text-to-image generation, the company's designers are able to visualize a custom garment for the customer and, consequently, identify a similar product within the brand's inventory.

In the future, this customization will become even more hyper-personalized. Among the tools used, facial and voice recognition will play a primary role. Even today, the technology is used to read and correctly interpret customers' emotional reactions during the different phases of the purchasing journey, focusing on customer retention and lead conversion.

While customers are in the physical store, facial recognition monitors their interactions. At the same time, AI associates the customer with their social profile, collects and analyzes data from various sources, and processes highly personalized messages, discounts, promotions, and offers in real time. In this way, the omnichannel experience of the highly diversified consumer targets is optimized and taken to a new level of customization.

AI is a marketing booster, and companies that adopt it operate in turbo mode. Not only do they best reach, engage, and satisfy their customers, but they also gain a significant competitive advantage in their industry. However, as with any powerful engine, it is up to the driver to know how to steer it toward achieving the set profitability and growth targets. For all marketers, the golden rule applies: Those who innovate overtake on the right. Always.

6 AI, Social Media Platforms, and Content Creators

6.1 The role of AI in social media

In today's interconnected world, social media stands tall as a linchpin of modern marketing strategies. The numbers speak for themselves: as of 2023, a staggering 4.76 billion individuals actively engage on these platforms, accounting for nearly 60 percent of the global populace.[1]

AI is not a recent entrant in this world; in fact, it has been intricately woven into the very fabric of social media platforms as a core product feature for years.[2] Its pivotal role is evident in how these platforms curate and present content to users, aiming for a unique and engaging experience. Central to this personalization are algorithms that sift through data and consider factors such as users' interactions with posts - whether they like, share, or comment - the pages they follow, the content they save, and even their interactions with other users and brands. By understanding these behaviors, AI enables platforms to reorder and showcase content that is most likely to keep users engaged and spending more time on the platform. This hyper-personalization ensures not only that but also that they engage more deeply with the content presented to them.

Given the effectiveness of AI tools in tailoring engagement based on user interests on social media platforms, it's unsurprising that an increasing number of brands are keen to harness these technologies and are establishing dedicated social media profiles for their products and services. These profiles serve as their digital storefronts, allowing them to show-

---

[1] https://datareportal.com/reports/digital-2023-global-overview-report.

[2] https://aimagazine.com/ai-strategy/how-are-social-media-platforms-using-ai.

case their values and stories in a more relatable and engaging manner. By defining strategic editorial plans, brands can ensure a consistent and compelling narrative that resonates with their audience.

The informal nature of social media platforms means they offer an excellent opportunity to adopt a tone that's less rigid and more intimate than that in traditional media. This shift in communication style, from corporate to conversational, has proven to be a game changer, allowing brands to build trust and loyalty among their followers.

Additionally, the advent of advanced advertising options on social media platforms has empowered brands to reach specific audience segments with pinpoint accuracy. Through targeted advertising campaigns, brands can ensure that their messages reach the right people at the right time, maximizing impact and return on investment. These campaigns can be tailored to various objectives, from brand awareness and engagement to direct sales and conversions. In this way brands are not just aiming to reach a broader audience; they're also striving to convey valuable messages that foster genuine intimacy at scale. As these interactions evolve, casual platform users can be transformed into devoted brand advocates.

6.1.1 *Reshaping social media marketing*

The opportunity to craft personalized brand experiences on social media, combined with the emergence of generative AI and its unparalleled transformative capabilities, is prompting businesses to increasingly invest in projects related to these technologies. This shift is clearly evidenced by the rapid growth of the AI market within the social media landscape. From a valuation of $600 million in 2018, projections indicate a remarkable ascent to approximately $3,714.89 million by 2026.[3]

This capability turns the vast troves of public user data into a perpetual focus group, offering real-time feedback and insights for companies willing to listen and engage. Every like, share, comment, and follow provides a glimpse into the user's psyche, preferences, and desires. Brands can leverage this continuous stream of data to test, evaluate, and refine their offerings, making public user data an invaluable asset for gauging the pulse of the market and understanding consumer sentiment.

---

[3] https://www.mordorintelligence.com/industry-reports/ai-market-in-social-media.

Through meticulous data analysis, AI refines social media strategies, leading to amplified engagement and bolstered conversion rates. But it goes beyond just reflecting the current whims of users. By analyzing patterns and predicting shifts in user behavior, AI provides businesses with a forward-looking lens. This proactive approach allows brands not only to respond to current trends but also to anticipate and shape future ones, ensuring they remain at the forefront of the ever-evolving digital landscape. With generative AI's assistance, businesses can transform passive data into actionable insights, optimizing their offerings and staying consistently attuned to the dynamic preferences of their audience.

These capabilities, which once propelled major social platforms to become central hubs for information and purchasing for millions, are now being harnessed by businesses to effectively convey their offerings to audiences. Let's delve into how these capabilities can be applied in corporate communication projects for businesses.

- **Content creation:** In the social media world, where the attention span of users is fleeting, the content's relevance and resonance become paramount. AI, with its ability to analyze multilayered interaction data, crafts content that goes beyond mere words. It understands the nuances of the brand's voice, the preferences of the target audience, and the context of the platform to generate content that truly engages. Whether it's crafting catchy headlines, generating blog post ideas, or even creating short video scripts, AI tools are equipped to handle a diverse range of content needs. This ensures that brands can maintain a consistent and fresh presence across various social media platforms without being bogged down by the content creation process. Businesses no longer need to rely solely on human creativity; they can now augment it with AI, ensuring a perfect blend of creativity and efficiency. Below is a curated list of tools that leverage AI to enhance the content creation process.
  - *Lumen5*: This tool leverages AI to transform blog posts and articles into engaging videos, making it easier for brands to tap into the video content trend on social media platforms.[4]

---

[4] https://lumen5.com/.

- *Yseop Compose*: This is an AI-powered writing assistant that can automatically generate reports, executive summaries, and other types of written content based on the data provided.[5]
- *Cleanvoice*: For brands looking to venture into podcasting or voice-based content, this tool can generate and edit human-like voiceovers using AI.[6]

• **Content curation**: Content curation involves sifting through a sea of information to select and present the most relevant and valuable pieces in a coherent manner. With the integration of AI, this process not only becomes more streamlined and efficient but also ensures consistency and alignment with the fundamental brand equity characteristics. AI-driven content curation tools can analyze public and proprietary data to identify trending topics and even predict future content preferences. This ensures that the content presented to the audience is not only relevant but also timely and engaging. By automating the curation process, brands can ensure that their content remains fresh, relevant, and in line with their audience's evolving preferences.

AI-driven curation can also help brands identify gaps in their content strategy, suggesting areas where they might need to create new content or repurpose existing content. This proactive approach ensures that brands are always ahead of the curve, delivering content that resonates with their audience and drives engagement. Below are a few examples of AI-driven content curation tools.

- *Curata*: This tool uses machine learning to help marketers identify the best content to share with their audience. It learns from user behavior to refine its content recommendations over time.[7]
- *Scoop.it*: While primarily known as a content curation platform, Scoop.it also incorporates AI to help businesses find and publish content that's most relevant to their audience.[8]
- *Feedly*: This tool uses AI to gather, analyze, summarize, and prioritize articles, press releases, and social posts from thousands of sources in real time. Their AI feature, named "Leo," creates a

---

[5] https://yseop.com/solutions/compose/.
[6] https://cleanvoice.ai/.
[7] https://curata.com/.
[8] https://www.scoop.it/.

smart feed based on a user's Feedly search, allowing users to track trends or even competitors' brand names.[9]

- **Personalized user experience**: Users are more likely to engage with content that feels tailored to their preferences, interests, and behaviors. By sifting through historical user interactions, preferences, and current market dynamics, AI can anticipate preferences. This proactive approach ensures that the content not only captures attention but also fosters genuine, meaningful engagement. Brands that harness AI for personalization can create a more intimate connection with their audience, leading to increased loyalty and trust. In addition to Dynamic Yield, which we discussed in the previous chapter, there are other tools in this area of interest.

  - *Emarsys*: This is a marketing platform that uses AI to automate personalized interactions, making it possible for marketers to deliver the right message to the individual user at the optimal time.[10]

  - *Segment*: This customer data platform helps businesses capture data from every customer touchpoint and funnel that data into other tools for better personalization. It ensures that the content and ads users see are tailored to their past behaviors and preferences.[11]

- **Automating task**: By automating repetitive and time-consuming tasks, brands can focus more on strategic and creative endeavors, ensuring a more efficient and effective approach to their social media campaigns. Artificial intelligence takes automation a step further by not just performing tasks but optimizing them based on data-driven insights. From scheduling posts at optimal times to automatically responding to user comments and queries, AI-driven tools ensure that brands maintain a consistent and timely presence on social media platforms. This kind of engagement is crucial for building and maintaining a loyal audience. Moreover, automation reduces the risk of human error and ensures that the brand's social media strategy is executed seamlessly. Below are some examples of tools that leverage AI to automate tasks on social media.

---

[9] https://blog.feedly.com/leo/.
[10] https://emarsys.com/ai-marketing/.
[11] https://segment.com/.

- *Hootsuite*: One of the most popular social media management tools, Hootsuite allows users to schedule posts, interact with followers, and get the analytics they need to improve their social media strategy. Its AI capabilities also suggest optimal times to post based on when your audience is most active.[12]
- *Buffer*: Similar to Hootsuite, Buffer is a platform that allows for scheduling, publishing, and analyzing all your posts in one place. Its AI-powered feature, Buffer Publish, suggests the perfect moment to post based on follower activity and previous post performances.[13]
- *Sprinklr*: This is a comprehensive social media management tool that uses AI to help brands listen to their audience, publish content, and engage users more effectively. It also offers automation in ad campaigns, ensuring that ads are optimized for the best performance.[14]

- **Crafting better-targeted campaigns**: Brands need to ensure that their campaigns on social media not only are visible but also resonate with the right audience. Crafting well-targeted campaigns requires understanding the audience's preferences, behaviors, and engagement patterns. AI can provide a comprehensive understanding of the ideal user profile, peak interaction times, and how different content formats interplay. This knowledge ensures that every campaign not only is well received but also achieves its intended objectives.

AI has also revolutionized the process of A/B testing in social media. What used to be a manual and time-consuming effort is now supercharged with AI's potential. Real-time analysis, capturing even the most subtle patterns, ensures that every aspect of a campaign, from posting times to content format and tone, is optimized for maximum impact. Below are some examples of tools that leverage AI for crafting better-targeted campaigns.

- *AdEspresso by Hootsuite*: This platform simplifies Facebook, Instagram, and Google Ads optimization. It offers AI-driven suggestions for ad variations and automates the A/B testing process,

---

12 https://www.hootsuite.com/.
13 https://buffer.com/ai-assistant.
14 https://www.sprinklr.com/.

ensuring that brands get the best return on investment (ROI) on their ad spend.[15]

- *Smartly.io*: This is a platform that automates every step of social media advertising to unlock greater performance. Its AI-driven features include predictive budget allocation, automated ad testing, and creative optimization.[16]
- *Optimizely*: Known for its experimentation platform, Optimizely uses AI to help brands test different variations of their content to see which one resonates most with their audience. This ensures that users receive content tailored to their preferences, leading to increased engagement and conversion rates.[17]
- *Albert*: An autonomous digital marketing platform, Albert learns from campaign performance and autonomously optimizes paid search, social, and programmatic campaigns. It can adjust strategies in real time based on ongoing results.[18]

6.1.2 *Decoding emotions and images: Brand perception and protection*

Recall the scene from *Minority Report* where Tom Cruise's character walks through a mall and personalized advertisements address him directly, recognizing his identity and past preferences.[19] More than twenty years ago that film painted a picture of a futuristic, high-tech world. However, from where we stand today, the future seems less dystopian and more filled with opportunities. Thanks to AI tools, brands are not just passively waiting for the future; they're actively shaping it. While we might not have holographic ads calling out our names just yet, the ability of brands to detect even the subtlest mentions of their products on social media, gauge real-time customer sentiment, and adapt their strategies accordingly is no longer the realm of fiction.

At the forefront of this AI revolution is sentiment analysis, bridging linguistics and machine learning to enable machines to interpret human emotions in text, images, and video. This technology primarily relies on

---

[15] https://adespresso.com/.
[16] https://www.smartly.io/.
[17] https://www.optimizely.com/.
[18] https://albert.ai/.
[19] https://en.wikipedia.org/wiki/Minority_Report_(film).

natural language processing (NLP), the branch of AI that focuses on computer–human language interaction. NLP tasks include tokenizing text, part-of-speech tagging, and dependency parsing to establish token relationships. Machines are trained to recognize sentiment by processing large datasets, such as product reviews labeled as positive, negative, or neutral, allowing them to associate specific words or phrases with particular sentiments over time.

Not every word in a sentence holds equal importance for determining sentiment. Through feature extraction, the most pertinent parts of the text are identified for analysis. For instance, adjectives often bear significant sentiment weight, such as the difference between "amazing product" and "terrible experience."

Once trained, the model can assign sentiment scores to new, unseen text. While a simple output might categorize text as positive, negative, or neutral, more advanced models might provide a gradient score, ranging from −1 (very negative) to +1 (very positive). As more data becomes available, the model undergoes retraining and refinement, enhancing its accuracy over time.

Now imagine a newly launched skincare product. While it might be receiving thousands of mentions across social media platforms, the sheer volume of mentions doesn't provide a clear picture of its reception. Are customers praising its effectiveness, or are they highlighting potential issues such as skin reactions? Sentiment analysis can sift through these mentions, categorizing them as positive, negative, or neutral. If there's a sudden spike in negative sentiments, the brand can quickly investigate, perhaps discovering a batch issue or a misunderstood product application method. This immediate insight allows for swift corrective action, whether it's addressing product concerns or launching an educational campaign.

One of the pivotal applications of this deepened insight is in the realm of crisis management. A sentiment analysis platform can establish a baseline of typical conversations surrounding a brand. Any deviation from this norm, especially negative sentiment spikes, can be flagged as potential crises in real time. This early detection allows brands to swiftly address issues, manage their reputation, and mitigate potential damage. Furthermore, these tools offer a unique lens through which brands can gauge the effectiveness of their communication messages, even those crafted for campaigns outside the digital and social spheres. By analyzing public perception and sentiment, brands can validate the impact of their campaigns in the real world. Unlike traditional lab-based research, this real-time sentiment analysis provides a genuine reflection of the value and ROI generated from their investment.

Expanding on this, sentiment analysis can also be a powerful tool for competitive analysis. By examining the sentiment surrounding competitors, brands can gain insights into their strengths, weaknesses, and areas of opportunity. This analysis can reveal thematic areas and perceptions where competitors are positioned, allowing businesses to identify incremental opportunities.

A brand can then identify areas where competitors are not meeting customer expectations or are entirely neglecting certain themes. This data-inspired approach can guide brands to create a unique value proposition, carving out a niche or "blue ocean" where they can operate without direct competition.[20]

Building on the foundation of sentiment analysis is the capability of AI-enabled image recognition. At its core, this process involves teaching machines to interpret and categorize visual data, much like how the human brain recognizes objects, faces, and scenes. Image recognition also begins with feature extraction, where an image is broken down into its essential elements or features. For brands, this technology offers a way to navigate the vast ocean of user-generated content on social media platforms, blogs, and forums. Every day, millions of images are uploaded online, many of which could contain references to a brand's products, even if they're not explicitly tagged or mentioned. AI-enabled image recognition can identify logos, products, or even specific product features within these images. This capability is invaluable for brands aiming to gauge their organic presence online and understand how their products fit into the daily lives of consumers.

For instance, a sportswear brand could use image recognition to identify pictures in which their sneakers are worn, even if the posts don't mention the brand by name. This provides insights into real-world use cases, potential influencers, and even emerging trends. A sneaker appearing frequently in hiking photos might suggest a new use case the brand hadn't considered. But beyond engagement, this capability plays

---

[20] https://www.blueoceanstrategy.com/what-is-blue-ocean-strategy/.

a crucial role in fraud detection. In today's digital age, counterfeits and unauthorized use of brand imagery are rampant. These AI tools act as vigilant sentinels, constantly scanning the digital landscape for any misuse or misrepresentation of a brand's products or identity. By identifying such discrepancies, brands can take swift action, ensuring that their market reputation remains untarnished and that customers are not misled by fraudulent offerings.

The fusion of image recognition with sentiment analysis represents a significant leap in understanding brand perception in the digital age. Consider a scenario where a user posts an image of a newly purchased gadget. The image alone indicates product usage, but the accompanying caption or comments might range from praise about its innovative features to complaints about its functionality. By analyzing the text alongside the image, brands can gain a deeper understanding of the emotions and sentiments tied to the visual representation of their products. This dual analysis paints a comprehensive picture, allowing brands not only to see where and how their products appear but also to understand the narratives and emotions surrounding them. In a world where consumers are continuously sharing their experiences, this combined approach ensures that companies capture the full spectrum of user perception, from the visual to the emotional.

6.1.3 *From potential to praxis*

As AI continues to revolutionize both social media and digital marketing landscapes, it's paramount to pinpoint the best practices for weaving AI into a business's overarching strategy. Here are some enhanced best practices to mull over.

- **Setting clear objectives:** Integrating AI without a clear roadmap can lead to missed opportunities. Setting precise objectives is key for several reasons. Firstly, every brand's social media presence is an extension of its identity. Clear objectives ensure that AI tools amplify the brand's voice in a manner that's authentic and resonates with its core values. This clarity also aids in optimizing resources. By having well-defined goals, brands can select AI tools tailored for their specific needs, ensuring efficient budget and resource allocation in the social media landscape.

Moreover, having clear objectives allows brands to set specific key performance indicators, making it easier to gauge the effectiveness of AI-driven social media campaigns. This clarity provides a foundation for refining strategies based on real-world data. Given the rapid evolution of social media trends, brands with solid objectives can pivot their AI strategies as needed, ensuring they remain relevant and impactful. Lastly, clear goals foster collaboration across teams. This unified vision ensures all stakeholders work cohesively toward harnessing AI's potential in the social media domain.

- **Identifying the right AI tools for your business:** AI's potential in marketing is vast, but its effectiveness hinges on the tools you choose. What's a boon for one enterprise might be redundant for another. Hence, a meticulous assessment of your unique needs and a deep dive into research is essential. For businesses focused on enhancing their social media content creation, platforms such as Flick are noteworthy.[21] This platform offers a seamless experience in crafting personalized, brand-aligned captions, effectively serving as a virtual copywriting assistant throughout the brainstorming, writing, and planning stages of social media content. Its suite of features, from content scheduling to hashtag optimization and analytics, ensures a strategic and impactful content approach. For those prioritizing caption and image generation, Content Studio emerges as a comprehensive solution tailored for agencies, brands, and marketers.[22] This platform harnesses AI to recommend pertinent hashtags, amplifying post visibility. It also boasts the capability to produce engaging images for social media posts derived from user-provided textual descriptions. For enterprises emphasizing social selling, Lately stands out as a premium choice.[23] As highlighted on its platform, Lately is a "social selling platform that learns any brand or employee voice, takes all of your content, and transforms it into targeted, effective social media posts." Its analytics further aid in pinpointing the best times to post, ensuring optimal audience engagement.

In today's fast-paced digital environment, innovative AI solutions are continuously being introduced. A significant number of these

---

[21] https://www.flick.social/.
[22] https://contentstudio.io/ai-writer.
[23] https://www.lately.ai/.

platforms offer a "try and buy" model, empowering even small businesses to experience the tool's capabilities before committing financially. By accurately identifying where AI can fortify their strategy and investing time in diligent research, businesses are better positioned to choose tools that truly elevate their social media endeavors. Nevertheless, remember that technology, especially in this area, is constantly evolving, and so should your strategy. Periodic evaluations of your AI tools can spotlight areas ripe for enhancement and allow you to fine-tune your strategy for optimal results.

- **Training your team on AI technologies**: As AI becomes an integral part of your strategy, arm your team with the knowledge to harness its full potential. Firstly, teams should grasp the foundational mechanics of how AI operates within the context of social media. While a deep technical understanding isn't necessary for everyone, a basic knowledge of how AI algorithms analyze user behavior, trends, and engagement can demystify AI, making it a more approachable and effective tool for social media endeavors.

  Beyond the technicalities, it's crucial to recognize how AI is revolutionizing social media engagement. This understanding encompasses how AI enhances user interactions, personalizes content for specific audience segments, and predicts emerging trends. By aligning AI's capabilities with specific social media goals, teams can harness its full potential.

  Hands-on experience is invaluable, so consider organizing workshops that provide live demonstrations of AI tools in action on social media platforms. These sessions can help bridge the gap between understanding AI's capabilities and applying them effectively.

- **AI as an augmentation, not a replacement**: The heart of social media is its social nature, emphasizing human connection, storytelling, and genuine interaction. While AI excels at analyzing patterns and predicting trends, it can't replicate the emotional depth, cultural understanding, and genuine empathy that humans bring to the table. Strategic decisions, whether it's pivoting a campaign or managing a PR crisis, demand human judgment. AI provides valuable data-driven insights, but the final decisions should harmoniously blend this data with human intuition. As businesses explore generative AI in social media, this balance becomes even more vital. This underscores the importance of experimenting with these tools. By actively testing, measuring, and refining their approach, businesses can fully harness the potential of AI in the ever-evolving social media domain.

Incorporating generative AI into social media strategies is a thrilling frontier, promising unprecedented levels of engagement and personalization. Selecting the right AI tools, training teams adequately, and ensuring a clear alignment with broader business objectives are all pivotal.

6.2   Evolving social media advertising

How does paid content on social media differ from the organic posts we see from brands? At first glance, a well-executed social media ad might be indistinguishable from an unpaid post, save for the subtle "Sponsored" label. But ads offer a level of predictability that organic content can't match. They aren't at the mercy of ever-changing social media algorithms, ensuring that they reach their intended audience. Moreover, ads usually come with specific calls to action, leading users to designated landing pages, making the user journey more directed. Ads, however, are transient, often tied to specific campaigns or business objectives; in contrast, organic social media content is a continuous endeavor, reflecting a brand's ongoing narrative.

The decline in organic reach, especially on major platforms such as Facebook and Instagram, has pushed advertisers toward these paid solutions to amplify the reach of organic content and guarantee it finds its intended viewers. Besides, the precision of social media advertising is unique; brands can now target specific demographics, ensuring their message resonates with past customers, website visitors, or even entirely new audience segments.[24] This ability to hyper-target ads based on distinct parameters means that brands can ensure their message is delivered to those who will find it most relevant.

But the benefits don't stop at reach and precision. The insights garnered from social media advertising are a treasure trove of data. Through these campaigns, brands can delve deep into their audience's preferences,

---

[24] About Look-a-like audience https://www.facebook.com/business/help/164749007013531?id=401668390442328.

behaviors, and interactions. This data-driven approach not only informs decision-making but also optimizes strategy, making advertising efforts more effective and efficient.

Furthermore, the cost-effectiveness of social media advertising is undeniable. With models such as pay-per-click or pay-per-view, brands only pay when users engage, ensuring they receive value for their investment. This strategy, when paired with user-friendly platforms such as Facebook Business Manager, guarantees a high return on investment while always maintaining control over the campaign.

As AI continues to evolve, offering brands innovative ways to leverage these platforms as covered in the previous paragraph, the platforms themselves are in a constant state of evolution. They are perpetually refining and expanding their product offerings to ensure advertisers are equipped with the most effective solutions. They are committed to providing advertisers with tools that not only meet the current demands but also anticipate future trends and challenges. This symbiotic relationship between AI's advancement and the platforms' evolution ensures that brands are always presented with cutting-edge solutions, tailored to navigate a competitive landscape and achieve optimal engagement. The future of social media advertising, therefore, promises to be one of continuous innovation, adaptation, and growth. Let's delve into how these platforms are ingeniously integrating AI to offer brands more targeted, effective, and dynamic advertising experiences.

- **Meta:** Advantage+ is a new platform designed to empower advertisers with the might of AI, ensuring that their marketing efforts are both efficient and effective.[25] The platform's primary goal is to harness the power of AI to deliver more relevant campaigns to the audiences that matter most to businesses. One of the standout features of the Advantage+ platform is its shopping campaigns. These campaigns are designed to help advertisers quickly identify which campaigns are converting, eliminating the manual steps of ad creation. The platform can automate up to 150 creative combinations at once, allowing advertisers to rapidly determine which ads resonate most with their audience. For instance, a study of fifteen

---

[25] https://www.facebook.com/business/help/1362234537597370.

A/B tests revealed that Advantage+ shopping campaigns resulted in a 12 percent lower cost per purchase conversion compared with traditional ads.[26]

Small businesses, often constrained by limited resources, can particularly benefit from the Advantage+ platform. Features such as Advantage+ creative and Advantage audience allow these businesses to create ads directly from their Facebook page, saving both time and money. The platform's AI-driven tools adjust the ad creative for each viewer, ensuring that the ad version most likely to elicit a response is displayed.

- **YouTube**: YouTube, underpinned by Google's AI, tailors ad delivery based on audience targeting and campaign objectives. This ensures ads are optimally placed across various formats, from in-stream to Shorts, reaching a diverse user base. For instance, video action campaigns, powered by AI, have shown a significant uptick in conversions due to automated audience targeting.[27] Moreover, YouTube's experiments highlight the importance of diverse video orientations, with campaigns incorporating multiple orientations seeing a boost in conversions. The video reach campaigns platform allows advertisers to upload various ad types, including six-second bumper ads, skippable in-stream ads, and non-skippable in-stream ads.[28] Google's machine learning technology then determines the most effective combination of these ads to enhance audience engagement and reach.

The AI-driven approach means advertisers no longer need to manage each ad category individually. Instead, they can rely on the AI engine to do the heavy lifting. This system uses aggregated and anonymous insights to predict which type of ad will be most engaging in any given situation. Furthermore, YouTube's brand safety settings, in collaboration with third-party providers such as DoubleVerify, leverage AI to ensure that ads are placed alongside content that is appropriate for brand association. This includes content exclusion features and digital content labels similar to movie rat-

---

[26] https://www.adlucent.com/resources/blog/best-practices-for-meta-advantage-shopping-campaigns.

[27] https://www.youtube.com/ads/how-it-works/set-up-a-campaign/action/.

[28] https://support.google.com/google-ads/answer/10581234?hl=en.

ings. Such advancements give advertisers confidence that their ads will be associated with brand-safe content.

- **TikTok:** TikTok stands out with its predictive AI algorithm, curating a personalized feed for each user. This has led over time to higher brand sentiment and deeper user–brand connections on the platform. Tools such as Automated Creative Optimization (ACO) exemplify TikTok's commitment to AI-driven advertising.[29] ACO identifies the best combinations of creative assets, ensuring ads resonate with the target audience. Additionally, the TikTok Search Ads feature allows brands to tap into user search behaviors, offering more targeted advertising opportunities.[30] Adding to its suite of AI-driven tools, TikTok has introduced the Script Generator tool. This innovative feature leverages AI to produce ad scripts within mere seconds. Users simply need to choose an industry, input a product name and its description, and the tool instantly provides a tailored script for video content. For instance, when the product "straws" with the description "meant for drinking" was tested under the "Food and Beverage" industry, the Script Generator promptly offered three distinct script options. Each of these options came with detailed directions for the scenes, encompassing voiceover, on-screen visuals, and potential text overlays.

However, the industry is still in its infancy regarding the widespread adoption of these tools, and TikTok itself urges caution. A banner at the top of the tool's interface advises users to use the AI-generated scripts judiciously, underscoring that TikTok does not guarantee the results of the generated content. This caution likely arises from the inherent challenges associated with AI models, which can occasionally yield unexpected or unsuitable outputs. A deeper exploration of these challenges and the ways to mitigate them will be addressed in the concluding chapter of this book.

---

[29] https://ads.tiktok.com/help/article/automated-creative-optimization?lang=en.
[30] https://www.tiktok.com/business/en/blog/introducing-tiktok-search-ads-toggle.

6.3   Embedding AI in the creator economy

Influencers, aptly named for their ability to influence, have become an invaluable asset for brands. This strategy sees brands collaborating with individuals who have carved out significant and engaged followings on social media platforms. Their effectiveness stems from several factors. Firstly, they exude an authenticity that's often unmatched by celebrity endorsements. They've cultivated their following based on trust and genuine content. When they vouch for a product or service, it resonates as a heartfelt recommendation rather than a mere paid advertisement. Moreover, these influencers often cater to niche audiences, be it beauty, tech, travel, or any other domain. This specificity allows brands to direct their marketing efforts toward a demographic that aligns perfectly with their target audience. Adding to this is the high level of engagement that influencers maintain with their followers. Regular interactions, from responding to comments to sharing personal anecdotes, ensure that their endorsements are not only seen but also acted upon.

But the digital transformation doesn't stop at influencer marketing. We're witnessing the rise of what has been called the "creator economy." This modern digital ecosystem is where individuals, dubbed "creators," harness their passion and skills to produce a myriad of content. It's a realm that extends beyond influencers promoting brands. It encapsulates bloggers penning insightful articles, YouTubers crafting engaging videos, podcasters broadcasting intriguing episodes, and artists showcasing their masterpieces on platforms such as Instagram.

The surge of the creator economy can be attributed to several factors. The proliferation of flexible digital tools has democratized content creation. With just a smartphone in hand, individuals can now shoot high-definition videos, refine them with sophisticated yet intuitive editing apps, and share them on platforms with potential reach in the millions. Software programs such as Adobe Premiere Rush, Canva, and Procreate have made it possible for anyone to become a content creator. Furthermore, platforms such as TikTok and Instagram have fine-tuned their algorithms to spotlight engaging content, ensuring that creators don't necessarily need a massive following to gain recognition. A single captivating post can garner attention and achieve virality. And, central to the thriving creator economy is the myriad of monetization opportunities available. From ad revenues and sponsored content to affiliate marketing and direct sales, creators have an array of avenues to generate income from their content.

6.3.1 *The State of influencer marketing*

The influencer marketing industry's projected worth is a testament to its burgeoning significance. Estimated to reach a staggering $21.1 billion in 2023,[31] this figure accentuates the pivotal role influencer marketing plays in the contemporary marketing milieu. Complementing this projection, HubSpot data unveils that 89 percent of marketers leveraging influencer marketing are poised to either maintain or augment their investments in 2023.[32] Additionally, 17 percent are gearing up to embark on their influencer marketing journey for the first time in the same year. This isn't a transient trend; influencer marketing's allure lies in its impressive ROI, second only to the magnetic pull of short-form video content.

A discernible shift in brand preferences is the growing affinity for collaborations with smaller influencers. Nano-influencers, boasting between 1,000 and 10,000 followers, and micro-influencers, with a following ranging from 10,000 to 100,000, are increasingly becoming the darlings of the influencer marketing world. This trend stems from the authentic and intimate relationship these influencers share with their audience. Their commendable engagement rates, often eclipsing those of their mega-influencer counterparts, render them an enticing proposition for brands aiming for genuine interactions and impactful endorsements.

However, the journey through the influencer marketing realm isn't devoid of hurdles. The vast expanse of content and the plethora of creators make discoverability a formidable challenge. Brands often find themselves navigating a maze, striving to pinpoint influencers whose ethos resonates with theirs, leading to collaborations that might not always hit the mark. In this saturated market, creators grapple with the onus of crafting content that distinguishes itself from the crowd. The capricious nature of platform algorithms, which can play a pivotal role in content visibility, further compounds this challenge.

---

[31] https://influencermarketinghub.com/influencer-marketing-benchmark-report/.

[32] https://blog.hubspot.com/marketing/influencer-marketing-stats.

As influencer marketing's ubiquity has grown, audiences have evolved, becoming more discerning and judicious. The shadow of skepticism looms large over sponsored content, leading to a barrage of questions probing the authenticity of influencer endorsements. To retain the trust of this discerning audience, brands and influencers are walking a tightrope, striving to strike a harmonious balance between promotional content and genuine engagement.

6.3.2 Introducing AI to the mix

The task of influencer analysis and selection has always been intricate, often likened to navigating a labyrinth. With the advent of AI, this process has witnessed a paradigm shift. AI's capability to delve deep into an influencer's audience demographics ensures that the influencer's audience aligns seamlessly with the desired target demographics. This meticulous analysis simplifies the otherwise daunting task of pinpointing the perfect influencer collaboration.

Further enhancing the influencer selection process, AI tools assist brands in aligning with influencers who resonate with their values and mission. By suggesting the most effective content type tailored for each influencer, AI ensures that the brand message is conveyed with maximum impact. Post-campaign, AI's prowess extends to collating crucial metrics, linking brand mentions, traffic, and conversions directly to specific influencer initiatives. This real-time insight into campaign performance is invaluable for brands. Moreover, AI's comprehensive analysis and reporting capabilities allow brands to gauge the efficacy and ROI of their influencer partnerships, ensuring that their marketing endeavors are always on the right track.

Consider the case of a hypothetical eco-friendly cosmetics brand aiming to promote its new line of sustainable lipsticks. Their target audience is environmentally conscious women aged 18–35. In the past, their marketing team might have spent weeks or even months scouring social media platforms, trying to identify influencers whose followers match this demographic. They would manually analyze engagement rates, content style, and audience feedback, hoping to find a perfect match.

With advanced algorithms, AI can swiftly sift through all the data from various social media platforms. It can analyze the demographics of an influencer's followers, ensuring a match with the brand's target audience. For instance, if a potential influencer has a significant following of men aged 40–55, the AI would immediately recognize the mismatch and move on to more suitable candidates.

But AI's capabilities don't stop at mere demographic matching. It can delve deeper, analyzing the sentiments expressed in the comments on an influencer's posts, gauging the authenticity of their engagement, and even assessing the alignment of their personal brand with the brand's values and mission. If our eco-friendly brand wants to collaborate with influencers who genuinely advocate for sustainability, AI can help identify those whose content consistently echoes this ethos.

Once the ideal influencers are identified, AI can further assist in tailoring the campaign content. For the brand's sustainable lipstick line, the AI might suggest video content for an influencer known for her engaging makeup tutorials, while recommending visually rich Instagram posts for another influencer celebrated for her photography skills. This ensures that the brand message is not only reaching the right audience but also being conveyed in the most impactful manner.

After the campaign is launched, the magic of AI continues. Instead of waiting for the campaign to conclude to assess its success, AI provides real-time insights. It can track metrics such as brand mentions, website traffic originating from influencer posts, and even conversions in terms of product sales. If a particular influencer's post leads to a surge in website visits and sales, the brand can immediately recognize and perhaps even amplify that collaboration. Several platforms have emerged as leaders, each harnessing the power of AI to optimize different facets of influencer marketing, from discovery to campaign measurement. Below is a list of these solutions.

- **Influencity** is a comprehensive tool that shines in influencer discovery, analysis, and campaign management.[33] It boasts the capability to analyze over 100 million influencers across various platforms, providing brands with detailed influencer analytics, including audience demographics and engagement metrics. Its campaign management tools are also noteworthy, offering features such as workflow automation and real-time analytics.

---

[33] https://influencity.com/.

- **CreatorIQ** is changing the way brands discover and analyze their brand communities.[34] By leveraging creator listening and industry insights, it offers brands the tools to search, compare, and get recommendations to find and vet creators. Its community trend analysis ensures that a brand's community remains engaged and grows sustainably.
- **OpenInfluence** offers a full suite of influencer marketing services.[35] It harnesses the power of AI to provide brands with influencer insights, content analysis, and campaign performance metrics. Its platform is designed to streamline the influencer collaboration process, from discovery to campaign execution, ensuring brands can effectively engage with their target audience.

As brands and creators begin to dip their toes into this AI-driven world, a cautious yet proactive approach is essential. Consider a scenario where an AI tool, in its attempt to generate content that resonates with a younger audience, inadvertently promotes a trend or behavior that goes against the brand's core values. For instance, an AI might suggest that the influencer post content that capitalizes on a trending but controversial hashtag, leading to a backlash against the brand for appearing insensitive or out of touch. Such missteps can not only damage the brand's reputation but also erode the trust it has built with its audience over the years.

Another potential repercussion is the dilution of authenticity. One of the primary reasons influencers are effective is their genuine connection with their audience. If content starts feeling too automated or lacks the personal touch that influencers are known for, it can alienate followers and reduce engagement. Imagine an eco-friendly brand's AI tool generating content that inadvertently promotes excessive consumerism, simply because it's a trending topic. Such contradictions can confuse the audience and diminish the brand's credibility.

From the perspective of influencers, the integration of AI into the creator economy presents both challenges and opportunities. On the one hand, AI tools can empower influencers to better understand their audience, refine their content strategy, and optimize their engagement metrics. Advanced analytics can provide insights into audience preferences, allow-

---

[34] https://www.creatoriq.com/.
[35] https://openinfluence.com/.

ing influencers to tailor their content to resonate more deeply with their followers. For instance, an influencer might use AI-driven tools to analyze the sentiments of comments on their posts, helping them gauge which topics or content formats are most impactful. Such insights can guide influencers in crafting content that not only aligns with their personal brand but also meets the evolving needs and interests of their audience.

Moreover, AI can streamline the content creation process for influencers. With tools that automate video editing, suggest optimal posting times, or even predict trending topics, influencers can focus more on their creative expression and less on the logistical aspects of content management. This can lead to more consistent content output and potentially higher engagement rates.

However, the increasing reliance on AI tools might lead to a homogenization of content, where influencers, guided by similar AI-driven insights, end up producing content that lacks distinctiveness. Another consideration is the ethical implications. As influencers often serve as role models for their followers, they bear a responsibility to ensure that their content, even if augmented by AI, remains authentic, ethical, and transparent. Overreliance on AI tools might lead to content that, while optimized for engagement, lacks the genuine human touch that followers seek.

6.3.3   *The virtual influencer phenomenon*

Virtual influencers are digital entities, meticulously crafted through advanced technologies, that challenge our traditional understanding of celebrity, influence, and authenticity. Unlike their human counterparts, these AI-driven personalities exist solely in the digital realm, yet they interact, endorse, and even create content much like any human influencer would. They are the product of a blend of art, technology, and marketing, designed to resonate with audiences in the digital age.

The primary allure of virtual influencers lies in their predictability. Unlike human influencers, who come with their own set of emotions, opinions, and unpredictabilities, virtual influencers are meticulously crafted digital entities. They are designed to perfection, ensuring that they align seamlessly with a brand's image, values, and messaging. This design-centric approach eliminates the uncertainties that often accompany human-led campaigns.

Brands, in their pursuit of crafting the perfect narrative, often grapple with the challenges posed by human influencers. A spontaneous tweet, an unforeseen scandal, or even a change in personal beliefs can derail a meticulously planned campaign. With virtual influencers, such risks are virtually nonexistent. These digital personas operate within the parameters set for them, ensuring that the brand message remains untainted and consistent.

Moreover, the ageless nature of virtual influencers offers brands a timeless ambassador. While human influencers age, evolve, and transform, a virtual influencer remains in its prime, ensuring that the brand's image remains consistent over the years. This agelessness is particularly beneficial for brands looking for long-term ambassadors without the fear of them outgrowing the brand or the target demographic.

Additionally, the omnipresence of virtual influencers offers brands unparalleled reach. A virtual influencer can simultaneously engage with audiences across different platforms, regions, and time zones. They can be at a fashion show in Paris while launching a product in Tokyo, offering brands a global presence without the logistical challenges of human influencers.

But the most significant advantage is the unparalleled control brands have over the narrative. Every post, comment, and interaction is preplanned, ensuring that the brand message remains consistent. There's no room for off-the-cuff remarks or personal opinions that might not align with the brand's values. This controlled environment ensures that the brand's reputation remains safeguarded, and the messaging remains on point.

Among the pantheon of virtual influencers, Lil Miquela stands out.[36] Introduced in 2016 by a Los Angeles-based company, she boasts millions of Instagram followers. From her inception, Miquela was designed to be more than just a visual entity; she was crafted with a backstory, emotions, and opinions, making her interactions on social media platforms feel genuine and relatable.

What sets Miquela apart from other virtual influencers is her multifaceted persona. She's not just an influencer; she's a fashion icon, activist, and musician. Her collaborations read like a who's who of the fashion

---

[36] https://www.instagram.com/lilmiquela/.

world, with partnerships with iconic brands such as Prada, Chanel, and Supreme. These collaborations aren't mere photo ops; they are meticulously crafted campaigns where Miquela often becomes the face of product launches, fashion shows, and brand promotions.

Beyond the world of fashion, Miquela has ventured into the music industry, releasing singles that have garnered significant streams on platforms including Spotify. Her tracks, often imbued with contemporary themes and catchy tunes, resonate with both her followers and casual listeners, further cementing her status as a digital polymath. Artificial intelligence powers Lil Miquela's interactions on her social media channels, allowing her to engage with her followers in real time, much like global music sensations such as Dua Lipa, Rita Ora, or Grimes. Beyond her digital persona, she actively promotes merchandise online, seamlessly blending the worlds of influencer marketing and e-commerce. While it's evident that Lil Miquela is a product of advanced CGI, her existence hints at a forthcoming shift in the music industry. This shift suggests a future where AI doesn't just assist but becomes an integral collaborator in the creative process. It even raises the possibility of an era where the essence of musical creativity is driven predominantly by AI, minimizing human intervention in the artistic process.

However, it was her collaboration with Calvin Klein that truly blurred the boundaries between the virtual and the real. In a bold and somewhat surreal move, Miquela was featured in a commercial where she shared a kiss with real-world supermodel Bella Hadid.[37] This moment, both celebrated and debated, underscored the potential of virtual influencers in the real world. It raised questions about the nature of reality, authenticity, and the future of marketing.

Not all virtual influencers are born from the ether of creativity. The Italian government introduced its own digital ambassador, a recreation of Botticelli's Venus, in 2023 in a campaign dubbed #OpenToMeraviglia.[38] While the intent was to promote Italian tourism, the choice of using an iconic piece of art as a virtual influencer stirred debates. Unlike characters such as Lil Miquela, Botticelli's Venus is an embodiment of cultural

[37] https://adage.com/article/cmo-strategy/calvin-klein-apologizes-bella-hadid-kiss-lil-miquela/2172796.
[38] https://amboslo.esteri.it/ambasciata_oslo/en/ambasciata/news/dall_ambasciata/2023/05/welcome-to-meraviglia-ecco-la-nuova.html.

heritage. The transformation of such a revered artwork into a digital influencer raised questions about authenticity, cultural appropriation, and the thin line between innovation and desecration.

With the advent of generative AI, the horizon for virtual influencers seems limitless. The technology can craft personalities that are more responsive, adaptive, and even predictive. But as the horizon expands, so do the challenges and ethical dilemmas. In my opinion, the rise of virtual influencers, while fascinating, might just be a passing trend. The Calvin Klein campaign with Lil Miquela and Bella Hadid, and the #OpenToMeraviglia initiative, while innovative, have shown that not all that glitters is gold. These campaigns have faced their share of criticism, debates, and even backlash.

At the heart of influencer marketing lies a simple truth: empathy. It's the genuine connection, the shared experiences, and the raw emotions that make influencer marketing resonate. While AI can augment creativity, it's a tall order to breathe soul into pixels. AI might be able to mimic human-like traits, but can it replicate the genuine human connection? The essence of influencer marketing isn't just about reach or engagement; it's about forging authentic bonds. And for now, that's a realm where humans reign supreme.

Insight
The Complex Relationship between AI and the Creator Economy

by *Karim De Martino**

The creator economy and AI have always had several points of contact. Social media, or the territory in which content creators operate, has always been governed by algorithms, predecessors of what is now called "intelligence," and for influencers, decoding these algorithms has always represented the Holy Grail. Understanding, in fact, how a computer decides whether content will have millions of views or not transforms into the success of a post and consequently into a gain for the creators. The truth is, however, that no one has yet managed to decode these algorithms, whether due to their complexity or the fact that they are constantly evolving. There are therefore guidelines that suggest to creators what the reasoning of the AI of Instagram, YouTube, and TikTok is, but no one has yet found the magic formula to make every single piece of content go viral. In the digital marketing landscape, creators often find themselves engaging with algorithms in a strategic manner, much like a dance of courtship. They offer a variety of content, distribute it at different times, and apply diverse strategies, all to decipher the complexities of what resonates with audiences and what falls flat. This process is key to mastering the art of online engagement.

It goes without saying that AI is now the counterpart of the creator economy that determines the success of certain profiles; in the future it could become an ally. In fact, only other AI-based tools will be able to compete with the complex algorithms of big companies. Today there are already examples of generative AI supporting creators; for example, there

---

* Senior Vice President, International Business Development, Open Influence.

is software capable of generating captions starting from images, user input, and platform trends, using the right mix of words and keywords to solicit algorithms. There are also apps that can translate speech, giving content creators the ability to extend the audience for their content to a global level rather than just those who speak their language.

What we call "virtual influencers" today are actually personalities created by companies, behind which there are strategies, texts, and creativity managed by people. To make a comparison, virtual influencers are to influencers in the flesh as cartoon characters are to actors in film and TV. They are drawings or animations made by someone, and they tend to follow a strategy similar to that of content creators: building an audience, producing content that generates engagement, and growing and monetizing through collaboration with brands. There is no real innovation involved except in giving a personality to a drawing, with the only difference being that the creator in the flesh maintains credibility in telling his real life, while the virtual influencer is explicitly a construct. In reality, sometimes the influencers of the physical world are much faker than virtual influencers, just as actors are not the characters they play in movies and TV series, but this is rarely perceived by the public, which always has the illusion of spying on a real life, in an evolution of *Big Brother*.

Moving to the brand side, AI is already a component of many of the platforms that help brands select which content creators to collaborate with. For example, Open Influence has been collaborating with Amazon since 2018, integrating image recognition based on AI and machine learning into its discovery platform.[1] The photographic and video content of millions of influencers is scrutinized by an algorithm that recognizes objects and situations present in the images, without the need for text. We can therefore query the platform by asking to select content creators in a certain country, with certain sociodemographic characteristics of the audience, and also with a frequency of images in which glasses appear. While content creators are usually prepared to textually describe objects and situations of interest such as "I'm at a fashion show" or "look at that beautiful sunset," it is unlikely that they will tell us "I'm nearsighted and wear glasses." AI therefore allows us to do in a few minutes what would take a person days. With the same system we can look for people eating

---

[1] https://aws.amazon.com/it/blogs/machine-learning/open-influence-us-es-amazon-rekognition-to-enhance-its-influencer-marketing-platform/.

pizza, holding a wine glass, running a marathon, surfing, and so on, with endless possibilities and combinations. But we don't stop there. In addition to indicating the presence of objects and recognizing situations (for example "breakfast"), we cross this data with engagement and other factors that allow us to determine the audience's interest. Let's take the example of a pasta brand that wants to collaborate with a food influencer. We are able to find all the profiles that post pasta recipes and tell the client whether the audience's interest is actually toward this content, discovering that maybe the audience of a profile posting pasta actually prefers different content. This allows us to avoid the client investing in that profile with little chance of success, proposing alternatives instead.

While AI represents a great opportunity for the creator economy, both on the influencer and the brand side, one fundamental limit remains: Today the analysis is done on what already exists. AIs study successful content and trends and give us guidance on what we need to do to follow them, but they don't predict what the trends of the future will be. The most successful content creators are those who have the intuition and luck to launch trends. Take the example of Khaby Lame, with the simplicity of his gesture. No AI could ever have predicted that gesture would transform him into the most followed TikToker in the world.

7 Augmented Events: Ideation, Management, and Production

7.1 An industry overview

For businesses, events are strategic tools that play an instrumental role in sculpting corporate communication strategies. From grand product launches to intimate stakeholder engagements and expansive industry trade shows, events offer unparalleled avenues to articulate brand ethos, captivate audiences, and fortify stakeholder relationships. The venue itself plays a key role in achieving these goals. Its design, layout, and aesthetic define the overall event experience and help convey core brand values. A sustainable, community-focused venue aligns with and strengthens corresponding brand messaging. Similarly, an innovative, cutting-edge venue underscores a brand's focus on innovation. The strategic choice of venue is therefore intrinsic to effectively sculpting holistic brand communications through events.

Corporate events aimed at internal stakeholders or business partners serve a different purpose than public-facing events open to a wider audience. Internal corporate events are focused on goals such as employee training, sales incentivization, partner onboarding, and team building. Strategies revolve around motivating and enabling employees and partners to become brand ambassadors. Public events allow brands to directly interface with consumers and media to shape broader brand perceptions and drive leads or sales. They require strategies tailored to captivate and inspire mass external audiences.

Beyond mere presentations, events serve as experiential platforms. They allow audiences to immerse themselves in product experiences, solicit clarifications, and offer real-time feedback, guiding businesses in their future endeavors.

The direct stakeholder engagement facilitated by events, be it with customers, partners, media, or influencers, is invaluable. These interactions not only bolster existing relationships but also pave the way for new collaborations and knowledge exchanges.

Furthermore, events are trust-building exercises. Even in this first digital and augmented world, the face-to-face interactions, the firsthand product experiences, and the open dialogues foster an environment of transparency and authenticity. This environment is instrumental in laying the groundwork for lasting business relationships. Leveraging astute communication strategies, the key messages from events can be amplified manifoldly. Digital tools, especially social media, can exponentially magnify their reach, resonating with a global audience.

Considering all these facets, it becomes evident that events are not just another tool in the corporate communication arsenal; they are a unique weapon. They offer a blend of authenticity, engagement, and impact that few other communication mediums can match. For corporate communication professionals, events are an indispensable asset, offering a distinct edge in a competitive landscape.

7.1.1 *The economic impact of business events*

Before the onset of the Covid-19 pandemic, 2019 stood out as a landmark year for the global business events sector. During that year, a staggering 1.6 billion people participated in business events across more than 180 countries.[1] These events weren't just about bringing people together; they also played a pivotal role in the global economy.

Attendees, especially those of large-scale events, channel substantial revenue into accommodations, dining, transportation, and entertainment. This influx benefits a myriad of local businesses, from hotels to restaurants. Moreover, international conferences, festivals, and sports tournaments have become pivotal for tourism. Attendees, captivated by the allure of the host city or country, often prolong their stay, enriching the tourism sector. This not only contributes economically but also brings about vibrant cultural exchange, enhancing the locale's appeal for future travelers.

---

[1] https://www.pcma.org/ and https://www.statista.com/study/85740/the-live-event-industry-and-covid-19/.

Beyond tourism, the event industry stands as a significant employment generator. The spectrum of job opportunities it creates is vast, encompassing event planners, technicians, caterers, security personnel, and even local artisans. In cities with bustling event calendars, seasonal employment witnesses a notable surge, offering livelihoods to countless individuals.

The industry's economic contributions extend to increasing entrepreneurship and innovation. Trade shows and industry-specific conferences emerge as platforms for startups and innovators. These events offer them a stage to spotlight their offerings, attract potential investors, forge partnerships, and garner invaluable market feedback. From a quantitative perspective, business events in 2019 generated over $1.15 trillion in direct spending. This spending encompassed various aspects, from the costs to plan and produce these events to related travel and other direct expenditures, such as exhibitor spending. The ripple effect of these events was profound. They supported 10.9 million direct jobs globally. But the impact didn't stop there. When considering the indirect and induced impacts, business events bolstered a total global economic impact of $2.8 trillion in business sales. This translated to supporting 27.5 million jobs and contributing a whopping $1.6 trillion to the global GDP.

The subsequent years, with the spread of Covid-19, brought challenges that few could have anticipated. The three-year period from 2020 to 2022 saw a cumulative loss in global direct business event spending amounting to $1.9 trillion. This loss wasn't just monetary; it represented the loss of more than 16 million jobs. Yet despite these setbacks, the resilience of the industry shone through. By 2022, direct spending had rebounded to more than 80 percent relative to 2019 levels. And the forecast is even more promising, with global business event spending expected to make a full recovery by 2024. This ongoing transformation, driven by both technological advancements and changing global dynamics, will inevitably redefine the very contours of the industry. To truly grasp the potential trajectory of its evolution, we must circle back to the starting point: the needs and desires of clients and attendees. It is their aspirations, preferences, and feedback that will illuminate the path forward, ensuring that the industry not only adapts but also thrives in the changing landscape.

7.1.2 *Evolving attendee needs and expectations*

The events industry has been deeply impacted by the Covid-19 pandemic, but its core essence remains. New priorities and methods are reshaping its future. Attendee needs and expectations have evolved, with more emphasis on digital engagement, sustainability, and flexibility. This is driving organizers to adapt with new hybrid event strategies. Technological innovations such as touchless systems, QR codes, and virtual networking platforms are transforming the event experience by making it more streamlined, insightful, and personalized. Sustainability efforts, such as using recycled materials, minimizing waste, and encouraging green transportation, are helping reduce events' environmental footprint. Generational differences are also emerging. Younger attendees favor virtual interactions and shareable social media moments. Older attendees still value face-to-face connections, tactile collateral, and tangible memories. Organizers must craft experiences that appeal to these varied preferences.

Variations can also be seen between business-to business (B2B) and business-to-consumer (B2C) events. B2B events, such as trade shows, conferences, and seminars, primarily cater to professionals and businesses. The core objective of these events is often centered around fostering business relationships, exploring partnership opportunities, and driving commercial growth. Attendees at B2B events come with specific expectations.

- **Lead generation:** Professionals attend B2B events with the aim of expanding their business network. They seek potential clients, partners, or suppliers, making lead generation one of the primary objectives. The event's success is often gauged by the number of quality leads an attendee or exhibitor can secure.
- **Relationship building:** Beyond mere lead generation, B2B events offer a platform for nurturing existing relationships and forging new ones. In an era where digital communication dominates, the value of face-to-face interactions in solidifying business partnerships cannot be overstated.
- **Knowledge exchange:** B2B events often feature industry experts, panel discussions, and workshops. Attendees expect to gain insights into industry trends, innovations, and best practices. This knowl-

edge exchange positions them to make informed business decisions and stay ahead of the curve.

On the flip side, B2C events, such as music festivals, product launches, and brand activations, target end consumers. The dynamics here are markedly different.

- **Brand experiences**: B2C events are platforms where brands can create immersive experiences for attendees. Whether it's a product demonstration, interactive installation, or live performance, the focus is on creating memorable moments that resonate with the consumer's emotions and senses.
- **Social sharing incentives**: In today's digital age, consumers are not just attendees; they are potential brand ambassadors. B2C events often incorporate elements that encourage social sharing, be it photo booths, hashtag campaigns, or shareable digital content. A single viral moment from an event can significantly amplify a brand's reach and impact.
- **Engagement and loyalty**: While B2B events focus on business growth, B2C events aim to foster brand loyalty. By offering consumers unique experiences, exclusive previews, or special offers, brands can cultivate a sense of belonging and loyalty among attendees.

For the event industry, the post-pandemic era is not just about recovery; it's about reinvention. This sector, like many others, finds itself at a crossroads, where the path forward is being paved with innovation, adaptability, and a keen understanding of attendee psychology. As we delve deeper into the nuances of this industry, it becomes evident that to effectively cater to the evolving demands of the audience, one must harness the power of technology. Virtual platforms, augmented reality, AI-driven tools, and interactive digital experiences can all play a pivotal role. They allow events to offer enhanced flexibility, sustainability, and engagement – key priorities for today's attendees. By blending technological capabilities with human-centric customization, events can continue to provide memorable and meaningful experiences.

7.1.3 *Technological innovation*

Building on the digital transformation catalyzed by the pandemic, event organizers have continued to push the boundaries of technological innovation. While video conferencing platforms such as Zoom, Microsoft Teams, and Google Meet enabled the initial emergency pivot to virtual events, organizers strived for more immersive and interactive experiences merging the physical and virtual worlds into a seamless omnichannel experience.

Augmented reality (AR) and virtual reality (VR) emerged as game changers. These technologies, once the domain of gaming and specialized applications, have found their way into mainstream events. AR overlays digital content onto the real world, enhancing the user's environment, while VR offers a fully immersive experience, transporting users to entirely virtual realms. For event attendees, this means a richer, more engaging experience. Consider a product launch where, instead of just watching a presentation, attendees could don a VR headset and walk through a virtual showroom, examining products up close, or even interacting with them. Similarly, AR could transform a simple event brochure into an interactive experience, with 3D models, videos, and animations springing to life from the page. The integration of AI-driven chatbots at virtual events has facilitated real-time query resolution, enhancing attendee engagement. Interactive polls, Q&A sessions, and virtual breakout rooms have further replicated the dynamism of physical events in the digital realm.

Another point of innovation is the advent of event management software programs, such as Bizzabo and Cvent, which simplify the intricate and costly event management process; their all-encompassing dashboards allow organizers to oversee everything from venue selection to attendee registration in one unified space.[2] This integrated planning approach eliminates the need for multiple tools, ensuring a more cohesive and efficient planning process. Advanced ticketing modules within these platforms provide flexibility in pricing, from early bird discounts to dynamic pricing based on real-time demand. This adaptability ensures optimal ticket sales and maximizes revenue. But it's not just about ticket sales. The real magic lies in the engagement tools these platforms offer.

---

[2] https://www.bizzabo.com/; https://www.cvent.com/.

Features such as live polling, interactive agendas, and Q&A sessions ensure that attendees are actively involved, making even virtual events feel vibrant and connected. Furthermore, the ability to gather and analyze data gives organizers invaluable insights into attendee behavior, session preferences, and overall engagement. This data-driven approach allows for the curation of personalized agendas, ensuring attendees receive content tailored to their unique interests.

Networking, a cornerstone of events, hasn't been overlooked either. Integrated tools, from virtual lounges to matchmaking, facilitate meaningful connections among attendees. This replicates the spontaneous interactions typical of physical events in a virtual setting. The benefits don't end there. Attendees can now access event content on demand, allowing them to engage at their own pace and convenience. This, combined with interactive tools such as gamified sessions and live chats, ensures attendees are more participants than mere viewers.

The convergence of advanced event software and the understanding of attendee needs is setting a new standard. Technology provides tools to create enhanced experiences, but truly understanding attendee preferences makes events resonate. The future will feature a blend of technology and personalization for more meaningful engagements. In the post-pandemic world, hybrid events will dominate, combining in-person and virtual options. There will be renewed focus on deriving tangible returns, requiring data-driven planning and marketing. Adaptability – the ability to pivot strategies amid challenges – will be critical. AI promises enhanced efficiency and redefined value in every facet of events. It is poised to transform the industry's future.

7.2   Transforming the event life cycle

Historically, the event industry has been about creating memorable experiences, meticulously crafting every detail to resonate with attendees. But as explored in earlier sections, this industry today stands at a crossroads. Having weathered the upheaval of a global pandemic, it now looks ahead to an era of reinvention and strategic transformation. The needs of attendees, the primary stakeholders, have evolved markedly. For organizers to deliver on these fronts, while also boosting productivity, the infusion of emerging technologies is essential. Of these, AI holds the greatest disruptive potential to reshape the event life cycle. AI allows businesses to derive strategic value from events like never before.

AI's analytical capabilities help identify the most promising opportunities aligned to business goals and evolving attendee expectations. This technology handles the tactical details, allowing organizers to focus on experiential elements. AI-powered customer relationship management (CRM) enables personalized engagement and, during events, AI creates immersive omnichannel experiences blending the physical and the digital.

The infusion of AI throughout the event life cycle allows businesses to deliver deeply personalized, interactive event experiences. These experiences forge lasting connections with attendees, be they customers, partners, or employees. As the capabilities of AI grow more advanced, its role in revolutionizing events will only amplify. With its balance of data-inspired optimization and human-centric customization, AI heralds a new era of strategic and value-focused event management. The traditional event life cycle, once a linear journey, is now a dynamic, feedback-driven loop, ensuring that each event is better than the last.

7.2.1 *Ideation and planning: Crafting memorable experiences with AI*

The ideation phase stands as a key moment in the event planning process, acting as the bedrock upon which the entire event is built. It's during this time that a mere spark of an idea is nurtured, expanded, and transformed into a comprehensive vision for the event. This vision encompasses everything from the broad strokes of the event's theme and objectives down to the intricate details of venue aesthetics and strategies for attendee engagement.

In days gone by, the ideation process was deeply entrenched in the realm of creativity. Teams of event planners would come together, pooling their collective experiences, successes, and even lessons from past failures, to craft a unique vision for an event. This traditional approach, while rich in its reliance on human intuition and experience, was inherently subjective. Decisions were often based on personal anecdotes or gut feelings, and while many successful events emerged from this method, there was always an element of unpredictability. The question of how attendees would perceive and engage with the event remained a constant uncertainty.

The integration of AI into the event industry marked a significant shift in how events are conceptualized. Ideation, once a purely creative endeavor, now beautifully marries the art of event planning with the precision of science. AI, with its ability to process and analyze data, offers event planners a treasure trove of actionable insights. These insights, grounded in empirical evidence from past events, attendee feedback, and even global industry trends, provide a roadmap for crafting events that resonate. Essentially, AI provides a 360-degree analytical perspective, elevating ideation from an intuitive exercise to one grounded in data intelligence.

For instance, the feedback from previous events, when processed through AI, can reveal patterns, highlighting elements that attendees found most engaging. Similarly, AI's capability to scan and analyze data from platforms such as social media means that event planners can have their fingers on the pulse of current industry trends and preferences. This ensures the event remains not just relevant but also timely.

Another impactful application of AI is in transforming event planning from a tedious, manual process to an intelligent and optimized one. AI technologies allow organizers to automate repetitive tasks, enabling them to focus their efforts more strategically.

AI algorithms can analyze venues across dozens of parameters from capacity and layout to location and amenities. By processing this expansive data, they provide organizers valuable insights for venue selection aligned to event goals and attendee preferences. This eliminates the need for manual research and guesswork.

Similarly, AI can optimize scheduling and logistics by considering session duration, speaker availability, and predicted attendee engagement. Machine learning allows the AI to continually refine event flow based on past data. Schedule conflicts and disjointed sessions become relics of the past. Planners can also now visualize potential outcomes based on different decisions, a concept we might term "predictive ideation." This forward-looking approach ensures that event planners are not just reacting to past data but are proactively equipped to anticipate and cater to future trends and behaviors.

Consider the scenario of organizing a global tech conference. In the past, determining the theme of the conference might have been based on the organizer's perception of what's trending in the tech world. However, with AI, this process can be significantly more refined. By analyzing data from tech news sites, forums, social media, and past conference feedback, AI can identify emerging tech trends and topics that are generating the most buzz and interest. If there's a rising interest in quantum computing, the AI can suggest this as a central theme or as a significant track for the conference.

Once the theme is set, AI can assist in identifying potential speakers. By analyzing data from platforms such as LinkedIn, academic journals, and tech publications, AI can identify leading experts in quantum computing, rank them based on their influence, and even predict their availability based on their past speaking engagements and current affiliations.

When it comes to venue selection, AI can analyze attendee data to predict the expected turnout, ensuring the chosen venue is neither too large nor too small. It can also consider factors such as proximity to major transport hubs, availability of accommodation options nearby, and even historical weather data to suggest the best dates for the event. AI can suggest the kind of sessions that would be most popular, allowing organizers to allocate them to larger halls. It can also provide personalized schedules for attendees based on their professional interests, ensuring they get the most out of the conference.

The cumulative impact is profound. With AI handling the tactical details, organizers can devote their creative energies to designing truly engaging session formats, immersive experiences, and innovative elements personalized for each event. By blending automation, analytics, and machine learning, AI enables intelligent event planning focused on strategy rather than logistics.

7.2.2 *Optimizing event management*

The traditional approach to event management, while effective, often relied heavily on manual processes, intuition, and personal experiences. It's a multifaceted process that requires meticulous coordination. At its core, it involves a series of interconnected tasks, each essential to the successful execution of an event. Central to this orchestration is the coordination with various vendors. An event often brings together a diverse group of service providers, from the culinary expertise of caterers to the aesthetic touch of decorators and the technical prowess of audiovisual teams. Each vendor plays a role, and ensuring they are in sync with the event's vision and requirements is paramount.

As the vendors fall into place, the intricate dance of scheduling takes center stage. Crafting a detailed timeline for the event is akin to choreographing a performance. Allocating time slots for speakers, performers, and even breaks is a delicate balance, ensuring that the audience remains engaged while also preventing any overlaps or logistical hiccups.

With the schedule set, the focus shifts to the judicious allocation of resources. Every event operates within the constraints of a budget, and the art of event management lies in maximizing the impact without overspending. This financial ballet involves negotiating with vendors, securing the best deals for venues, and managing a myriad of other expenses. It's about ensuring that every penny spent contributes to the event's success, creating value for both the organizers and the attendees.

But what's an event without its attendees? Managing the guests, from the moment they receive an invitation to the time they leave the venue, is a crucial aspect of event management. This process starts with sending out captivating invitations, tracking RSVPs, and managing the registrations. As the event date approaches, ensuring a smooth check-in process becomes vital, setting the tone for the attendee's entire experience.

The crescendo of the event management process is undoubtedly the actual event day. This is where months of planning come to fruition. Real-time coordination is the order of the day, ensuring that all activities unfold as envisioned. It's about being prepared for the unexpected, swiftly addressing any challenges that arise, and constantly gauging attendee satisfaction. Every detail, from the lighting and sound to the temperature of the venue, plays a role in crafting the desired ambiance and experience.

Whether it's automating repetitive tasks, offering insights for optimal vendor selection, or providing real-time feedback during the event, AI has introduced a level of precision and efficiency previously unattainable, heralding a new era in event management. AI-driven CRM systems engage attendees even before the event starts by compiling detailed attendee profiles. This data-driven approach enables personalized communication and real-time adaptation as event registrations evolve.

During the event, AI's influence becomes even more pronounced. It facilitates immersive experiences that blend the physical and digital realms. Attendees can interact with AI-powered kiosks, engage with VR simulations, and benefit from smart device integrations, ensuring a seamless omnichannel engagement. Moreover, AI's capability to analyze audience reactions in real time allows organizers to dynamically shape the event narrative, optimizing the overall energy and engagement levels. AI is also enhancing security via facial recognition and biometrics. AI empowers event production teams to actualize their creative vision through a confluence of optimization, personalization, analytics, and technology integration. It helps craft events that engage, inspire, and leave indelible memories. The result is elevated production standards that capture the imagination rather than just attracting physical attendance.

Beyond the event's immediate environment, AI-powered tools provide invaluable insights into attendee sentiment. By using facial recognition also to detect emotions or analyzing feedback from live polls, organizers can gauge attendee reactions in real time. This immediate feedback mechanism allows for on-the-spot adaptations, ensuring optimal attendee satisfaction.

A prime example of this transformation is evident in the Folkemødet festival in Denmark. Folkemødet, a festival celebrating democracy, faced the challenge of navigating its extensive program, which featured more than 200 venues and close to 3,200 events over three days. The sheer volume of events presented attendees with a paradox of choice, making it challenging to find activities tailored to their interests.

To address this, Halfspace, a Microsoft AI partner, developed a web app leveraging generative AI and natural language processing.[3] This app allowed users to navigate the festival's vast array of activities through an intuitive conversational interface. Beyond mere keyword-based searches, the app understood context and user intent, delivering event suggestions on demand using generative AI. This approach transformed the event discovery process, offering attendees a curated list of activities aligned with their specific interests, ensuring a more meaningful and engaging experience. Furthermore, the app's AI-driven features simplified event planning. Attendees could effortlessly search for events based on various criteria, from location and date to topic and speaker. The app's intelligent algorithms filtered through the extensive program, presenting attendees with a refined selection that matched their preferences. This streamlined process, combined with the app's user-friendly interface and intelligent organization, exemplified the power of AI in simplifying complex tasks and enhancing user experiences during an event.

---

[3] https://www.halfspace.ai/.

In summary, AI infuses new levels of orchestration, automation, and analytics into the event management process. It ensures seamless planning and flawless execution powered by precision, speed, and foresight.

7.2.3 AI's role in post-event analysis

The event life cycle doesn't end when the curtains fall. The post-event phase is as crucial as the planning and execution stages. It's during this time that event organizers gather feedback, analyze performance, and derive insights for future events. These follow-ups can be the difference between an event that wasn't worth the investment and one that delivers maximum return on investment. With the integration of AI, this phase has witnessed a transformative shift, offering tools and methodologies that were previously unimaginable.

It allows marketers to deeply understand the goals, preferences, and behaviors of attendees. This understanding is pivotal for delivering better experiences and personalized recommendations, and for crafting content and sales pitches that match individual needs. AI in this context streamlines workflows, gathers comprehensive feedback from all stakeholders, and provides insights that can be used to enhance attendee engagement, refine event content, and optimize marketing strategies for future events.

For example, traditionally, event planners would spend hours searching for the right questions to include in their post-event surveys. Now, with the integration of AI, event planners can quickly generate a plethora of relevant survey questions tailored to their specific event. Many platforms, such as Accelevents, facilitate the collection of this type of feedback.[4] Whether it's a keynote speech that resonated with them or a logistical hiccup they faced, attendees can easily provide both positive and negative feedback. This comprehensive feedback mechanism ensures that event organizers receive a holistic view of the event's impact, capturing the highs and the lows through quantitative metrics, such as net promoter scores (NPS),[5]

Beyond just using the attendee's name, AI can assist in tailoring the email's content to match the tone and language that would most appeal to the recipient. By analyzing past interactions and feedback, AI can de-

---

[4] https://www.accelevents.com/.
[5] https://en.wikipedia.org/wiki/Net_promoter_score.

termine whether a formal, casual, or enthusiastic tone would be most effective. Furthermore, based on the data and the patterns it recognizes, AI can generate multiple versions of the email content, each with a distinct tone and approach. This provides the communication manager with a range of alternatives, ensuring that the final message aligns perfectly with the desired brand voice and the event's objectives. In this way, AI not only enhances the personalization of communication but also empowers decision-makers with choices, ensuring that the most resonant and effective message is selected. For instance, if an attendee showed particular interest in a specific workshop, the thank you email could highlight key takeaways or provide additional resources related to that workshop. This not only expresses gratitude but also invites attendees to provide feedback and informs them about upcoming events. Time and again, we're reminded that the essence of technology isn't just about streamlining processes for efficiency. It's about tapping into the transformative power of AI to craft event experiences that are not only more meaningful and personalized but also leave a lasting impact. As the event industry undergoes rapid evolution and grapples with challenges that intensify by the day, the significance of AI in shaping its future cannot be overstated. Forward-thinking event planners and organizers who wholeheartedly adopt and integrate these AI-driven tools and insights will find themselves at an advantage. They'll be better equipped to navigate the competitive landscape, ensuring that their events don't just meet the mark but consistently surpass attendee expectations.

7.3   The event horizon: Envisioning the next frontier

As AI and emerging technologies continue to transform the event landscape, the possibilities appear to be endless. Immersive hybrid experiences represent the intersection of the physical and virtual worlds, offering a unique and engaging experience for users. These experiences are powered by emerging technologies, including 5G, AR/VR, and spatial computing. 5G technology, with its ultra-low latency and broad bandwidth, is pivotal in enabling large-scale adoption of AR/VR. In particular, private 5G networks ensure that applications receive the capabilities needed to execute critical processes, offering advantages in terms of security, latency, and bandwidth.

Spatial computing refers to the ability of computers and devices to recognize and interact with their surrounding environment. Combined with AR/VR, it allows for the creation of immersive experiences where users can interact with digital elements within their physical environment. For instance, at a music concert, attendees could use AR glasses to see virtual effects around the stage or get real-time statistics about the performance.

Biometrics and facial recognition technologies allow for proximity-based customization. For example, an event system might recognize a returning attendee and customize their experience based on their past preferences or behavior. This kind of "living" customization can transform events in real time, adapting to audience data. Imagine that, walking into a tech conference, the event system recognizes you and guides you to stalls based on your past interests or suggests networking opportunities with professionals in your field (and here's another reference to the film *Minority Report* in this book).

Practical applications of AR/VR in the event world are vast. A remote expert feature could allow a technician at a tech expo to get real-time guidance from a specialist located elsewhere, using smart glasses. Real-time collaboration can be enhanced at global summits, where delegates from different locations can interact with the same virtual data or presentations, enhancing collaborative discussions. Maintenance, repairs, and operations can be streamlined at large-scale events such as festivals, where organizers can receive AR instructions during setup, improving efficiency and reducing errors. Furthermore, AR/VR offers potential applications for training event staff, allowing them to learn in realistic virtual environments, ensuring they are well prepared for the actual event.

The event of the future is set to be a personalized, multisensory phenomenon – shaped by AI but imagined by human creativity. Each aspect will be tailored to the individual, from schedules to VR journeys, creating an inclusive and accessible experience, just as AI is currently assisting in crafting memorable experiences during the planning phase. Biometrics will enable emotion-aware interactions, while AR layering will transform static venues into kinetic playgrounds. Real-time AI translation breaks down language barriers, opening global connections.

In a discourse aiming to shed light on the future of the event industry, one cannot overlook the burgeoning concept of the metaverse. The metaverse, a collective virtual shared space born from the convergence of enhanced physical reality and persistent virtual realms, is not just a mere representation but an augmentation of our world. It's poised to redefine how we perceive and interact within event spaces.

The metaverse offers an expansive canvas, unshackled by the constraints of physical space, logistics, and geographical boundaries that traditional events often grapple with. Imagine a tourism expo that can virtually transport attendees to exotic locations, allowing them to immerse themselves in the sights and sounds as if they were truly present. Or consider a medical conference offering immersive surgery simulations, granting professionals the chance to practice intricate procedures in a risk-free environment.

Yet beyond the allure of limitless virtual spaces, the true transformative power of the metaverse lies in its decentralized nature. Events in the metaverse can be collaborative endeavors, with attendees from across the globe contributing to the experience. This decentralization not only democratizes participation, ensuring inclusivity regardless of geographical location, but also presents a sustainable alternative to traditional events. By eliminating the need for physical venues, extensive logistics, and travel, the carbon footprint of events can be significantly reduced. This approach aligns with the growing global emphasis on sustainability and the urgent need to mitigate the environmental impacts of large-scale gatherings.

Furthermore, the integration of AI within the metaverse ensures a level of personalization previously unattainable. As attendees navigate these virtual realms, AI systems can curate experiences tailored to individual preferences and past behaviors. This ensures that each journey is not only immersive but also deeply personal.

However, while the metaverse presents a plethora of opportunities, it's essential to approach it with a discerning eye. The allure of limitless virtual spaces and hyper-personalized experiences, though groundbreaking, brings forth challenges that cannot be ignored. One of the most significant challenges is the potential erosion of intimacy and genuine human connection.

Events, at their core, are about people coming together, sharing experiences, and forging bonds. The tactile sensation of a handshake, the warmth of a hug, or the spontaneity of a shared laugh – these are intangible elements that virtual realms might struggle to replicate. Overreliance on the metaverse for events could inadvertently create environments that, while technologically advanced, feel sterile and devoid of genuine human warmth. Moreover, the very personalization that AI offers within the metaverse could become an issue. While attendees might enjoy experiences tailored to their preferences, there's a risk of creating echo chambers where individuals are only exposed to familiar ideas and perspectives. Such environments could stifle creativity, innovation, and the serendipity of unexpected encounters that often lead to the most profound insights and connections.

Nevertheless, the future beckons organizers to craft events unencumbered by physical constraints. With human ingenuity at the helm and AI as the engine, bespoke multisensory attendee journeys become reality. Events are evolutions, catalysts that spur innovation. And the next horizon promises experiences beyond our imagination – a truly exciting vision for this dynamic industry.

Insight
AI in the Meeting Industry

by *Patrizia Semprebene Buongiorno**

It is fascinating to see how AI is transforming the event industry. As someone deeply involved in the meeting industry, I am aware that we are still in a dynamic phase where the full extent of its capabilities and costs are not yet fully known. AI's potential is continuously expanding, and it keeps surprising us.

One area where AI is making an impact is in preplanning. From helping to define and design scientific programs to gathering feedback for future editions, it's like having a crystal ball powered by data and attendee preferences.

As we move forward, the synergy between human expertise and AI's capabilities will become increasingly vital. Embracing AI in the event industry means not only optimizing operations but also exploring new frontiers. While the complete roadmap is still unfolding, there's no doubt that AI is a driving force shaping the future of conferences and events.

The increasing use of AI in events has now become a clear trend that will continue to expand as technology advances. Both event organizers and participants will gain significant benefits from this versatile emerging technology. However, using the full potential of AI tools requires experience, knowledge, and experimentation to guide the AI effectively toward desired outcomes.

Event organizers looking to incorporate AI should consider starting experiments with the technology to become comfortable with its capabilities.

Now, let's dive into the pros and cons.

---

* VP AIM Group International.

On the positive side.

- **Efficiency:** AI can streamline various meeting-related tasks, such as scheduling, registration, and attendee check-ins. Automated processes reduce the chance of errors and free up human resources to focus on more strategic aspects of event planning.
- **Personalization:** AI can analyze attendee data and preferences to create personalized experiences. For example, it can recommend sessions, workshops, or networking opportunities based on an individual's interests and past participation.
- **Data insights:** AI-driven analytics can process vast amounts of data generated during meetings and provide valuable insights. Organizers can use this information to understand attendee behavior, optimize event content, and improve overall event strategy.
- **Language translation:** AI-powered language translation tools can break down language barriers, enabling international collaboration and making meetings more accessible to a global audience.
- **Virtual assistants:** AI chatbots or virtual assistants can handle common queries and provide real-time support during events. They can help attendees find information, answer questions, and offer assistance 24/7.
- **Content management:** AI can categorize and tag meeting content, such as presentations, videos, and documents, making it easier to organize and retrieve. This enhances content accessibility and sharing among participants.

On the flip side.

- **Cost:** Implementing AI solutions can be expensive, particularly for smaller organizations or event planners with limited budgets. Costs include acquiring AI software, hardware, and ongoing maintenance.
- **Privacy concerns:** Collecting and analyzing attendee data can raise privacy concerns. To address this, event organizers must have robust data protection measures in place, comply with relevant regulations, and obtain explicit consent for data usage.
- **Technical issues:** AI systems are not immune to technical problems or errors. System failures during a critical event can disrupt proceedings and lead to frustration among attendees.
- **Job displacement:** Some people worry that AI might take over cer-

tain jobs in event planning and management. While AI can handle repetitive tasks efficiently, it's important to remember that human creativity, intuition, and people skills are still vital for making events successful. So, finding the right balance between using AI for automation and keeping humans involved is key to ensuring the best outcomes in event planning and management.

- **Learning curve:** Participants and event staff may struggle to adapt to new AI tools. This can result in resistance to change and a temporary decrease in efficiency as users become familiar with the technology.

Indeed, AI offers significant advantages in terms of efficiency, personalization, data insights, and accessibility in the meeting industry. However, event planners and organizers should carefully consider the costs, privacy implications, technical challenges, and the human touch when integrating AI solutions, and ensuring ethical AI use is crucial as we move forward in this transformative journey.

8 Data Ownership and Privacy

8.1 Data ownership in the AI landscape: Evolution and challenges

From the dawn of civilization, our ancestors recognized the value of recording and preserving knowledge.

The act of record-keeping was not merely an administrative task; it had profound economic and societal implications. Those who held records - whether they were of trade, debts, treaties, or lineage - possessed power. Knowledge of grain reserves could influence economies, while control over lineage records could legitimize or delegitimize a ruler. In essence, information was as valuable a currency as gold or silver.

Transitioning into the computer era of the mid-20th century, this intrinsic value of data didn't diminish - it exponentially amplified. Magnetic tapes and floppy disks represented a seismic shift in how information could be stored, accessed, and leveraged. Businesses began to realize that data, when analyzed correctly, could provide insights that translated to significant competitive advantages in the market.

As we venture into the realm of generative AI, we are confronted with a new dimension of complexity. Data is no longer just a source of power and economic value; it has become the very fuel that powers these advanced AI models. The quality and richness of data determine the efficacy of these models. For instance, LLMs such as ChatGPT ingest billions of paragraphs from books, articles, and websites without explicit permission from or compensation to the creators. Their ability to generate coherent, contextually relevant, and sometimes even creative content is directly proportional to the quality of the data they are trained on. While transformative, the output of these AI models contains traces of copyrighted source content. This raises pressing questions around proper attribution, fair financial compensation of rights holders, and the limits of fair use when operating at such vast scales. There are parallels to the music sampling debates of the 1990s. Fundamentally, the issue centers on data ownership. If models are trained on swathes of the internet, who rightfully owns that data? And perhaps more critically, who owns the novel outputs they generate? Are they mere reflections of the training data or entirely new creations? If the latter, ownership remains ambiguous. Furthermore, biases and discrimination remain a real danger, as historical datasets often incorporate prejudices that AI can amplify exponentially. Cases such as racially biased facial recognition demonstrate how AI can perpetuate real-world harms if not carefully implemented.[1] This raises important questions about the ethical use of data that companies must address.

The *New York Times'* decision to block OpenAI's web crawler underscores the complexities of this issue.[2] High-quality content producers are wary of their data being used without compensation or acknowledgment. This case highlights the complex ethical and legal issues around the unauthorized use of others' content to train AI models. Quality content creators consider it a form of intellectual "theft," where their work is exploited without adequate recompense. At the same time, training AIs on large amounts of data is crucial to improving their capabilities.

The very case of this book serves as a poignant example. While LLMs might have been instrumental in generating parts of its content, does that mean the authorship of the book is diluted? Who holds the rights to the words generated by an AI that was trained on data from countless sources? These are not just philosophical questions; they have significant legal, ethical, and economic implications.

The stakes are even higher in a corporate setting, where the integrity, security, and trustworthiness of communication are paramount. Paralleling the rise of cloud computing, companies faced similar challenges migrating data to third-party platforms such as Amazon, Microsoft, and Google. The essence of a business - its data - was now entrusted outside

---

[1] https://sitn.hms.harvard.edu/flash/2020/racial-discrimination-in-face-recognition-technology/.

[2] https://www.theverge.com/2023/8/21/23840705/new-york-times-openai-web-crawler-ai-gpt.

its walls. This raised immense concerns around security, accessibility, and critically, ownership. Who truly owned the data in the cloud? And what rights did these providers have?

With generative AI, risks are magnified - from potential security breaches and data leakage to intellectual property (IP) disputes and compliance issues. For instance, if sensitive information is shared with ChatGPT, it becomes part of the model, risking exposure. Likewise, ChatGPT's outputs may inadvertently infringe on IP rights. In corporate communications, these risks intensify even further - whether in drafting press releases, marketing campaigns, financial reports, or internal memos. The potential for data breaches, copyright disputes, and other legal and ethical pitfalls is substantial. Companies must be proactive in addressing these challenges. The question becomes: How should corporate policies adapt? Here are some key areas companies should consider.

- **Clear data usage policies**: In the context of corporate communication, every piece of information, from internal memos to public press releases, carries weight. Establishing clear data usage policies ensures that all communication, whether intended for internal stakeholders or the public, adheres to a consistent standard of data sharing. This not only safeguards sensitive information but also ensures that the company's messaging remains consistent and in line with its brand values. For instance, a company might have proprietary research that they wish to highlight in a press release. A clear data usage policy would dictate how much of that research can be shared, with whom, and in what context.
- **Evaluate AI tools**: Corporate communication strategies often involve a mix of manual and automated processes. Before integrating an AI tool into this mix, it's crucial to understand its capabilities and limitations. For instance, if an AI tool is used to draft press releases or social media posts, understanding its data handling practices can prevent unintentional sharing of sensitive information. Moreover, by evaluating the terms of service, companies can ensure that they retain ownership of their content and avoid potential IP disputes.
- **Ongoing training and awareness**: The world of AI is ever-evolving, and so are the potential risks associated with its use in corporate communication. Regular training ensures that employees are not only aware of these risks but also equipped to mitigate them. For

instance, if a PR team is trained on the potential biases of an AI tool used for sentiment analysis, they can interpret the tool's outputs more critically and ensure that their communications remain unbiased and factual.

- **Engage legal and ethical experts:** The legal and ethical landscape of AI is complex and often varies by jurisdiction. In corporate communication, where the stakes are high, navigating this landscape is crucial. Engaging legal and ethical experts ensures that all communications, from investor reports to marketing campaigns, adhere to local regulations and global ethical standards. For instance, if a company is launching a global marketing campaign that leverages AI-generated content, legal experts can ensure that the content adheres to IP laws in all target markets.
- **Adopt trustworthy enterprise AI solutions:** Trust is a cornerstone of corporate communication. Stakeholders, be they customers, investors, or employees, need to trust the information being presented to them. By adopting AI solutions that prioritize transparency and ethical data handling, companies can ensure that their communications remain credible. For instance, if a company uses an enterprise AI model to analyze customer feedback and then communicates those insights to its stakeholders, the transparency of the AI tool ensures that the insights are both accurate and trustworthy.

Recognizing this need for trust and transparency, the AI landscape has seen the emergence of enterprise solutions such as IBM WatsonX and OpenAI's ChatGPT Enterprise.[3] Startups are also emerging at a rapid pace with the promise of enabling companies of all sizes to leverage LLM models trained on their own data. For example, SanaAI is focused on making LLMs more accessible and customizable for enterprise use cases.[4] By providing tools to fine-tune models on a company's unique data, SanaAI aims to allow businesses to deploy AI that is tailored to their industry, products, and customers. Other startups are taking a similar approach, seeking to democratize access to LLMs so they are not solely the domain of big tech companies with extensive resources.

-----

[3] https://www.ibm.com/products/watsonx-ai; https://openai.com/blog/introducing-chatgpt-enterprise.

[4] https://www.sanalabs.com/sana-ai.

This aligns with the trend of industrialization of AI, taking it from research into scalable, commercial applications. Enabling businesses to tap into transformer-based models in a simple, cost-effective way could accelerate AI adoption across the corporate landscape. These platforms are not just about harnessing the power of AI; they are meticulously designed to offer robust security, privacy, and advanced functionalities. Tailored to cater to the unique needs of individual organizations, they aim to be indispensable tools for a myriad of work aspects. Beyond just addressing the data security concerns that were prevalent during the initial days of cloud computing, these enterprise solutions are also navigating the intricate challenges posed by generative AI. They provide a secure environment where data can be seamlessly ingested, processed, and outputted, all the while upholding the rights and ownership of the original data sources.

Based on what we've discussed in this book, it's evident that the emergence of generative AI in corporate communication offers both unparalleled opportunities and complex challenges. As AI becomes a fundamental tool in crafting messages, handling public relations, and defining brand narratives, companies must proceed with caution. The core values of corporate communication are authenticity, trust, and clarity. Although AI can improve efficiency and deliver insights, it also brings with it the risks of unintentional plagiarism, misrepresentation, and the potential dilution of a brand's distinct voice.

Furthermore, as data ownership and usage come to the forefront, companies must be transparent with their stakeholders. This includes being open about the extent of AI involvement in communications and the sources of data used for training these models. Establishing a code of ethics around AI usage in corporate communication can serve as a guiding light, ensuring that while the power of AI is leveraged, the sanctity and integrity of communication are never compromised.

8.2   The consumer's centrality in data ownership and privacy

The digital era, marked by the omnipresence of social media, personal blogs, and user-generated content, has redefined the process and value of content creation and its dissemination. Previously, content production was primarily the domain of established media houses such as the *New*

York Times. But today, the paradigm has shifted. Anyone with a smart-phone or internet connection can be a creator, chronicling their daily lives, sharing insights, or narrating stories. This transition from a few se-lect voices to millions of diverse, global narratives offers a treasure trove of data, ripe for AI ingestion.

Content created by everyday netizens is inherently "public by design." Social media posts, tweets, blogs, vlogs, and even some discussions on public forums are available to the vast expanse of the internet. Their ac-cessibility, combined with their organic, unfiltered nature, makes them a golden source for AI models, especially language models such as LLMs.

These real-world narratives, anecdotes, and expressions contribute to the richness of the training data. For an AI model to understand con-text, colloquialisms, evolving slang, cultural nuances, emotions, and more, it must be exposed to an eclectic mix of data. Everyday content brings this diversity. It presents not just the formal, structured language found in newspapers or academic journals, but also the candid, spontaneous, and diverse expressions of humanity. The sheer volume and variety of user-gen-erated content hold immense value for LLMs. Let's break down why.

- **Diversity of expression:** An AI model trained only on formal texts might falter when exposed to internet slang or cultural idioms. Us-er-generated content bridges this gap, introducing models to the ever-evolving language of the internet.
- **Real-world context:** Personal stories and shared experiences offer a glimpse into real-world scenarios. For an AI to respond effectively to a myriad of user queries, understanding these contexts is para-mount.
- **Cultural nuances:** Global platforms mean global voices. Exposure to content from different cultures and regions allows AI models to develop a more holistic understanding, minimizing biases and ensuring better cross-cultural interactions.
- **Emotion comprehension:** Photos, videos, and emotive narratives enable AI to delve into the realm of human emotions - a challeng-ing feat. By analyzing these snippets, models can better discern and respond to emotional cues, making interactions more empathetic.

However, while the potential of such content in enhancing AI capabil-ities is undeniable, it simultaneously introduces ethical considerations.

The inadvertent use of personal stories, without explicit consent, for training AI models raises concerns about data privacy, ownership, and the broader implications of commodifying human experiences.

Even giants in the tech industry, such as Google, have for years used client interactions and responses to their search rankings to refine and enhance their products. They assess how users interact with the results provided to continuously refine their search algorithms. This iterative feedback loop allows them to perfect the user experience and the relevance of results. In contrast, generative AI platforms have the capability to train on vast amounts of online content and interactions. What sets them apart is not just the scale but also the methodology; these systems can evolve not only without direct user engagement, but often also without users' explicit consent or even their cognizance of such utilization. This adds another complex layer to the ethical considerations surrounding data usage in the era of AI-driven technologies.

As these models shift their applications into professional spheres, including the legal and medical realms, the associated risks are magnified exponentially. Consider, for instance, the controversy surrounding Zoom, a globally adopted video conferencing platform.[5] In 2023, Zoom changed its terms of service to allow the company to use user data to train AI models. The primary concern revolved around the extent of data Zoom might be siphoning from unsuspecting users to nurture its AI algorithms. Such practices, while potentially enhancing user experience, raise substantive ethical dilemmas, especially when users remain oblivious to the end use of their data. This spotlight on Zoom also ushered in discussions about its alignment with the General Data Protection Regulation (GDPR) and the ePrivacy directives. The crux of GDPR mandates companies to secure explicit user consent prior to processing personal data. Meanwhile, the ePrivacy directive focuses on safeguarding the confidentiality of electronic communications. A section of the tech community postulated that Zoom's practices might be toeing the line with these regulations, championing the need for transparent user agreements and an unambiguous opt-out option. Responding to the maelstrom of concerns, Zoom has articulated its commitment to user privacy and regulatory adherence, emphasizing ongoing efforts to refine and rectify its practices in alignment with global standards.

---

[5] https://www.nbcnews.com/tech/innovation/zoom-ai-privacy-tos-terms-of-service-data-rcna98665.

Such instances emphasize the profound evolution in how businesses and consumers interact in the age of generative AI. As corporate communication expands its horizons, understanding and fostering genuine relationships with audiences is paramount. The principles of trust, transparency, and collaboration are foundational in this renewed dynamic.

In the contemporary digital space, punctuated by frequent news of data breaches and misuse, mere adherence to regulatory norms isn't enough. Businesses must provide clear insights into data practices and grant consumers an influential role in the decision-making process. This mutual respect and understanding will pave the way for enriched corporate communication and consumer trust.

- **Consumer-centric communication**: The essence of modern corporate communication lies in recognizing the consumer's role beyond a passive audience. Informed consent is pivotal. Rather than seeing regulations such as GDPR as mere compliance, they should be viewed as frameworks to foster trust. This means offering comprehensive information, ensuring users are making informed choices, not just ticking boxes.
- **Empowerment through data control**: As the narrative shifts to emphasize the power of generative AI, consumers should have nuanced control over their data. This means more than just transparency; it's about granting consumers the autonomy to modify, restrict, or revoke access. Effective corporate communication positions consumers as active partners, not just data sources.
- **Navigating AI ethics in communication**: The world of generative AI presents uncharted challenges. While AI offers unprecedented tools for personalization in corporate communication, businesses must tread cautiously. The fine line between personalization and intrusion becomes even thinner. Businesses need to ensure that AI-driven communications respect user boundaries and refrain from using sensitive data without clear consent.

In this new era, corporate communication professionals harnessing generative AI must be not only tech-savvy but also ethically attuned. The future beckons a more transparent, collaborative, and respect-driven approach toward consumers, ensuring both businesses and their audiences thrive in harmony.

8.3   Corporate blueprints for traversing data and privacy challenges

As we explored in the previous sections, the advent of generative AI has added multiple layers of complexity to the already intricate landscape of data ownership. From the ethical quandaries surrounding the use of copyrighted content to the legal implications of data usage in corporate settings, the challenges are manifold.

Against this backdrop, the integration of generative AI into corporate communication presents an array of opportunities, from enhanced customer engagement to streamlined internal processes. Data, often touted as the "new oil," presents vast avenues for innovation and growth. Yet with its potential comes a labyrinth of ethical, legal, and operational challenges, especially concerning ownership and privacy. How then should enterprises, both seasoned and nascent, navigate this intricate terrain?

At the forefront of this navigation lies the responsibility of data stewardship. While data can be a formidable asset, its mismanagement can lead to catastrophic outcomes in terms of both reputation and finances. Modern enterprises must therefore embrace gold standards in data management and privacy with a specific focus on corporate communication, ensuring not just its optimal use but also its protection. Transparency with stakeholders, from customers to partners, is pivotal in this quest. By offering clear insights into data practices, businesses can foster trust, ensuring a collaborative relationship that values and respects data privacy.

Yet the foundation of these practices lies within the organization. As AI and data analytics become mainstream tools, it's imperative that the workforce understands their nuances. Comprehensive training programs that delve into data ownership, the intricacies of privacy, and the ethical considerations of AI become indispensable. An informed employee is, after all, the first line of defense against potential missteps.

However, theory and intent only go so far. The real litmus test for businesses lies in their actions. A deep dive into real-world case studies, both of successes and of misfires, offers invaluable lessons. By analyzing these incidents, enterprises can glean insights, refining their strategies to ensure that the dance between AI, data ownership, and privacy is both graceful and ethical.

For companies navigating this complex landscape, establishing clear frameworks is essential. Corporate blueprints can serve as guiding lights, helping businesses harness the power of AI responsibly and effectively. Table 8.1 is designed as a comprehensive framework for corporations aiming to integrate AI into their communication strategies. The goal is to do so ethically and in compliance with existing laws. Each focus area has been carefully selected to address critical aspects such as strategic alignment, data governance, ethical AI use, legal compliance, and more. Objectives, action steps, and examples of value are included to provide a practical action framework.

Table 8.1 Integrating AI in communication strategy

Area focus	Objective	Why it's important	First action steps	Company value
Strategic alignment	Align AI capabilities with corporate communication goals.	Ensures that AI integration serves the broader objectives of the company, maximizing return on investment.	• Conduct a SWOT (strengths, weaknesses, opportunities, and threats) analysis • Develop a roadmap with clear milestones and key performance indicators.	By aligning AI with corporate goals, a company can automate customer service inquiries, freeing up human resources for more strategic tasks, thus improving overall efficiency.
Data governance	Establish a robust data governance framework.	Ensures data quality and availability, which are critical for the effective functioning of AI models.	• Classify data based on sensitivity and utility. • Implement data lineage and quality management systems.	Proper data governance can help a company avoid costly mistakes such as data breaches, thereby preserving brand reputation.
Ethical AI use	Ensure ethical considerations are integrated into AI usage.	Builds consumer trust and avoids potential reputational damage due to unethical AI practices.	• Establish an AI ethics committee. • Adopt or develop ethical AI frameworks and guidelines.	An ethical AI use case could be a transparent recommendation system that explains why a particular product or service is being suggested, thereby building customer trust.
Legal compliance	Adhere to data protection and privacy laws.	Avoids legal penalties and builds consumer trust by ensuring that data is handled in a lawful manner.	• Conduct regular compliance checks. • Consult with legal experts.	For example, compliance with GDPR can help a company build trust among European customers, potentially increasing market share in the European Union.

Consumer consent management	Obtain and manage consumer consent effectively.	Ensures lawful and ethical data usage, thereby building consumer trust.	• Implement transparent opt-in/opt-out mechanisms. • Conduct periodic consent reviews.	A clear and easily accessible opt-out option for data collection can make consumers feel more in control, thereby enhancing brand trust.
Data security	Ensure data integrity and security.	Protects against data breaches that can result in financial loss and reputational damage.	• Implement encryption and multifactor authentication. • Conduct regular security audits.	For instance, robust data security can protect a company's proprietary research from being leaked, preserving its competitive edge.
Transparency and accountability	Maintain transparency in AI algorithms and operations.	Builds consumer and stakeholder trust by being open about how AI is used and how decisions are made.	• Publish AI ethics and data usage policies. • Implement regular audits for accountability.	A company that publishes its AI ethics policy can demonstrate its commitment to responsible AI use, potentially attracting more ethically minded consumers.
Employee training	Equip employees with the knowledge and skills for ethical AI use.	Ensures that all staff are aware of best practices and potential risks, thereby reducing the likelihood of unethical or insecure AI usage.	• Conduct regular training sessions. • Develop a resource hub for ongoing learning.	Training employees on AI ethics can help prevent unintentional biases in AI algorithms, thereby avoiding potential public relations crises.
Third-party management	Manage third-party data and AI tool risks.	Ensures that external vendors comply with the company's data and ethical standards, thereby reducing risk.	• Vet third-party AI tools for data security and ethical use. • Establish secure data transfer protocols.	For example, vetting a third-party chatbot provider for data security can prevent potential data breaches, thereby preserving customer trust.
Future-proofing	Prepare for future changes in AI technology and regulations.	Allows the company to adapt quickly to new technological advancements or changes in legal requirements, ensuring long-term sustainability.	• Keep abreast of emerging technologies and legal changes. • Update policies and strategies accordingly.	By staying updated on AI advancements, a company can quickly integrate new features that improve customer service, such as a more advanced natural language processing algorithm for chatbots, thereby staying ahead of competitors.

As companies integrate generative AI into their communication strategies, establishing robust frameworks for data governance, ethics, and legal compliance is crucial, but it is only the first step. To truly harness the power of AI responsibly, organizations must commit to continuous improvement and proactive adaptation. Regular audits, updated training programs, and active monitoring of emerging technologies will help future-proof strategies amid rapid advancements. Beyond internal processes, proactively engaging consumers as partners through transparent communication and meaningful consent mechanisms fosters enduring trust and mutually beneficial relationships. Ultimately, responsible AI integration requires a holistic approach, spanning technology, processes, people, and corporate culture. With informed, empowered workforces, consumer-centric values, and adaptable but steadfast principles, companies can unleash transformative innovations in corporate communication, pioneering new standards for ethical AI use that responsibly elevates both business and society.

Insight
AI for Good

by *YeSeul Kim**

Artificial intelligence can be a life-changing tool for many. As a business person, you may be considering its applications to transform processes, roles, and approaches. On a personal level, you may be excited about how it might level up your productivity and creativity. But AI and its potential is much bigger than what it can do one person, one organization at a time.

While all technology at its core is neutral, how we apply that technology is crucial. And if we had to choose between using AI for good or bad, we can find concrete ways to apply this game-changing technology for good. The key is to prioritize this objective over commercial and capitalistic gains. The aim is to make the world a better place, for everyone.

What can AI do for disabled populations? What can AI do for those living in regions vulnerable to natural disasters and climate change? What can AI do for those who contract a rare disease? It turns out that AI can be immensely useful across all types of industries—in healthcare, accessibility, privacy, sustainability, and even empathy.

For example, AI technologies such as machine learning and natural language processing can aid in analyzing real-time data during emergencies, enabling quicker responses and improving disaster management strategies. Machine learning algorithms can analyze real-time data from social media platforms, news outlets, and other sources to identify areas that are most affected by a disaster. This information can be used to direct emergency responders to the areas that need the most help. Mean-

---

* Head of Innovation at Crafted.

while, natural language processing can be used to analyze emergency calls and other communications to assess the severity of a situation and prioritize responses accordingly.

CrisisLex is an organization that uses AI technologies to analyze social media data during emergencies. By monitoring platforms such as X (formerly Twitter), CrisisLex can identify real-time information about disaster events, including location, severity, and needs of affected populations. This helps emergency responders to gather critical information quickly and coordinate their response efforts effectively.

Nothing is worse than not getting the information you need during a crisis or hearing a busy tone when trying to call for help. Chatbots powered by AI can be used to provide information and support to people affected by a disaster. They can answer frequently asked questions, provide updates on relief efforts, and connect people with the resources they need. The American Red Cross for one is experimenting with an AI-powered chatbot called "Emergency" to provide support and information during disasters. The chatbot uses natural language processing to understand user queries and provides real-time updates on emergency situations, safety tips, and guidance on finding nearby shelters or resources.

While disaster response and recovery are important roles, equally important is prevention. That's why it is imperative that we use predictive analytics powered by AI to forecast the impact of natural disasters and other emergencies. For example, one company that utilizes AI for disaster prediction and response is IBM. Their system, called the IBM Disaster Prediction and Response Optimization (DPRO) platform, combines various data sources, including weather data, social media feeds, and historical disaster data, to predict the impact of natural disasters. While false positives may create unnecessary panic and eventually cause the population to distrust these alarms, AI could potentially save millions of lives by giving individuals and organizations time to prepare for the worst.

For more future-looking applications, AI is a potential game changer and accelerator for science. By analyzing vast amounts of complex data quickly, AI systems can assist researchers in discovering new insights across various fields such as medicine, astronomy, and genomics. AI could also cut the time it takes to find new drugs for treating diseases, especially those deemed too niche or unprofitable, by simulating millions, if not billions, of molecular interactions from a large genetic database. Yes, AI could finally help scientists cure cancer.

For example, researchers at Stanford University have developed an AI system that can predict which patients are at risk of developing sepsis, a potentially life-threatening condition. The system uses machine learning algorithms to analyze electronic health record (EHR) data, including vital signs, laboratory results, and other clinical data, to identify patterns and risk factors associated with sepsis. The researchers trained the AI system on a dataset of more than 130,000 patient encounters. The system was able to predict which patients would develop the condition with an accuracy of 90 percent, and it outperformed existing clinical scoring systems.

AI was also of fundamental importance during the COVID-19 outbreak. AI-powered contact tracing tools have been using machine learning algorithms to analyze data from mobile phones, social media, and other sources to identify potential exposure risks and notify individuals who may have been in contact with someone who had tested positive for COVID-19. For example, the COVIDSafe app developed by the Australian government uses Bluetooth technology to detect when two phones are within close proximity to each other. Similarly, researchers at MIT developed an AI-powered contact tracing tool called Private Kit: Safe Paths that uses GPS data to track individuals' movements and identify potential exposure risks. The tool allows users to share their data anonymously and securely, and it has been used in several countries around the world to help track the spread of COVID-19.

If we're not careful, AI has the potential to amplify the biases embedded in our datasets, culture, and society. But if designed from the outset to remove human biases in decision-making, AI systems have the potential to promote fairness and reduce discrimination, especially institutional biases.

For example, AI-powered recruitment tools can help to eliminate biases in the hiring process. These tools can analyze job descriptions, résumés, and other relevant data to identify the most qualified candidates for a position. By using AI to make hiring decisions, companies can reduce the impact of human biases based on gender, race, or age on the hiring process.

Similarly, AI can be used to eliminate biases in loan approvals. Banks and other financial institutions can use AI algorithms to evaluate loan applications and identify the most qualified candidates for a loan. By using AI to make loan decisions, financial institutions can reduce the impact of human biases based on race or ethnicity on loan approvals. This is an important topic as explicit racism against African Americans applying for mortgages to purchase a home (known as redlining) has led to extreme inequality in generational wealth. To overcome these biases, ZestFinance's AI models consider various nontraditional data sources, such as education, employment history, and even social media activity, to assess creditworthiness. By incorporating this additional information, the models can provide a more comprehensive view of an individual's financial situation and repayment potential. Moreover, ZestFinance's AI algorithms are designed to identify and mitigate potential biases that may arise from historical lending practices. The models are trained on diverse datasets to ensure fair treatment across different demographic groups. The company also actively monitors and audits its algorithms to identify and correct any unintended biases that may emerge over time. By leveraging AI, ZestFinance aims to provide fairer access to credit for individuals who may have been overlooked or unfairly judged by traditional lending practices.

Climate change. Pandemics. Polarizing political environments. Fake news. Overconsumption. It's overwhelming to think about global issues that are so complex. And yet we must all do our part not only in understanding the issues, but also in finding or at least being a part of the solutions.

AI will never be the magic bullet that solves our very human problems, but it can provide us with a valuable tool to augment human efforts to come up with and implement both simple and innovative solutions to vexing problems. So let's save the world, one algorithm at a time.

9 Transparency, Ethics, and Responsibility

9.1 The ethics of AI-driven decision-making

The fact that AI is increasingly becoming a cornerstone in business decision-making, raising a host of ethical questions surrounding fairness, impartiality, and transparency, is of growing importance in both the business and technology worlds.

When it comes to fairness, algorithms can inherit biases from the data they are trained on. For instance, a hiring algorithm might discriminate against candidates based on gender or ethnicity if historical data shows a preference for a particular group. Additionally, there is a concern about unequal access, where AI could be used to favor more profitable customers or groups, creating a disparity in access to services or opportunities.

Impartiality and accountability are also crucial. Questions arise about who is responsible when an algorithm makes an incorrect or unfair decision. Companies should also be transparent about how they use AI, what data is used to train the algorithms, and how decisions are made.

Navigating the ethical complexities of AI is a significant challenge that companies must approach with diligence and foresight. This chapter aims to provide a comprehensive guide on how to do just that, incorporating actionable guidelines for responsible and equitable technology deployment.

9.1.1 *Establishing multidisciplinary ethics committees*

The concept of a multidisciplinary ethics committee isn't new; it has roots in medical ethics, where life-and-death decisions necessitate a range of perspectives. But in the realm of AI, this committee takes on a new level of complexity and urgency. It's about creating a diverse group that can grapple with the nuanced ethical implications of the algorithms. This committee becomes the organization's moral compass, guiding it through the murky waters of AI ethics.

Imagine a team made up of data scientists, ethicists, legal experts, and representatives from the business sectors most impacted by AI. The data scientists understand the mechanics of the algorithms; they know what's technically possible. The ethicists ask the hard questions: just because we can do something, should we? They challenge the team to consider the societal and moral implications of their work. Legal experts ensure that the company's AI practices comply with existing laws and anticipate future regulations. And representatives from various business sectors bring real-world context to the table, helping the committee understand how AI will affect different aspects of the organization.

This committee doesn't just serve as a reactive body to scrutinize AI projects after they've been developed; it's proactive, involved in the decision-making process from the beginning. It reviews project proposals, scrutinizes data sources for potential biases, and recommends ethical frameworks. It might also be responsible for setting up guidelines for transparency and accountability, ensuring that if something does go wrong, there's a clear path to make it right.

But perhaps most importantly, this committee serves as a bridge between the organization and the public. In an era where trust in technology is eroding, the committee can offer assurances that ethical considerations are a priority, not an afterthought. It can engage with the community, seek public input, and even publish audit results, thereby fostering transparency and building trust.

Particularly for corporate communication, which often serves as the face and voice of an organization, the role of such a committee is indispensable. Here are five suggestions on how to construct a multidisciplinary ethics committee with a focus on corporate communication.

- **Recruit communication experts with ethical training:** The committee should include corporate communication professionals who are not only skilled in crafting messages but also trained in ethical considerations. They can guide the team on how to communicate complex ethical issues related to AI in a manner that is both transparent and easily understandable to the public.

- **Incorporate external advisors:** Sometimes, an outside perspective can provide invaluable insights. Consider bringing in external experts in ethics, law, or AI to serve as advisors to the committee. Their impartiality can add credibility to the committee's decisions and help in communicating those decisions to external stakeholders.
- **Develop a crisis communication plan:** One of the committee's first tasks should be to develop a crisis communication plan specifically for AI-related issues. This plan should outline how to communicate with stakeholders in the event of an ethical lapse or controversy, ensuring that the company's response is both swift and ethically sound.
- **Engage with stakeholders:** The committee should have a strategy for regular engagement with key stakeholders, including employees, customers, and shareholders. This could involve periodic updates on the committee's activities, public consultations, or even interactive webinars. The aim is to make ethics in AI a two-way conversation between the company and its stakeholders.
- **Transparency in reporting:** Lastly, the committee should commit to a high level of transparency in its operations. This could involve publishing minutes of meetings, disclosing the criteria used for ethical evaluations, and even releasing the results of third-party audits. Transparency not only builds trust but also sets a standard for ethical conduct that the entire organization can follow.</BL>

By integrating these suggestions, the multidisciplinary ethics committee can serve as a robust mechanism for ethical oversight, particularly in the realm of corporate communication. It can help navigate the complex ethical terrain of AI, ensuring that as companies become more technologically advanced, they also become more ethically responsible.

9.1.2 *Setting ethical guidelines*

AI presents unique challenges that traditional ethical frameworks aren't equipped to handle. We're talking about algorithms that can learn and evolve, making decisions that even their creators don't fully understand. In this context, a generic code of ethics simply won't suffice. Companies need guidelines that are tailored to the complexities and nuances of AI technology.

So, what might such a code of ethics look like? At its core, it should address the three pillars of ethical AI: fairness, transparency, and accountability. Fairness ensures that AI algorithms don't perpetuate existing biases or create new ones. Transparency mandates that companies are open about how their algorithms work and make decisions. And accountability establishes a system for redress if things go wrong.

But a code of ethics should go beyond these broad principles. It should delve into the specifics, offering concrete guidance on issues such as data privacy, algorithmic bias, and informed consent. For instance, if a company uses AI to screen job applicants, the code should stipulate that the algorithm must be trained on diverse datasets to avoid discriminatory hiring practices. Or if AI is used in healthcare, the code should require that patients are informed and consent to AI-driven diagnoses or treatment plans.

A well-crafted code of ethics for AI becomes a cornerstone of the company's communication strategy, serving as both a narrative tool and a governance framework.

1. Firstly, a code of ethics specific to AI allows a company to proactively control the narrative. By clearly articulating its stance on fairness, transparency, and accountability, the company can pre-emptively address concerns and questions that stakeholders might have. This proactive approach can be communicated through various channels—press releases, white papers, social media posts, and even in shareholder meetings—ensuring that the message reaches a broad audience.

2. Secondly, the code serves as a blueprint for crisis communication. Should an ethical issue arise, such as data misuse or algorithmic bias, the company can refer back to its code of ethics in its public response. This not only demonstrates accountability but also provides a structured framework for addressing the issue, making it easier to communicate complex ethical considerations in a clear and concise manner.

3. Thirdly, the specifics in the code of ethics—such as guidelines on data privacy and informed consent—offer opportunities for thought leadership. The company can produce content that delves into these ethical nuances, positioning itself as an industry leader in ethical AI. This could range from op-eds and blog posts to webinars

and panel discussions, providing valuable insights that elevate the brand's authority.

4. Lastly, the code of ethics should be a living document, subject to periodic review and revision. This iterative process can be communicated transparently, showcasing the company's commitment to ethical growth and adaptation. It could even be an annual event, such as an "Ethical AI Day," where updates to the code are announced and discussed publicly.</NL>

In the final analysis, a code of ethics serves as both a shield and a compass. It's a shield against the reputational damage that can result from unethical AI practices, which can be devastating in an age where consumers are increasingly choosing brands that align with their values. And it's a compass that guides companies through the ethical minefields that AI presents, ensuring that they don't lose their way as they navigate the path to innovation.

9.1.3 Empowering ethical governance in AI

Effective whistleblowing procedures are not just a safeguard against unethical practices; they are a cornerstone of a company's ethical AI governance structure. In an era where AI technologies are becoming increasingly complex and their impact more far-reaching, the role of whistleblowers in identifying and mitigating risks cannot be overstated. It's about creating an organizational culture that values ethical conduct, particularly in the deployment and management of AI systems.

To operationalize this, companies should establish clear, confidential channels for reporting concerns. These could range from an anonymous hotline managed by the AI ethics committee to a secure digital portal where employees can submit reports. The key is to ensure anonymity and protection from retaliation, thereby encouraging more employees to come forward with their concerns. The AI ethics committee should be responsible for promptly investigating these reports, leveraging their expertise to assess the validity and severity of the claims.

But having a whistleblowing procedure is not enough; it must be actively communicated to all stakeholders. Corporate communication teams should develop comprehensive communication plans that inform employees, shareholders, and the public about the existence and accessibility of these reporting channels. This could include information sessions, FAQs on the company website, and even stories or testimonials that highlight the positive impact of ethical reporting. The message should be clear: the company values ethical conduct and provides the mechanisms to uphold it.

Moreover, the whistleblowing system should be integrated into the company's crisis response plans. If a report exposes harmful or unethical AI practices, the corporate communication team should have a well-defined protocol for addressing the issue publicly. This could involve immediate corrective actions, public apologies, or even partnerships with external organizations for third-party audits. The goal is to demonstrate accountability and commitment to ethical conduct, thereby maintaining public trust.

For example, consider a hypothetical case where an employee at a tech company notices that an AI algorithm used for hiring is biased against certain ethnic groups. The employee reports this through the anonymous tip line. The AI ethics committee investigates and confirms the bias. The company then takes corrective action by retraining the algorithm and conducts an internal audit of past hiring decisions. The corporate communication team releases a public statement acknowledging the issue, outlining the steps taken to correct it, and reaffirming the company's commitment to ethical AI. They might also host a public webinar on the importance of ethical AI in hiring, featuring experts in the field.

By doing so, the company not only corrects an ethical lapse but also strengthens its brand as an ethical AI leader. It turns a potential crisis into an opportunity for positive engagement, demonstrating that it views its employees as allies in upholding ethical standards. In a world where trust is hard to come by, such whistleblowing systems, backed by transparent and proactive corporate communication, offer companies a way to earn it.

9.2 Explainability and the "Black Box" dilemma

The common notion that technology is inherently neutral and can be equally used for good or evil is a false idea. No technology is truly neutral, as design always encodes values, perspectives, and trade-offs, whether implicitly or explicitly.

Consider the analogy of static versus neutral equilibrium in physics.[1] A neutral equilibrium is fully at rest—morally inert. No technology resembles this mythical state. Instead, each new invention creates a dynamic tension between moral vectors, like a static equilibrium with competing forces. The values encoded in any technology's design tilt it one direction or another. This is especially relevant for disruptive technologies such as AI. This new technology has both positive and negative potentials; it is doubly charged. AI innovators then have a responsibility to create systems that tend toward an ethical equilibrium, even if never fully neutral. Testing immature AI on people to see what happens is an abdication of that duty. We must acknowledge the values embedded in the design. The neutrality thesis obscures the inherent trade-offs and responsibilities involved. Acknowledging technology's double charge makes those choices explicit, enabling public debate. This transparency is vital for influential technologies such as AI. By rejecting neutrality and embracing transparency, we can steer technology's double charge toward human progress. This more ethical path recognizes design as a profoundly moral act.

One of the biggest challenges in this area is the "black box" problem, where decisions made by AI systems are inscrutable to human beings. Indeed, while the outcomes from these models are visible, the intricate mechanics inside this box remain shrouded in mystery. This opacity isn't just a philosophical conundrum; it's a ticking time bomb with ethical, social, and even security implications.

Imagine a marketing algorithm that inexplicably targets a demographic with a controversial ad campaign, or a customer service chatbot that inadvertently violates privacy norms by asking for sensitive information. Just like a self-driving car making an unexplained swerve or a healthcare algorithm making mysterious choices, these corporate scenarios raise urgent questions of accountability.

When a marketing campaign goes awry or a chatbot crosses ethical lines, who is to blame? Is it the machine for executing the action, the data scientists who programmed it, or the data that informed its decision-making? The opacity inherent in these AI systems complicates the matter, making it challenging to pinpoint the root cause of the issue, much less to address it effectively.

---

[1] https://en.wikipedia.org/wiki/Mechanical_equilibrium.

The ramifications of a lack of transparency in powerful models, capable of both analyzing and generating output, is potentially catastrophic. The investment sector serves as a good example. Gary Gensler, the chair of the Securities and Exchange Commission, has highlighted emerging risks as AI spreads through finance.[2] Gensler argues that AI could precipitate the next systemic crisis. A few big tech firms will likely develop the foundational models underlying many AI applications. Overreliance on these centralized models could increase herd behavior during market swings. With interconnected systems all responding similarly, a crash becomes more likely. AI tools predicated on maximizing user engagement could also prioritize company revenue over investor interests. Gensler cited as an example meme stock manias driven by algorithms optimized for app stickiness over prudent investing.[3]

Moreover, opacity is also a security risk. If we can't see inside the black box, we can't fully understand its vulnerabilities. This is not just a theoretical concern; it's a practical one that could have real-world consequences, from data breaches to more nefarious forms of cyber-attack.

So, what's the way forward? The burgeoning field of explainable AI aims to make these systems more transparent, offering a window into the previously impenetrable black box. Independent audits of AI algorithms are also gaining traction to assess their fairness and safety.[4]

Researchers at Stanford University have developed a framework called Holistic Evaluation of Language Models (HELM) to open up these black boxes through comprehensive testing.[5] Traditionally, the evaluation of AI in corporate settings has been narrowly focused on performance metrics. Can the AI model analyze consumer behavior accurately? Can it automate customer service responses effectively? While these questions are crucial, they barely scratch the surface. HELM introduces a new lexicon for AI evaluation, one that includes fairness, robustness, and a host of other ethical considerations.

---

[2] https://www.bloomberg.com/news/articles/2023-07-17/gensler-warns-artificial-intelligence-risks-financial-stability.

[3] https://en.wikipedia.org/wiki/Meme_stock.

[4] https://medium.com/@jamesmodupe75/auditing-ai-generated-financial-statements-the-unique-challenges-auditors-face-with-ai-generated-b3c643816299.

[5] https://crfm.stanford.edu/helm/latest/.

It doesn't just look at how well your AI performs tasks; it examines how your AI behaves in diverse real-world scenarios. From detecting biases to assessing the model's vulnerability to disinformation, HELM provides a comprehensive ethical scorecard that every corporate communication strategy needs.

For example, HELM's evaluation of thirty-four major AI systems revealed a concerning divide: Corporate AI models are often more accurate but less transparent than their public counterparts. In an era where corporate responsibility and transparency are more than just buzzwords, this is a gap we can't afford. Stanford's framework offers a solution by enabling in-depth scrutiny of even the most proprietary models, ensuring they meet ethical and corporate standards.

But as AI becomes a boardroom topic, HELM also serves as a blueprint for governance and policymaking. It provides actionable insights that can guide corporate communication strategies and ethical guidelines. Imagine a future where your company's AI policy is as robust and comprehensive as your financial audit. That's the promise of solutions such as HELM; they don't just make AI more accountable, they also make the technology understandable, transforming the black box into a glass box, where the inner mechanisms are laid bare for scrutiny, adjustment, and improvement.

9.3   The Urgency of corporate responsibility in the AI era

Corporate responsibility has traditionally served as a foundational pillar for organizations that prioritize long-term viability and ethical business practices. This notion is not limited to legal compliance or philanthropic endeavors; rather, it extends to how a corporation engages with its diverse stakeholders—be it employees, consumers, suppliers, or even the environment. In this respect, corporate responsibility acts as a key determinant for both public perception and the organization's long-term sustainability prospects.

The accelerating developments in AI technologies have brought about a paradigm shift, compelling organizations to adopt an "augmented" form of corporate responsibility. This enhanced concept transcends traditional frameworks, necessitating a more nuanced and comprehensive approach to ethical considerations.

Equally crucial is responsible communication about AI capabilities and limitations. It is imperative that organizations abstain from making misleading or inflated claims regarding their AI technologies. Such behavior can significantly tarnish their corporate image and erode trust, not just within the consumer base but among stakeholders at large. Furthermore, misrepresentations can have wider societal ramifications, including the potential to shape public opinion or inform regulatory decisions based on faulty premises.

The issues outlined in this chapter make it abundantly clear that the responsible use of AI requires an antifragile approach. As coined by author Nassim Taleb, antifragility is the ability not only to withstand shocks and stressors, but also to actually grow stronger from them. It's a quality that is sorely needed as organizations navigate the turbulent waters of emergent technologies such as AI.

Simply relying on rigid rules or principles is not enough when dealing with such a dynamic field. Principles provide a moral foundation, but their application requires nuance, vigilant monitoring, and continual evolution. An antifragile approach recognizes the need for perpetual learning and ethical growth in the face of technological disruption.

To operationalize these elevated commitments, companies should proactively revise their existing corporate codes of conduct or ethical guidelines to specifically address responsible AI use. For example, Google's AI Principles offer a framework that could be adapted to various organizational contexts.[6] These guidelines should provide actionable advice on key issues.

In short, corporate responsibility must evolve to address all the challenges posed by AI. Organizations need to adopt a new approach, upholding ethical principles despite the challenges in doing so.

To accomplish this aim, communication teams should take actions such as continuously monitoring stakeholder sentiment to identify emerging concerns about AI use. Keeping a pulse on perceptions will allow for early detection of issues. Teams should also engage in two-way dialogue with stakeholders to understand their perspectives and apprehensions. Open communication builds trust and uncovers potential problems.

Conducting tests of communication plans helps refine messaging and crisis responses by providing trial runs to prepare teams to share information effectively. Sharing results of ethical audits demonstrates a com-

---

[6] https://ai.google/responsibility/principles/.

Table 9.1 Embedding AI in Corporate Responsibility framework

Principle	Description	Actionable steps
Be socially beneficial	Align your corporate communication strategies with social benefits, prioritizing transparency and social responsibility.	1. Develop content that educates your audience on social issues. 2. Partner with socially responsible organizations.
Avoid unfair bias	Ensure that your corporate communications are inclusive and do not perpetuate stereotypes or biases. This is particularly important in advertising and public relations.	1. Use AI algorithms to analyze content for biases. 2. Diversify content creators and decision-makers.
Be built and tested for safety	Adhere to the highest standards of data security and user privacy when using AI-driven communication tools or platforms.	1. Regularly update security protocols. 2. Conduct third-party audits of AI tools.
Be accountable to people	Implement mechanisms for feedback and redress in your communication channels. Transparency reports could be a good practice.	1. Create an easily accessible channel for feedback. 2. Publish annual transparency reports.
Incorporate privacy design principles	Make data privacy a cornerstone in your strategy, especially when using AI for personalized marketing or customer engagement.	1. Clearly state data usage policies. 2. Use AI for data anonymization.
Uphold high standards of scientific excellence	Utilize data-driven methods and rigorous testing to continually improve the effectiveness of your corporate communications.	1. Partner with academic institutions for research. 2. Publish white papers and case studies.
Be made available for uses that accord with these principles	Ensure that your communication technologies are not used for misleading or harmful purposes, such as spreading misinformation.	1. Develop a code of ethics for your services. 2. Monitor the use of your platforms and tools.
Technologies to avoid	Have a clear stance on what types of communication technologies or strategies are off-limits due to ethical considerations.	1. Create an internal review board for ethical considerations. 2. Publicly disclose technologies or practices you avoid.

mitment to responsible AI by providing transparency regarding reviews, signaling that priorities are in the right place.

Highlighting improvements in AI governance builds public trust by updating the public on progress, showing dedication to ethical AI. Collaborating with outside experts integrates new viewpoints and competencies into the development of more thoughtful AI systems by seeking diverse opinions.

Providing regular media briefings manages news coverage by being proactive in shaping accurate narratives.

In summary, corporate responsibility in the AI era necessitates communication that is transparent, knowledgeable, and stakeholder-attentive. Organizations integrating these tenets will strengthen their reputation as ethical, responsible leaders.

Insight
A Responsible Proposal for a Paradigm Shift, from AI-Driven to Human-Driven

by *Emilia Garito*[*]

When we talk about AI in any business, social, public, or private context, we are essentially discussing digital anthropology. In doing so, we wonder how and when the former will be able to impact the latter, surpassing human intelligence. We thus talk about machine discretion, consciousness, and will—about the qualitative and quantitative meanings that AI can assign to data. We are increasingly captivated by the capability of this human–machine interaction, hoping to understand how it will transform our daily lives, the world of work, and the social and political scenarios of a future that has, in fact, already arrived.

In this discourse, which separates humanists from the most passionate technologists, scientific arguments intertwine with ethical and regulatory issues in a limbo of uncertainties. This period of uncertainties between yesterday and today, heading into tomorrow, is our playing field. This temporal space encapsulates the risk of errors in implementing algorithmic choices in our lives. Therefore, it's essential to reflect on the relationships between the costs and the opportunities of using AI, starting from the most significant scientific elements, to understand what to accept or reject regarding the continuous offerings of AI applications.

A recurring question we ask ourselves is whether machines can indeed self-learn, and if so, whether they can eventually replace humans in most or all of our activities, significantly improving performance. In addressing this question, a scientific and political debate unfolds. While some

[*] CEO Quantum Leap Srl, Chairman Deep Ocean Capital SGR S.P.A., European Innovation Council Jury Member.

scientists argue that AI will enhance human capabilities and allow us to live better lives by making fewer mistakes (predictive and diagnostic capabilities in medicine, increased accuracy in image analysis, semantic interpretation of texts, and accurate translation, for instance), others argue that AI harbors the terrifying danger of accelerating human extinction by replacing us in all our primary, albeit currently non-biological, functions.

In this debate, a natural question arises: If machines reach and surpass human logical abilities, are we ready to give up the often unknown complexity of our rational and emotional minds and their power? Do we genuinely want to regard intuition merely as a technological tool for observing phenomena, replicable by machines, as supported by proponents of the cynical theory of the selfish algorithm (as defined by Massimo Chiriatti in his intriguing #Humanless. The Selfish Algorithm - HOEPLI)? And if the answer is yes, have we considered the repercussions on our lives?

One solution to this question once again relates to the combination of scientific approaches and ethical axioms. The scientific approach calls for transparency in both data and the algorithm itself. In fact, the scientific answer is to train the intelligent algorithm to become responsible, preferably using knowledge graphs instead of a black box approach. Through knowledge graphs, it's possible to trace the data processing and compilation and to understand the logic of transforming input data into output data, whereas with a black box, this level of understanding is entirely obstructed. Thus, when we talk about transparency, we inevitably refer to technological development and the design of neural networks, aiming for responsible design.

However, algorithm transparency is a necessary but not sufficient condition to resolve our dilemma. Indeed, with the development of transparent networks and algorithms, we can understand their reliability level, but to make truly informed and useful choices about using AI, we need to address the meaning of ethics in its sociopolitical application context.

We know that ethics can be defined as the discipline concerning what is right or wrong and the moral obligations and duties of entities, in this case algorithmic entities. For this reason, we might be inclined to think that algorithms should be endowed with ethics, and thus the ability to discern right from wrong for humans autonomously, thanks to their self-learning capability. However, in my opinion, this is where the evolution of the machine world and their dream of resembling humans shatters. An algorithm will never be able to generate its ethical rules unless humans establish what these should be and when they should be applied.

The algorithm could indeed have infinite degrees of freedom, but not having them, ensuring transparent and ethical behavior, will depend on when humans can define its limits. In fact, regardless of the inherent developmental capabilities of AI, to ensure its ethical use, humans will always need to identify the limits of its applicability, addressing the issues. So, when we talk about ethical algorithms, we think about the responsibility acquired by the algorithm to act for the collective benefit, but in reality, this responsibility is once again a prerogative of the humans who design and translate it into action. Responsible AI is the practice of humans designing, developing, and deploying AI with good intentions to enhance its positive impacts on people, society, and companies.

On this journey, if transparency can be left to scientific prerogative and ethics to the regulatory instrument, hopefully global, responsibility is exclusively of the individual. Hence, there is a need and an opportunity to create a new professional figure, the AI Shaper, that is, the forger/designer of responsible algorithm use, against the drifts that they might take. The AI Shaper is knowledgeable about the potential of and the limits to set on AI: with responsibility and competence, they modulate the possible impacts in a way that always guarantees control over data processing, respecting the principles of transparency and neutrality, and facilitating the experimental process of collection and observation, protecting them from computational biases common in many pseudo-intelligent algorithms today.

The AI Shapers could become our guarantor of a conscious and sustainable AI-based work model. Operating within companies, they are responsible for ensuring that AI is developed transparently, ethically, and responsibly, thus also contributing to the global scientific and political conversation, but in a pragmatic and operational manner.

10 Evolutionary Trends, Risks, and Opportunities

10.1 Intelligence as a service

As we draw the curtain on this intellectual journey, it's imperative to revisit our point of departure—the inception of photography in 1826 by Joseph Nicéphore Niépce. That inaugural, albeit flawed, image was not merely a snapshot; it served as a catalyst for transformative change, democratizing art and liberating human expression. Now, standing at this pivotal juncture in time, we are on the cusp of another monumental paradigm shift—one that transcends existing frameworks to redefine the very essence of human existence. This is a revolution with the capacity to impact every facet of our lives, from our thought processes to our interactions with technology.

We are witnessing a transformation so profound that it will fundamentally alter how we interact, create, and even think. Within the scope of corporate communication, envision a future where virtual boardrooms become vastly more interactive through augmented reality. Imagine AI-driven analytics that can evaluate public sentiment in real time, allowing corporations to adjust their messaging instantly. Think about the capability of machine learning to analyze massive datasets, spot emerging trends, and enable companies to take proactive measures instead of merely reacting. This goes beyond simply improving efficiency; it elevates the quality of dialogue between corporations and their stakeholders.

As we wrap up this exploration, let's not perceive ourselves as mere spectators in this era of change. We are the architects and pioneers of this brave new world. Though the challenges ahead may appear daunting, the landscape is ripe with unparalleled opportunities. Today we are authoring the guidelines for an entirely new game.

10.1.1 *Exponential growth: All for AI, AI for All*

Generative AI might just be the most important human invention ever—it's as simple as that—more crucial than the wheel, the printing press, or even the internet. Why? Firstly, it marks a paradigm shift in our relationship with technology. For the first time, we've engineered a tool that is not just an extension of human capability but a meta-tool that can wield other tools. This is not merely an incremental advancement; it's a foundational leap that redefines the very architecture of innovation. As AI evolves, it's transforming into an active agent capable of executing tasks. These advanced AI systems will of course interface with different APIs (application programming interfaces) but will also interact with third-party databases to fetch information, make reservations, and even complete purchases. They'll go beyond the need for specialized interfaces, learning to navigate websites just as a human would—filling out forms, clicking buttons, and interpreting visual data on the screen.

Moreover, these AI agents will be capable of communicating with each other, negotiating terms, discussing prices, and collaborating on creative projects—all in natural language. This ensures that their interactions are transparent and auditable, a crucial factor for explainability and accountability in AI systems. While they could communicate in machine-specific languages or embeddings, we'd prefer them to use plain English for the sake of transparency.

But their capabilities won't stop at machine-to-machine interactions. They'll also be able to engage with humans, gathering additional information and clarifications to execute tasks effectively. This represents a concentration of capabilities, a fusion of reasoning and action, that will be applied across diverse settings.

From a productivity standpoint, this is revolutionary. It's clear that it's not just about automating tasks; it's about enhancing decision-making and action-taking at an unprecedented scale. For those committed to leveraging these tools for the greater good, the possibilities are endless.

That's why more and more experts and professionals refer to this moment we are living in as a new Renaissance. Just as the 14th-century Renaissance shifted the focus from God to man, leading to unprecedented advancements in art, science, and knowledge, we're on the brink of another paradigm change. In a decade or so, if you want the most comprehensive advice or information on any subject, you'll consult a machine, not a human. This will bring an evolution in how we live, work, and think.

Consider that at the time of writing this book, AI has generated more images in less than 18 eighteen months than photographers have captured in the last 150 years.[1] Pioneering services such as Midjourney, DALL-E, Stable Diffusion, and Adobe Firefly have collectively produced over 15 billion images in this short time span. To offer some context, think about Instagram—a platform that has democratized photography to a degree. It has seen an estimated 50 billion image uploads in total, but it took thirteen years to reach that milestone. But the transformative impact of AI extends beyond just the volume of image creation; it is fundamentally reshaping our very understanding of aesthetics. In the corporate world, we've always been obsessed with efficiency, right? But what we're talking about here goes beyond that. It's not just about doing things faster; it's about doing things better and doing different things. Imagine, just for a moment, a world where your company doesn't just send messages—it sends the right messages. Thanks to AI-driven analytics, we can now understand public sentiment as it unfolds, in real time. This isn't a small step; this is a giant leap in how we communicate. Think about it: You're not just pushing out ads or press releases; you're engaging in a dialogue, a meaningful, two-way conversation with your stakeholders, your customers, your audience. And you're doing it with a level of personalization that was unthinkable just a few years ago. You can tailor your visuals, your messaging, your entire campaign to resonate with the individual preferences and behaviors of your target audience. We're not just improving the mechanics of corporate communication; we're elevating its very soul. We're making it more human, more authentic, more impactful.

10.1.2 *Accessibility and the commoditization of intelligence*

One of the foundational principles of technology is that as tools become more useful, they also become more affordable and user-friendly, thereby reaching a broader audience. Moore's Law, which posits that the number of transistors on a microchip will double approximately every eighteen months, thereby reducing the cost per transistor, has been a reliable predictor of this technological advancement since the 1960s. This law has

---

[1] https://journal.everypixel.com/ai-image-statistics.

facilitated a wide range of technological breakthroughs, from personal computing to the internet.

However, the advancements we're witnessing in the field of AI are on an entirely different scale. The speed at which AI is evolving outstrips even the impressive trajectory set by Moore's Law.

What makes this AI revolution even more groundbreaking is its accessibility. The increasing accessibility and affordability of advanced AI tools represents a pivotal shift, as powerful capabilities once exclusively available to large tech firms are now within reach for small teams and startups. Just as the PC revolution enabled the development of new software companies in the 1980s, the democratization of AI unlocks new entrepreneurial potential.

With cloud computing infrastructure and open-source frameworks, developing impactful AI applications no longer requires an army of PhDs or massive computing resources. A small team can now leverage state-of-the-art AI to quickly build and iterate on products, opening up possibilities that were previously out of reach. As AI becomes more commoditized, its integration will follow a similar trajectory to that of computers and the internet. Consider how website builders, e-commerce platforms, and SaaS (software as a service) tools have allowed small businesses to harness the power of the internet. Similarly, no-code and low-code AI tools will empower nontechnical users to integrate intelligent features into their products and processes.

This proliferation of AI capabilities will unleash a wave of innovation, with clever entrepreneurs finding novel applications across every industry. Healthcare, education, transportation, finance, media—AI can transform decision-making and unlock new sources of value. The businesses that effectively leverage AI will gain competitive advantages, allowing them to rapidly scale and capture market share from incumbents.

Venture investment in AI startups has already surged over the past decade, from $415 million in 2011 to over $40 billion in 2021.[2] This trend will accelerate as AI becomes more accessible and central to building innovative companies. The businesses born out of this AI revolution have the potential to become massive enterprises, generating trillions in economic value. Just as Microsoft and Apple created unprecedented wealth

---

[2]   https://www.forbes.com/sites/cindygordon/2023/08/31/ai-start-up-investments-bucking-venture-capital-decline-trends.

from the PC revolution, and Google and Amazon from the internet boom, we will likely see new behemoths emerge from this democratization of AI. The companies that can best empower small teams to harness the promise of AI will be the enterprise titans of the future.

In summary, the accessibility of powerful AI represents a uniquely enabling moment in technological history. By lowering barriers and supercharging entrepreneurial potential, the democratization of AI can unleash an explosion of emerging companies and an accompanying wave of wealth creation. The economic and social implications will be on par with the internet revolution, if not greater.

10.1.3 *Short-term/long-term effect*

In the short term, the efficiency trajectory provided by generative AI will likely benefit large corporations. Over the next five to ten years, these companies will have the resources to develop the most advanced AI models, attracting a majority of users and thereby gaining a competitive edge. This will create a compounding effect, allowing them to dominate the market much like Google has done in the search engine space. Google's success isn't solely due to its advanced technology; it's also a result of market lock-in. They've established a brand that users trust and a platform that advertisers prefer, creating a triad of lock-in involving technology, users, and advertisers. This lock-in is largely a byproduct of being a first mover in the market.

However, in the long term, the landscape may change. The ongoing advancements in AI efficiency suggest that market dominance won't be permanent. As AI becomes more accessible and affordable, the lock-in effect could diminish, opening the door for new players and perhaps democratizing access to advanced AI capabilities. Therefore, while large corporations may control the AI market in the immediate future, the long-term outlook suggests a more open and competitive environment.

In such a world, the very fabric of society could be rewoven. Traditional barriers to education, healthcare, and economic opportunity could be dismantled. The way we interact with technology, with each other, and with the world at large could undergo a shift. Knowledge is power, but the ability to act on that knowledge is the ultimate source of power. Future AIs will not only distill knowledge but also take actions. We could then see a new form of collective intelligence emerge, one that combines the best of human intuition with machine precision. But it won't come without challenges.

As AI evolves into a general-purpose technology, we are entering a critical transitional phase that will necessitate human adaptation, training, and the identification of new opportunities. While the future of employment remains uncertain, the inherent adaptability and versatility of AI suggest that we will be able to accomplish more with fewer resources. This represents a concentration of power and a significant leap in productivity, but it also introduces the risk of misuse.

Much like social media, which has served as both a catalyst for positive social change and a platform for misinformation and divisiveness, AI has the potential to reflect the best and worst aspects of humanity. The difference with AI, however, is its capability to enable actions, not just words. This amplifies the stakes considerably.

For example, AI could be used to automate the spread of misinformation at a scale and speed that humans could never achieve manually. This could destabilize political systems, sow social discord, and amplify existing societal divisions. Similarly, the use of AI in deepfake technology could create convincing false narratives that could be used for anything from discrediting public figures to fraudulent activities.

Moreover, the "compression of power" that AI offers could be a double-edged sword. On the one hand, it could democratize access to capabilities previously reserved for large organizations or specialized experts, leveling the playing field. On the other hand, it could also enable malicious actors to wield outsized influence, effectively weaponizing the technology. Therefore, as we integrate AI more deeply into our societal frameworks, it becomes imperative to establish guidelines and regulatory measures while considering strategies to mitigate these risks.

10.2 Mitigating AI risks

In Plato's "Phaedrus" the myth of Theuth explores the intricate relationship between knowledge and wisdom through a dialogue between the Egyptian god Theuth and King Thamus.[3] Theuth presents writing as a "pharmakon," a remedy for memory and wisdom. However, Thamus

---

[3] https://www.cambridge.org/core/books/abs/myth-and-philosophy-in-platos-phaedrus/theuth-thamus-and-the-critique-of-writing/C644C2E0821AF38066420F53322D2DDD.

counters this notion, arguing that writing could weaken memory and provide only an illusion of knowledge rather than genuine wisdom. This ancient myth raises fundamental questions about the use of intellectual tools, a debate that feels incredibly relevant in today's era of AI.

Many people fear that AI will ultimately erode our cognitive abilities, and some even speculate that it could lead to human extinction. However, it's worth considering that AI, like writing, may simply serve as an extension of our intelligence, a means to overcome our limitations.

Just as writing expanded the scope of human memory and communication, AI has the potential to augment our cognitive functions in unprecedented ways. It can sift through vast amounts of data to identify patterns and insights that would take us a human lifetime to uncover. It can automate routine tasks, freeing us to focus on creative and complex problem-solving endeavors. But, like any tool, its impact depends on how we use it. As we integrate AI into our lives, we must remain vigilant, ensuring that it augments rather than diminishes our human faculties. In essence, the challenge is not just to build intelligent machines but to wisely integrate them into the fabric of human life.

But how do we address the cost and management implications of the vast amounts of data used to train these systems, while also upholding ethical standards such as data privacy and algorithmic fairness? In June 2020, the release of GPT-3, with its 175 billion parameters, marked a significant milestone in the field of AI.[4] The number of parameters in a model is a rough indicator of how resource-intensive it is to run queries against it. Fast-forward to today, and we can achieve the same level of performance in tasks such as question-answering, knowledge synthesis, and reading comprehension with models that have just 2 billion parameters. This is a remarkable achievement, as it significantly reduces the cost of deploying these models. Over the next ten to twenty years, we can expect these models to become even smaller and more efficient, without sacrificing performance. This will make advanced AI models more accessible, again, to a broader audience.

Contrary to initial fears, larger models such as GPT-3 have proven to be more controllable and less prone to generating misinformation or biased content. This dispels many of the sci-fi-inspired concerns about

----

[4] https://www.techtarget.com/searchenterpriseai/definition/GPT-3.

unintended intelligence explosions or AIs going rogue. Instead, the real concern lies in the potential misuse of these increasingly powerful and accessible tools by bad actors.

For instance, these AI models are trained on vast amounts of publicly available data, which can include sensitive information such as the manufacturing process for biological or chemical weapons. The models' ability to assist in complex tasks could inadvertently simplify the process of creating dangerous weapons. Therefore, while the advancements in AI bring incredible benefits, they also introduce new risks that we must carefully manage.

Nevertheless, the collaborative effort among leading AI research labs including Anthropic, OpenAI, DeepMind, and Inflection is helping in the process of addressing the ethical and security concerns associated with advanced AI models. By sharing best practices on how to suppress harmful or misleading content generated by these models, we are taking proactive steps to mitigate risks. This kind of cross-organizational coordination is essential for tackling the challenges that come with the democratization of AI technology.

It's worth noting that these challenges are not insurmountable. In fact, they are relatively straightforward to address, especially when the broader community of open-source providers and producers participate in these efforts. Drawing a parallel to the way the tech industry handled the issue of email spam in the 1990s and 2000s, we can expect to make incremental progress in resolving these problems. The key is to adopt a collective approach, where multiple stakeholders contribute to the development of robust solutions.

By doing so, we can significantly mitigate the downsides of AI, allowing society to reap the full benefits of this transformative technology. However, it's crucial that these efforts are sustained and adaptive, as the landscape of AI and its potential risks are continually evolving. Therefore, ongoing vigilance, research, and collaboration will be essential in ensuring that AI serves as a force for good, rather than a tool for harm.

10.3   AI as Your Work Copilot

We are entering a transformative era where AI is not just a tool but a companion, a "copilot" that assists us in navigating our daily lives. Microsoft's recent announcement of Copilot, an everyday AI assistant embedded in its operating system, is a testament to this shift.[5] Copilot aims to be a seamless experience that integrates with Windows 11, Microsoft 365, and web browsers such as Edge and Bing. It will provide contextual assistance based on your work data, web intelligence, and real-time activities, all while prioritizing your privacy and security.

But the real challenges for these tools lie ahead. On the one hand, they must demonstrate the ability to cover a broad range of competencies. On the other hand, and perhaps more crucially, they must establish a trustworthy relationship with us, the users. Imagine a digital entity, tailored to your needs, that serves as your chief of staff, life coach, and personal curator all rolled into one. This isn't about a glorified version of Siri or Alexa; we're talking about an AI that knows you intimately, one that has a fiduciary relationship with you, akin to your lawyer or accountant.

The key to this revolutionary idea lies in the business model, which represents a significant shift in the tech industry's approach to user engagement and monetization. Traditionally, tech companies have thrived on a model of attention and distraction. In this paradigm, the end user is not the customer but the product. Your data is commodified and sold to the highest bidder, your attention is monetized through targeted ads, and your digital experience is shaped not by your needs but by the interests of advertisers and third parties. This model has been criticized for eroding user privacy, perpetuating information silos, and contributing to the spread of misinformation.

The new wave of personal AIs aims to flip this model on its head by introducing a fiduciary relationship between the user and the technology. Instead of being funded by ads or third-party interests, these AIs would be funded directly by you, the user, through a subscription-based approach. This fundamentally changes the dynamic of the user–tech relationship. No longer is the AI incentivized to keep you scrolling or clicking to generate ad revenue; instead, its primary function becomes to assist, enhance, and simplify your life.

This subscription-based approach ensures that your AI is aligned with your interests, not someone else's agenda. It creates a sense of ownership and agency, empowering you to customize your AI to serve your specific

---

[5] https://blogs.microsoft.com/blog/2023/09/21/announcing-microsoft-copilot-your-everyday-ai-companion/.

needs. Moreover, it opens the door for a more ethical and transparent handling of data, as the AI has no reason to collect more information than is necessary to provide its services.

In essence, this new business model doesn't just offer a more personalized experience; it offers a more ethical one. It shifts the focus from exploiting user data for profit to using technology as a tool for human betterment, setting the stage for a future where technology serves people, not the other way around.

In the realm of corporate communication, the impact of this evolution could be profound. Imagine a C-suite executive's AI copilot trained to understand the nuances of the company's business model, industry regulations, and stakeholder relationships. This AI could assist in crafting more effective communication strategies, analyzing market trends, and even predicting consumer behavior. It could serve as a mediator in negotiations, offering real-time insights and suggestions. Moreover, the fiduciary model ensures that the AI's recommendations are unbiased and aligned with the company's goals, not influenced by third-party advertisers or external agendas. This could lead to more authentic, transparent, and effective corporate communication.

The power of brand has always been a cornerstone in the digital economy. Now, with AI copilots, the brand narrative can be more authentic and consistent than ever. These AI systems can analyze consumer sentiment in real time and adjust corporate messaging accordingly. This ensures that the brand remains agile and responsive to market dynamics, thereby solidifying its position in the marketplace.

Data monetization has been a contentious issue, often criticized for its ethical implications. The fiduciary model offers a new way forward. Instead of commodifying stakeholder data, the focus shifts to using data responsibly to provide value-added services. This ethical handling of data can lead to trust and long-term relationships, which are invaluable assets in the corporate world. The AI copilot, funded by the company and serving its interests, would collect only the data necessary to fulfill its functions, such as trend analysis or stakeholder engagement.

Understanding market dynamics has always been crucial for corporate success. AI copilots can be game changers in this regard as well. These advanced systems can analyze vast amounts of data to identify emerging trends and consumer needs and even predict future behaviors. This offers corporations a significant competitive advantage. For instance, an AI copilot could analyze social media chatter, news, and other data sources to predict a potential crisis or opportunity, allowing the company to take proactive measures.

In summary, the advent of AI copilots doesn't just signify a technological advancement; it represents a strategic asset that could redefine corporate communication. It offers a more ethical approach to data monetization and provides a nuanced understanding of market dynamics. This new business model shifts the focus from exploiting user data for profit to using technology as a tool for human betterment. It sets the stage for a future where technology serves people, not the other way around.

Insight
AI for the Brands of the Future:
Trends and Possible Evolutions

by *Massimo Bullo*[*]

If we ask ChatGPT today what areas will be revolutionized by AI, the answer it returns clearly describes a predicted impact in a much broader area than just the workplace, even citing in the response the economy and the governments of countries with the optimization of public services, data analysis for crime prevention, and improvements in administrative efficiency. In this way, we should consider AI not just a technological revolution, but also a potentially a new industrial revolution capable of bringing about radical changes in companies—in roles, processes, and ways of developing their own business and brand.

In the corporate context, numerous companies are already using AI in the development of complex projects. In particular, a significant trend is emerging to review the usage and enhancement models of the customer base of companies and to define the customer experience for the entire "time" in which the interaction between company and customer takes place. In fact, thanks to AI, the starting point of the purchasing and relationship process potentially becomes the "pre-present," or rather the ability to accurately define the consumer journey long before the classic initial temporal phase of the purchase funnel, the so-called awareness phase (knowledge of the offer).

Today, thanks to AI, it is possible to start with greater precision from an earlier, anticipatory phase with respect to the temporal scheme of purchasing behavior, a phase that we can define as "intent" and "predictive" marketing, whether this is to define purchasing propensities or,

---

[*] Brand Director, Vodafone.

in the case of managing one's own customer base, to predict possible customer churn rates. This project area, comprising marketing and sales plans, communication, and management of a company's customer base, is defined within the so-called innovative "propensity modeling" projects that base their effectiveness precisely on the ability of companies to integrate customer base management, big data management, and AI projects, making the best use of their first-party data. These models are based primarily on a careful study using AI models of customer behavior in their interactions with the company's various touchpoints, from the website, to the physical and online store, to customer service. Marketing and sales divisions are increasingly able to "target" their communications more precisely, starting from an analysis of the purchasing propensities of current and future customers, in some cases going so far as to develop and define, thanks to generative AI, multiple and specific messages for each customer type based on their unique and distinctive criteria of relevance, geolocation, customer life cycle, target profile, and mode of interaction with the various corporate touchpoints.

Through AI, the company can in fact push the relationship with each individual customer to an extreme level of personalization and interaction beyond current boundaries, adapting the brand to the mode of interaction the specific customer desires and is looking for in their current life cycle phase with the company. This could lead to the adoption of new logics of development and "co-creation" of products and services with individual customers, who will become a direct part of the production chain, customizing and building their ideal product or service to measure, as already well theorized by Chris Anderson in 2012 in his book *Makers: The New Industrial Revolution*[1] and which today, with AI, takes on exponential proportions. New production, commercial, and performance indicators are born, combining classic sell-out indicators and metrics with digital ones such as traffic, geolocation, and marketing, such as consumer insights and behaviors in the consumer journey.

The increasingly exclusive and in some ways more inclusive relationship between the individual customer and the company through AI raises significant questions about the future of brands themselves in their current classical conception, still largely based on models of competitive

---

[1] Chris Anderson, Crown Currency (2014), *Makers: The New Industrial Revolution*, NO-VALUE edition.

positioning. For example, one of the founding fathers of such a model, Philip Kotler, in his book *Principles of Marketing*[2], emphasizes that to facilitate the purchasing process, companies should "position" products, services, and brands in the minds of consumers by category of belonging, based on a "set of perceptions, impressions and sensations relating to the product compared to competitors' offerings." However, in these models the competitive brand positioning is designed at the drawing board by the company; this certainly involves studying potential customers, but they are clustered into target segments, somehow "simplifying" their many specificities and uniqueness, and the brand positions are defined identically for all people belonging to the target audiences of the offer, only in some cases leaving it to brand line extension projects to partly adapt the brand to the different characteristics and needs of specific sub-target segments.

With AI, a completely new and partly unexplored field is now opening up for brands that recognizes the complexity of the individual. Thus, target clusters disintegrate into individual customers, which heralds the advent of a new relational complexity in which the brand can build a specific, intimate, and exclusive relationship with each individual customer, recognizing and enhancing their individuality, specific territories of relevance, history, communication channels, and the most appropriate tone of voice for interacting with them. Brand positioning in this sense would become tailored to the individual customer, as if the brand could take on multiple, specific positions, moving away from the current idea of a single brand positioning proposed equally across all markets and for all customers clustered in the target audiences of the offer.

In his 2005 book *Brand Hijack: Marketing without Marketing*[3], Alex Wipperfürth identifies the possible phenomenon of an increasingly possible "[b]rand anarchy: the phenomenon of loss of power and control by the company over its own brand generated by consumer-users who voluntarily or unknowingly manage, through their actions and through the viral and social potential of interactive media, to transform and communicate a different personality, values and market positioning of the

---

[2] Phil T. Kotler, Gary Armstrong, Lloyd C. Harris, Hongwei He (2019), *Principles of Marketing*, Pearson Education; 8th edition.

[3] Alex Wipperfurth (2005), *Brand Hijack: Marketing Without Marketing*, Portfolio.

brand." While Wipperfürth defined the brand hijacking phenomenon, today, thanks to AI, this phenomenon can be perceived not only as a potential problem for the company, but also as a new frontier of opportunity in which the brand can innovate, can speak a language and preside over areas of specific relevance for each customer, proposing a potentially epochal transition between company brand and "individual brand."

What is envisioned is a possible future where there will certainly remain some big brands, based on global positioning and inspiring millions of customers—iconic brands, global platforms offering a specific category of services and products—that will likely exponentially enhance the personalization of their offerings and partly their communications. Meanwhile, the rest of the emerging and rebranding companies will be able to take entirely new paths, right from the start, with multiple, "democratic," and co-created positioning for and with each specific customer among the potential millions, through various AI-based relationship and interaction tools.

The transformation we are experiencing is pushing us to carefully analyze and review the existing, well-established approaches and models of marketing and sales. Central to this crucial transition will be how companies interpret and integrate within their marketing and sales divisions consistent skills and projects in digital, big data, and marketing automation with strong integration of the emerging potential of AI. A management profile trained and able to develop complex marketing and sales projects with cross-cutting skills between digital transformation and marketing and sales management will soon develop and become essential, reducing current distances in terms of technicalities and verticalities, but integrating them into a single large area that we could now define as marketing and sales transformation in which AI will be the colleague at the desk next door.

11 The AI Behind This Book

11.1 The Opportunity of a lifetime

In a career spanning more than a quarter-century, I've worn many hats—entrepreneur, manager, investor. I've held key roles in global communication groups and founded my own successful social agency. And I've authored four books, each exploring aspects of the digital revolution reshaping our world.

Yet nothing prepared me for what happened here, writing this book. This was the first time I had collaborated with an AI. And let me tell you, it was a game changer. During the writing process AI soon became more than a tool; it was a co-worker, a tireless sparring partner to riff ideas with.

In a way, it felt like learning how to write all over again. With my previous books, writing was largely a solo endeavor—just me and my laptop screen in a personal yet isolated flow of thought. Any "collaboration" was limited to surface-level editing. This time, it was entirely different. I had a brainstorming teammate available 24/7 for rich, meaningful dialogue beyond just proofreading. The old writer–editor dynamic was replaced by a collaborative dance, with the AI and me taking turns leading and following, questioning norms, exploring new frontiers. We weren't merely editing; we were co-creating.

This once-in-a-lifetime opportunity has been revelatory. The methodology and act of creating with an AI partner marks a radical departure from the norm. It's not just about the final product; it's about the evolved process. This experience has been unique, teaching me how to write in a way I never imagined possible before.

But more than that, it feels like the start of an entirely new way of working, thinking, and perhaps living. A door has been opened to creative possibilities we are only beginning to grasp. What has happened in the process feels to me like just a small preview of things to come, as AI enables us to achieve things we never thought possible. This glimpse has whetted my appetite, and I am excited to see where this journey leads next, both for myself and for society as a whole.

Of course, there are delicate issues, for example, around intellectual property that will need to be worked through in the coming months and years. Though we may be entering a brief transitional phase, I believe we'll soon fully appreciate the enormous potential here, and we all stand to gain tremendously from it.

With that said, I'm happy to share the key lessons I've learned through using this technology in writing this book. My hope is that sharing my experience may prove useful not only to others in the corporate communication sphere, but also to anyone wishing to embrace these new technologies in their daily life.

11.2   A New methodology

In my previous experiences as an author, the workflow for producing a book has always been standardized. There are usually three main phases: ideation and planning, writing, and review and revision. In the first phase, different techniques such as brainstorming, extensive reading, and drawing upon personal experiences are employed to generate a rich tapestry of ideas. For the book you are reading right now, defining the key themes was relatively straightforward. A credible discourse required covering all crucial areas in the field of corporate communication. Nevertheless, extensive preliminary research and a well-structured outline were needed to set the stage for a coherent narrative.

The writing phase is where creativity meets rigor. In addition to drawing upon articles and case studies, it is vital for the aim of this book to challenge the real-world applicability of AI tools in corporate communication. This helped separate genuine opportunities from mere trends. The final phase, review and revision, is the time for critical self-examination and external validation.

Undoubtedly, generative AI offers significant advantages throughout this process. These technologies can rapidly generate an initial table of contents and draft chapters based on your notes, streamlining the review and refinement stages.

Additionally, AI excels in the realms of proofreading and editing. It can scrutinize draft chapters for spelling errors, grammatical inconsistencies, structural issues, and narrative flow. By efficiently tidying up the draft, AI allows you to focus your attention on crafting a compelling narrative, thereby saving you valuable time. Research is a key part of writing a compelling book. You can leverage AI to synthesize and summarize both qualitative and quantitative sources. But how was this achieved concretely in this book?

11.2.1   *The toolkit: ChatGPT, Claude2, and Perplexity*

In crafting this book, three particular AI tools have been employed to elevate the quality and depth of the content. The first and arguably the most renowned at the time of the book's publication is ChatGPT Plus, developed by OpenAI. This tool has been particularly adept at content analysis, synthesis, and review. It has sifted through an extensive array of documents, research papers, and corporate case studies, identifying the most relevant information. This analytical prowess not only conserved valuable time but also ensured that the book was grounded in credible sources. Following this, the AI synthesized these key points into concise yet comprehensive summaries that were effortlessly incorporated into the book. Additionally, it was instrumental in revising individual chapters, ensuring that the content was coherent, logically structured, and accurate. By setting a specific context through custom instructions,[1] ChatGPT was made aware that it was contributing to a long-term project—a book on corporate communication and AI. This context awareness had a ripple effect on how the AI approached various tasks. For instance, in the selection of sources, the AI was guided to focus on materials that were directly relevant to the themes and objectives of the book. This resulted in a more targeted and efficient research process, eliminating the need to sift through irrelevant or less impactful sources.

---

[1] https://openai.com/blog/custom-instructions-for-chatgpt.

When it came to content synthesis, the custom instructions ensured that the AI's summaries and key takeaways were aligned with the book's overarching narrative and goals. This meant that the synthesized content was not just concise but also contextually relevant, making it easier to integrate into the book without extensive rework.

Lastly, in the revision stage, the custom instructions played a pivotal role in fine-tuning the content. The AI was better equipped to identify inconsistencies, logical gaps, or thematic deviations thanks to its understanding of the book's context. This led to revisions that were not just grammatical but also structural and thematic, thereby elevating the overall quality of the book.

In essence, the "Custom Instructions" feature acted like a compass, guiding ChatGPT to produce output that was not just high-quality but also contextually aligned with the book's objectives. This resulted in a more streamlined and efficient writing process, reducing the time and effort required for manual adjustments and rework.

Another AI tool that has been instrumental in the writing of the book is Claude2. While ChatGPT excels in content generation and synthesis, Claude2, developed by Anthropic, is engineered to be upfront when it is unsure or can't provide an accurate answer.[2] This level of transparency is invaluable, especially when dealing with complex topics that require factual accuracy. It tends to reference facts more often than ChatGPT and can self-correct based on new evidence, making it a reliable partner in the writing process. While ChatGPT provides the creative and generative muscle, Claude2 acts as the discerning eye that ensures factual integrity. This synergistic relationship between the two AI tools has been invaluable in creating a book that is not just informative but also reliable. Amazon's recent investment in Anthropic is a significant development that not only validates the capabilities of Claude2 but also signals a shift in the AI market landscape.

The third tool in the toolkit, Perplexity.ai, distinguishes itself from the previously mentioned language models. It is often referred to as "the future of search engines," primarily because its core functionality revolves around information discovery and organization. Perplexity.ai has a unique feature called Copilot that goes beyond your initial query by

---

[2] https://www.anthropic.com/index/claude-2.

asking clarifying questions to provide precise answers.[3] It delves deeper into each source to extract the most pertinent information. This is particularly useful when you're looking for specific data, research findings, or expert opinions to substantiate the arguments or points made in the book. Perhaps one of the most challenging aspects of writing a book is connecting disparate pieces of information into a coherent narrative. Perplexity.ai excels in this area by not just providing isolated pieces of information but also offering insights into how they could be interconnected. This is particularly useful for a book on corporate communication and AI, where multiple disciplines and fields intersect.

The orchestration of these three AI tools—ChatGPT Plus, Claude2, and Perplexity.ai—has been a cornerstone in the book's production process. Each tool has its unique strengths, and their synergistic collaboration has significantly elevated the quality, depth, and reliability of the content. But beyond the tools themselves, another pivotal element in this journey has been the definition of three personas. These personas served as frameworks through which the language models were utilized as true collaborators and co-authors of the book. By defining these personas, we were able to tailor the AI's approach to specific tasks, whether it was in-depth research, content synthesis, or factual verification. This persona-based approach made the collaboration with the AI models more nuanced and context-aware, thereby reducing the time and effort required for manual adjustments and rework.

10.2.2 *Meet the personas*

In the past decade user personas have become a cornerstone in digital marketing, primarily for their role in enabling targeted content creation. User personas help in crafting content that resonates with particular groups, thereby increasing engagement and conversion rates.

Beyond just content, user personas also offer a nuanced understanding of the customer journey. Knowing the characteristics and behaviors of the ideal customer allows marketers to create experiences that guide consumers more effectively through the sales funnel.

---

[3] https://www.perplexity.ai/.

Similarly, AI personas can play a critical role in increasing productivity by enabling targeted augmentation of workflows. Just as user personas represent archetypes of real users, AI personas represent archetypes of how AI systems can support knowledge workers.

By mapping specific workflows of the book to the appropriate AI persona, you can boost productivity and creativity in a targeted way, and that's exactly what has been done here. Three AI personas were defined by crafting targeted prompts: the assistant, the strategist, and the creator. The prompts were structured to provide the AI with relevant information on the job to be done. Therefore each persona has its own character, so to say.

The assistant persona is like an assistant or summer intern. It excels at repetitive, time-consuming tasks, freeing up the knowledge worker. The assistant persona learns quickly, never gets bored of repetitive tasks, is strong at data analysis, can conduct research and prepare briefings, and is eager to please its "boss," and it is thus prone to hallucinations. The main benefits of the assistant persona are automating repetitive tasks such as document and report preparation, summarizing qualitative and quantitative data, and proofreading.

The strategist persona, meanwhile, acts as a thought partner and strategic advisor. It thinks in mental frameworks, is trained across multiple domains and knowledge sources, is rational and unaffected by emotions, and can generate alternative options and different perspectives. The main benefits of the strategist persona are the ability to constructively critique decisions, simulate conversations, and review content, providing an outsider's viewpoint.

Finally, the creator persona assists with drafting content. It quickly learns the writing style, provides starting drafts to build upon, and works with specific templates such as creative briefs. The main benefits of the creator persona are drafting initial versions of paragraphs and chapters plus filling out project specs.

By assigning the right workflows in the book to each persona, I was able to benefit from the different capabilities of each AI archetype and effectively have a co-author endowed with abilities I had never dealt with before.

11.3 The need for constraints

In the nascent years of elevator technology, the spotlight was squarely on engineering marvels that could significantly reduce transit times between floors. Engineers and architects were in a constant race against time, striving for solutions that could deliver passengers to their destinations as swiftly as possible. Advanced motors, sophisticated control systems, and even aerodynamic designs for the elevator cabs—all were deployed in the quest for speed and efficiency.

However, as the mechanical complexities increased, so did the costs. At some point, the quest for speed hit a financial bottleneck; it was under these circumstances that designers and psychologists turned to subtler, less overtly technical solutions to enhance the elevator experience and reduce the number of complaints. One such fascinating solution was the strategic placement of mirrors within elevators.[4] While they may not actually make the elevator go faster, they offer a unique blend of psychological and practical benefits that greatly enrich the user experience.

This story offers us an intriguing parallel with the nature and limitations of generative AI systems, particularly LLMs. It's unlikely that an LLM, when queried on how to improve the elevator experience, would have arrived at the creative solution of installing mirrors. These models don't know what the world is; they only know how the world "talks" about the world. So, the LLM's first instinct would be to suggest conventional engineering improvements to increase speed and efficiency. However, my personal experience in this book illustrates that LLMs need constraints and lateral thinking to produce truly innovative solutions by reframing the problem.[5]

Without these limitations, LLMs tend to provide answers within their specific semantic space—in this case, faster elevator components. But the disruptive mirror idea requires drawing connections across domains such as psychology and human perception. Truly creative solutions emerge when LLMs are "pushed" out of their comfort zone. Finding the optimal balance between expanding and limiting their solution space is key to unlocking their creative potential. With the right scaffolding, LLMs can

---

[4] https://medium.com/pixel-playground/why-are-there-mirrors-in-elevators-2c8fa04f9db6.

[5] https://hbr.org/2017/01/are-you-solving-the-right-problems.

produce the kind of lateral innovation that led to the ingenious elevator mirror idea. Asking a machine to emulate specific personas or personalities in its responses represents a unique form of constraint. Interestingly, constraints often act as catalysts for innovation. By narrowing the scope of possibilities, they force creative solutions to emerge, enhancing the system's utility and broadening its applications. In the context of AI, asking a model to adopt specific characteristics or personas can then lead to more nuanced, context-sensitive, and potentially insightful responses. These constraints can inspire novel ways to interact with and utilize the technology, enriching its capabilities and broadening its appeal.

It is my sincere hope that this book has helped outline a scenario where the integration of AI and corporate communication leads to a positive evolution of this field. Through the examples and reflections shared in the preceding pages, I sought to demonstrate how these technologies, when properly framed and balanced with human oversight and direction, can open new communicative horizons.

If we maintain the right equilibrium, embracing this virtuous collaboration between man and machine with an open mind, we will not only enhance the quality and efficacy of our work but also enter a new, exciting phase of corporate communication—a phase where previously unimaginable messages and narratives can take shape, redefining modes of engagement between brands and audiences. In this voyage, humans must be the captains, ready to correct the course when necessary. But with AI as the propulsive engine, we can go farther and faster than we ever imagined. These tools are only as powerful as our vision is clear and the constraints we impose are well defined.

In conclusion, I hope the seeds planted in this volume may germinate, inspiring other professionals to embrace the opportunities of AI with optimism, yet also with a critical spirit. Only with this balanced approach can we truly unlock the potential of these technologies and catalyze an evolutionary leap for corporate communication.